GW00545305

OSHO PURNIMA DISTRIBUTION
" GREENWISE "
VANGE PARK ROAD
VANGE, BASILDON
ESSEX, SS16 5LA
Tel. 071 284 1415

TM

Published by
Rajneesh Foundation International
Rajneeshpuram, Oregon 97741, U.S.A.

Bhagwan Shree Rajneesh

AND NOW, AND HERE
Volume 1

Discourses from
the Meditation Camp
at Dwarka, Gujarat, India

Editors: Swami Satya Vedant, Ph.D., M.M., D.Litt.M.
    (RIMU), Acharya
  Swami Krishna Prem, M.M., D.Phil.M. (RIMU), Acharya
Design: Ma Prem Tushita
Direction: Ma Yoga Pratima, M.M., D.Phil.M. (RIMU),
    Arihanta
Copyright: 1984 Rajneesh Foundation International
Published by: Ma Anand Sheela, M.M., D.Phil.M.,
    D.Litt.M. (RIMU), Acharya
  Rajneesh Foundation International, President
  P.O. Box 9, Rajneeshpuram,
  Oregon 97741, U.S.A.

First Edition: July 1984 — 10,000 copies

Printed in U.S.A.

ISBN 0-88050-709-8

Library of Congress Catalog Number   84-42798

CONTENTS

INTRODUCTION

I can remember the first time I became aware that I was going to die. I was nine years old, and so frightened that I got sick to my stomach and had a fever. My mother tried to figure out what I'd eaten that had made me so sick. I couldn't tell her what it was. I knew no one could help me, no one could tell me I wasn't going to die. So I just lay on the bed shivering in utter fear until finally, after a little while, the fear left as suddenly as it had come. I didn't know that probably everyone I'd ever known was shaking inwardly with the same fear. No one ever mentioned death. They closed it out of their lives, they thought. And so I grew up, shrinking, withdrawing, fearful . . .

And there we all are, terrifyingly mortal, clinging tenaciously to whatever comes our way. In our quest to stay alive we gather things, people, ideas. We cling to dead loves, we delude ourselves into positions of power, we run after anything that will give us a sense of permanency on this earth. But in doing so we have chosen just half of life. We have become schizophrenic. It never occurs to us to look at what we are running from. It never even occurs to us that we are running from anything . . .

In the fall of 1969, Bhagwan Shree Rajneesh gave a series of discourses at a meditation camp at Dwarka, in Gujarat, India. To the seekers gathered around him, he spoke of life and death. He told them that the only way to ever live life fully was to experience death, accept death, embrace death, understand death in all its aspects. He led them in meditations that would allow them to experience their nothingness. He exhorted them to inquire into every corner of their lives and their universe and find death dancing, hand in hand with life, its partner and its self.

This book presents these discourses. He is speaking to you and me. He is giving us the key to life, showing us the witness, showing us the divinity of all things, asking us to put aside our hopes and assumptions and desires, and drown in His ocean.

His ocean is unknown to us, and yet somehow we yearn for it. We can sense its freshness on the breeze.

When I think back to being nine years old, I think how amazing it would have been had there been someone to tell me, yes it is true, you *are* going to die . . . And instead of turning away from it in fear, someone would have been there to take my hand and say: Look — here is death. Just befriend it, just open up your whole body and soul to it. Just die to all the anguish your separateness has given you, and then all the joy of life is given to you.

As He tells us, ". . . the one who learns the art of dying becomes an expert in the art of living as well . . ."

I know I am beginning to understand it, somehow, and somehow I am learning the tremendous freedom it gives.

Ma Krishna Gopa, M.M. (RIMU), Siddha

AND NOW, AND HERE
Volume 1

Discourses from
the Meditation Camp
at Dwarka, Gujarat, India
from October 28 to 31, 1969

NO BIGGER LIE THAN DEATH

Evening
October 28, 1969

We become free from that which we have known. We also triumph over that which we have known. Our failure and defeat are only because of our ignorance. Defeat is because of darkness; when there is light, defeat is impossible—light itself will bring triumph.

The first thing I would like to tell you about death is that there is no bigger lie than death. And yet, death appears to be true. It not only appears to be true but even seems like the cardinal truth of life—it appears as if the whole of life is surrounded by death. Whether we forget about it, or become oblivious to it, everywhere death remains close to us. Death is even closer to us than our shadow.

We have even structured our lives out of our fear of death. The fear of death has created society, the nation, family and friends. The fear of death has caused us to chase money and has made us ambitious of higher positions. And the biggest surprise is that our gods and our temples have also been raised out of the fear of death. Afraid of death, there are people who pray on their knees. Afraid of death, there are people who pray to God with folded hands raised towards the sky. And nothing is more false than death. That is why whatever system of life we have created, believing death to be true, has become false.

How do we know the falsity of death? How can we know there is no death? Until we know that, our fear of death will not go. Until we know the falsity of death, our lives will also remain false. As long as there is fear of death, there cannot be authentic life. As long as we tremble with the fear of death, we cannot summon the capacity to live our lives. Only those can live for whom the shadow of death has disappeared forever. How can a frightened and trembling mind live? And when death seems to be approaching every second, how is it possible to live? How *can* we live?

No matter to what extent we may remain oblivious to death, it is never really forgotten. It makes no difference if we put the cemetery outside the town—death still shows its face. Every day someone or other dies; every day death occurs somewhere, and it shakes the very foundation of our lives.

Whenever we see death happening, we become aware of our own death. When we cry over somebody's death, it is not just for that person's death alone, but also for the hint we get of our own. Our suffering from pain and sorrow is not only over someone else's death but also over the apparent possibility of our own. The occurrence of every death is, at the same time, our own death. And so long as we remain surrounded by death, how can we live? Like that, living is impossible. Like that, we cannot know what life is—neither its joy, nor its beauty, nor its benediction. Like that, we cannot reach the temple of God, the supreme truth of life.

The temples which have been created out of the fear of death are not the temples of God. The prayers which have been composed out of the fear of death are not prayers to God either. One who is filled with joy of life, he alone reaches the temple of God. God's kingdom is filled with joy and beauty, and the bells of God's temple ring only for those who are free from all kinds of fears, for those who have become fearless.

Because we like to live in fear this seems difficult. But this is not possible—only one of the two things can be right. Remember, if life is true then death cannot be true—and if death is true then life will be nothing but a dream, a lie; then life cannot be true. These two things cannot exist simultaneously. But we hold on to both together. There is the feeling that we are alive and there is also the feeling that we are dead.

I have heard about a *fakir* who lived in a far-away valley. Many people would go to him with questions. Once a man came and asked him to explain something about life and death. The *fakir* said, "You are welcome to know about life; my doors are open. But if you want to know about death then go somewhere else, because I have never died nor will I ever die. I have no experience of death. If you want to know about death then ask those who have died, ask those who are already dead." Then the *fakir* laughed and he said, "But how will you ask those who are already dead? And if you ask me to give you the address of a dead person, I cannot do it. Because ever since I have come to know that I cannot die, I have also come to know that no one dies, that no one has ever died."

But how can we believe this *fakir*? Every day we see someone dying; every day death happens. Death is the supreme truth; it makes itself apparent by penetrating the center of our being. You may shut your eyes, but no matter how far away it is from you, it still remains apparent. No matter how much we escape from it, run away from it, it still surrounds us. How can you falsify this truth?

Some people do, of course, try to falsify it. Just because of their fear of death people believe in the immortality of the soul—just out of fear. They don't know; they simply believe. Every morning, sitting in a temple or a mosque, some people repeat, "No one dies; the soul is immortal." They are wrong in believing that just by repeating this, the soul will become immortal. They are under the impression that death can be falsified by repeating, "The soul is immortal." Death never becomes false by such reiterations—only by knowing death can it be falsified.

This is very strange, remember: we always accept the opposite of what we go on repeating. When someone says he is immortal, that the soul is immortal—when he repeats this—he is simply indicating that he knows, deep down, he will die, he will have to die. If he knows he will

not die then there is no need to go on about immortality; only one who is frightened keeps on
repeating it. And you will see that people are
more scared of death in those countries, in those
societies which talk the *most* about the immortality of the soul. This country of ours talks
untiringly about the immortality of the soul, and
yet is there anyone on earth more scared of
death than us? There is no one more afraid of
death than us! How can we reconcile these two?

Is it ever possible for people who believe in the
immortality of the soul to become slaves? They
would rather die; they would be ready to die because they know there is no death. Those who
know that life is eternal, that the soul is immortal, would be the first to land on the moon! They
would be the first to climb Mount Everest! They
would be the first to explore the depths of the
Pacific Ocean! But no, we are not among those.
We neither climb the peak of Everest nor land on
the moon nor explore the depths of the Indian
Ocean—and we are the people who believe in
the immortality of the soul! In fact, we are so
scared of death, that out of the fear of it we go on
repeating, "The soul is immortal." And we are
under the illusion that perhaps by repeating it, it
will become true. Nothing becomes true by repetition.

Death cannot be denied by repeating that
death does not exist. Death will have to be
known, it will have to be encountered, it will
have to be lived. You will have to become ac-
quainted with it. Instead, we keep running away
from death.

How *can* we see it? We close our eyes when we

see death. When a funeral passes by on the road, a mother shuts her child behind closed doors and says, "Don't go out; someone has died." The cremation ground is put outside the town so it rarely meets your eyes, so that death won't be there, right in front of you. And if you ever mention death to somebody, he will forbid you to talk about it.

Once I stayed with a sannyasin. Every day he would talk about the immortality of the soul. I asked him, "Do you ever realize that you are coming closer to death?" He said, "Don't say such ominous things. It is not good to talk about such things." I said, "If, on the one hand, a person says that the soul is immortal, but also, he finds it ominous to talk about death, then this fouls up the whole thing. He shouldn't see any fear, any omen, anything wrong in talking about death—because for him there is no death." He said, "Although the soul *is* immortal, I, nevertheless, do not wish to talk about death at all. One should not talk about such meaningless and threatening things." We are all doing the same thing—turning our backs on death and escaping from it.

I have heard...

Once a man went mad in a village. It was a hot afternoon and the man was walking along a lonely road all alone. He was walking rather fast, trying not to be scared...it is possible to be scared when someone is already there, but how can anyone be scared when there is no one around? But we do feel scared when there is no one around. In fact, we are afraid of ourselves, and when we are alone the fear is even greater.

There is no one we fear more than ourselves. We are less afraid when accompanied by someone and more afraid when left all by ourselves.

That man was alone. He became scared and began running. Everything was still and quiet— it was afternoon; there was no one around. As he began to run faster, he sensed the sound of running feet coming from behind. He grew frightened—maybe someone was following him. Then, afraid, he glanced behind out of the corner of his eye. He saw a long shadow chasing him. It was his own shadow—but seeing that some long shadow was pursuing him, he ran even faster. Then that man could never stop, because the faster he ran, the faster the shadow ran after him. Finally the man went mad. But there are people who even worship madmen.

When people saw him running like that through their villages, they thought he was engaged in some great ascetic practice. Except in the darkness of night, when the shadow would disappear and he would think there was no one behind him, he never stopped. With daybreak he would start running again. Then he didn't even stop at night—he figured that in spite of the distance he had covered during the day, while he rested at night the shadow had caught up with him and would follow him in the morning once again.

So even at night he continued running. Then he went completely mad; he neither ate nor drank. Thousands of people watched him run and showered flowers upon him, or someone might hand him a piece of bread or some water. People began worshipping him more and more;

thousands paid their respects to him. But the man became more and more crazy, and finally one day, he fell down on the ground and died. The people of the village where he died made his grave under the shade of a tree, and they asked an old *fakir* of the village what they would inscribe on his gravestone. The *fakir* wrote one line on it.

In some village, someplace, that grave is still there. It is possible you may pass it by it. Do read the line. The *fakir* wrote on the gravestone: "Here rests a man who fled from his own shadow all his life, who wasted his whole life escaping from a shadow. And the man did not even know as much as his gravestone does— because the gravestone is in the shade and does not run, hence no shadow is created." We also run. We may wonder how a man can run from his shadow, but we too run from shadows. And that which we run away from starts pursuing us itself. The faster we run, the faster it follows— because it is our own shadow.

Death is our own shadow. If we keep running away from it we will not be able to stand before it and recognize what it is. If that man had stopped and seen what was behind him, perhaps he would have laughed and said, "What kind of a person am I, running away from a shadow?" No one can ever escape from a shadow; no one can ever win a fight with a shadow. This does not mean, however, that the shadow is stronger than we are and that we can never be victorious—it simply means that there *is* no shadow, that there *is* no question of being victorious. You cannot win against that which does not exist. That's why people keep facing defeat by death—because death is merely a shadow of life.

As life moves forward, its shadow moves along with it too. Death is the shadow that forms behind life, and we never want to look back, to see what it is. We have fallen, exhausted, so many times—after having run this race again and again. It is not that you have come to this shore for the first time, you must have been here before—maybe it was not this shore; then some other shore. It may not have been this body; then some other body—but the race must have been the same. The legs must have been the same; the race must have been the same.

Through many lives we live, carrying the fear of death, and yet we are neither able to recognize it nor to see it. We are so scared and frightened that when death approaches, when its total shadow closes in on us, out of fear we become unconscious. Generally, no one remains conscious at the moment of death. If, even once, one were to remain conscious, the fear of death would disappear forever. If, just once, a man could see what dying is like, what happens in death, then the next time he would have no fear of death because there would *be* no death. Not that he would be victorious over death—we can achieve victory only over something which exists. Just by knowing death, it disappears. Then nothing remains over which to be victorious.

We have died many times before, but whenever death has occurred we have become unconscious. This is similar to when a physician or a surgeon gives anesthesia before an operation so you won't feel the pain. We are so very afraid of dying that at the time of death we become unconscious willingly. We become unconscious just a little before dying. We die unconscious, and then we are reborn in a state of unconsciousness. We neither see death, nor do we see birth—and hence we are never able to understand that life is eternal. Birth and death are nothing more than stopping places where we change clothes or horses.

In olden times there were no railroads and people traveled in horse-drawn carriages. They traveled from one village to another, and when the horses grew tired they exchanged them for fresh horses at an inn, and they changed them again at the next village. However, the people changing the horses never felt that what they were doing was like dying and being born again, because when they changed horses they were fully conscious.

Sometimes it used to happen that a horseman would travel after drinking. When he would look around in that state, it would make him wonder how everything had changed, how everything appeared so different. I have heard that once a drunk horseman even said, "Could it be that I am changed too? This doesn't seem to be the same horse I was riding. Could it be that I have become a different man?"

Birth and death are simply stations where vehicles are changed—where the old vehicles are left behind, where tired horses are abandoned and fresh ones are acquired. But both these acts take place in our state of unconsciousness. And one whose birth and death happens in this

unconscious state cannot live a conscious life—
he functions in an almost half-conscious state, in
an almost half-awakened state of life.

What I wish to say is that it is essential to see
death, to understand it, to recognize it. But this
is possible only when we die; one can only see it
while dying. Then what is the way now? And if
one sees death only while dying, then there is no
way to understand it—because at the time of
death one will be unconscious.

Yes, there is a way now. We can go through
an experiment of entering into death of our own
free will. And may I say that meditation or
samadhi is nothing else but that. The experience
of entering death voluntarily is meditation,
samadhi. The phenomenon that will automatically occur one day with the dropping of the
body—we can willingly make that happen by
creating a distance, inside, between the self and
the body. And so, by leaving the body from the
inside, we can experience the event of death, we
can experience the occurrence of death. We can
experience death today, this evening—because
the occurrence of death simply means that our
soul and our body will experience, in that journey, the same distinction between the two of
them as when the vehicle is left behind and the
traveler moves on ahead.

I have heard that a man went to see a Mohammedan *fakir*, Sheikh Fareed, and said, "We have
heard that when Mansoor's hands and legs were
cut off he felt no pain...which is hard to believe.
Even a thorn hurts when it pricks the foot.
Won't it hurt if one's hands and legs are cut off?
It seems that these are all fantastic stories." The

man also said, "We hear that when Jesus was hanged on the cross he did not feel any pain. And he was permitted to say his final prayers. What the bleeding, naked Jesus—hanged on a cross, pierced with thorns, hands stuck with nails—said in the final moments can hardly be believed!"

Jesus said, "Forgive these people, they don't know what they are doing." You must have heard this sentence. And the people all over the world who believe in Christ repeat it continuously. The sentence is very simple. Jesus said, "O, Lord, please forgive these people, because they know not what they are doing." Reading this sentence, people ordinarily understand Jesus is saying that the poor people didn't know they were killing a good man like him. No, that was not what Jesus meant. What Jesus meant was that "These senseless people do not know that the person they are killing cannot die. Forgive them because they don't know what they are doing. They are doing something which is impossible—they are committing the act of killing, which is impossible."

The man said, "It is hard to believe that a person about to be killed could show so much compassion. In fact, he will be filled with anger." Fareed gave a hearty laugh and said, "You have raised a good question, but I will answer it later. First, do me a little favor." He picked up a coconut lying nearby, gave it to him and asked him to break it open, cautioning him not to break the kernel. But the coconut was unripe, so the man said, "Pardon me, I cannot do this. The coconut is completely raw, and if I break open the shell the kernel will break too." Fareed asked him to put that coconut away. Then he gave him another coconut, one which was dry, and asked him to break that one open. "Can you save the kernel of this one?" he asked. And the man replied, "Yes, the kernel can be saved."

Fareed said, "I have given you an answer. Did you understand?" The man replied, "I didn't understand anything. What relation is there between a coconut and your answer? What relation is there between the coconut and my question?"

Fareed said, "Put this coconut away too. There is no need to break it or anything. I am pointing out to you that there is one raw coconut which still has the kernel and the shell joined together—if you hit the shell, the kernel will also break. Then there is the dry coconut. Now how is the dry coconut different from the raw coconut? There is a slight difference: the kernel of the dry coconut has shrunk inside and become separated from the shell; a distance has occurred between the kernel and the shell. Now you say, even after breaking open the shell, the kernel can be saved. So I have answered your question!"

The man said, "I still don't get it." The *fakir* said, "Go, die and understand—without that you cannot follow what I am saying. But even then you will not be able to follow me because at the time of death you will become unconscious. One day the kernel and the shell will be separated, but at that moment you will become unconscious. If you want to understand, then start learning now how to separate the kernel from the shell—now, while you are alive."

If the shell, the body, and the kernel, the

consciousness, separate at this very instant, death is finished. With the creation of that distance, you come to know that the shell and the kernel are two separate things—that you will continue to survive in spite of the breaking of the shell, that there is no question of *you* breaking, of *you* disappearing. In that state, even though death will occur, it cannot penetrate inside you — it will occur *outside* you. It means only that which you are not will die. That which you are will survive.

This is the very meaning of meditation or *samadhi*: learning how to separate the shell from the kernel. They can be separated because they *are* separate. They can be known separately because they *are* separate. That's why I call meditation a voluntary entry into death. And the man who enters death willingly, encounters it and comes to know that, "Death is there, and yet *I* am still here."

Socrates was about to die...The final moments were approaching; the poison was being ground to kill him. He kept asking, "It is getting late, how long will it take to grind the poison?" His friends were crying and saying to him, "Are you crazy? We want you to live a little longer. We have bribed the person who is grinding the poison; we have persuaded him to go slowly."

Socrates went out and said to the man who was grinding the poison, "You are taking too long. It seems you are not very skilled. Are you very new to this? Have you never ground it before? Have you never given poison to a condemned person?"

The man replied, "I have been giving poison

my whole life, but I have never seen a crazy man like you before. Why are you in so much of a hurry? I am grinding it slowly so that you may breathe a little more, live a little longer, remain in life a little more. You keep talking like a crazy man, saying it is getting late. Why are you in such a hurry to die?''

Socrates said, ''I am in a great hurry because I want to see death. I want to see what death is like. And I also want to see, even when death has happened, whether *I* survive or not. If I don't survive, then the whole affair is finished— and if I *do* survive, then death is finished. In fact, I want to see who will die with death—will death die or will I die? I want to see whether death will survive or whether I will survive. But how can I see this unless *I* am alive?''

Socrates was given the poison. His friends began to mourn; they were not in their right senses. And what was Socrates doing? He was telling them, ''The poison has reached up to my knees. Up to the knees my legs are totally dead —I will not even know if you cut them off. But my friends, let me tell you, even though my legs are dead, *I* am still alive. This means one thing is certain—I was not my legs. I am still here, I am totally here. Nothing within me has faded yet.'' Socrates continued, ''Now both my legs are gone; up to my thighs everything is finished. I wouldn't feel anything if you cut me right up to the thighs. But *I* am still here! And here are my friends who go on crying!''

Socrates is saying, ''Don't cry. Watch! Here is an opportunity for you: a man is dying and in- forming you that he is still alive. You may cut off my legs entirely—even then I won't be dead, even then I will still remain. My hands are also drifting away; my hands will die too. Ah! How many times I identified myself with these hands —the same hands that are leaving now—but I am still here."

And, like this, Socrates continues talking while dying. He says, "Slowly, everything is becoming peaceful, everything is sinking, but I am still intact. After a while I may not be able to inform you, but don't let that make you think I am no more. Because, if I am still here, even after losing so much of my body, how then would an end come to me if a little more of the body is lost? I may not be able to inform you— because that is only possible through the body —but still I will remain." And at the very last moment he says, "now, perhaps I am telling you the final thing: my tongue is failing. I won't be able to speak a single word further, but still I am saying, 'I exist'." Until the final moment of death he kept saying, "I am still alive."

In meditation, too, one has to enter slowly within. And gradually, one after another, things begin to drop away. A distance is created with each and every thing, and a moment arrives when it feels as if everything is lying far away at a distance. It will feel as if someone else's corpse is lying on the shore—and yet *you* exist. The body is lying there and still *you* exist— separate, totally distinct and different.

Once we experience seeing death face-to-face while alive, we will never have anything to do with death again. Death will keep on coming, but then it will be just like a stopover—it will be like changing clothes, it will be like when we take new horses and ride in new bodies and set out on a new journey, on new paths, into new worlds. But death will never be able to destroy us. This can only be known by encountering death. We will have to know it; we will have to pass through it.

Because we are so very afraid of death, we are not even able to meditate. Many people come to me and say that they are unable to meditate. How shall I tell them that their real problem is something else? Their real problem is the fear of death...and meditation is a process of death. In a state of total meditation we reach the same point a dead man does. The only difference is that the dead man reaches there in an unconscious state, while we reach consciously. This is the only difference. The dead man has no knowledge of what happened, of how the shell broke open and the kernel survived. The meditative seeker *knows* that the shell and the kernel have become separate.

The fear of death is the basic reason why people cannot go into meditation—there is no other reason. Those who are afraid of death can never enter into *samadhi*. *Samadhi* is a voluntary invitation to death. An invitation is given to death: "Come, I am ready to die. I want to know whether or not I will survive after death. And it is better that I know it consciously, because I won't be able to know anything if this event occurs in an unconscious state."

So, the first thing I say to you is that as long as you keep running away from death you will continue to be defeated by it—and the day you stand up and encounter death, that very day death will leave you, but you will remain.

These three days, all my talks will be on the techniques of how you can encounter death. I hope that, these three days, many people will come to know how to die, will be able to die. And if you can die here, on this shore...

And this is an incredible seashore. It was on these very sands that Krishna once walked—the same Krishna who told Arjuna in a certain war, "Don't be worried; have no fear. Don't be afraid of killing or of being killed, because I tell you that neither does anyone die nor does anyone kill." Neither has anyone ever died, nor can anyone ever die—and that which dies, that which can die, is already dead. And that which does not die and cannot be killed—there is no way of its dying. And that is life itself.

Tonight, we have unexpectedly gathered on this seashore where that very Krishna once walked. These sands have seen Krishna walk. People must have believed that Krishna really died—since we know death as the only truth; for us everyone dies. This sea, these sands, have never felt that Krishna died; this sky, these stars and the moon have never believed in Krishna's death.

In fact, nowhere is there any room for death in life, but we have all believed that Krishna died. We believe so because we are always haunted by the thought of our own death. Why are we so preoccupied with the thought of our death? We are alive right now, then why are we so afraid of death? Why are we so very afraid of dying?

Actually, behind this fear, there is a secret which we must understand.

There is a certain mathematics behind it, and this mathematics is very interesting. We have never seen ourselves dying. We have seen others dying, and that reinforces the idea that we will have to die too. For example, a raindrop lives in the ocean with thousands of other drops, and one day the sun's rays fall on it and it turns into vapor, it disappears. The other drops think it is dead, and they are right—because they had seen the drop just a little while ago, and now it is gone. But the drop still exists in the clouds. Yet how are the other drops to know this until they themselves become the cloud? By now that drop must have fallen into the sea and become a drop again. But how can the other drops know this until they themselves set out on that journey?

When we see somebody dying around us, we think the person is no more, that yet another man has died. We don't realize that the man has simply evaporated, that he has entered the subtle, and then set out on a new journey—that he is a drop which has evaporated, only to become a drop once again. How are we to see this? All we feel is that one more person is lost, that one more person is dead. Thus, somebody dies every day; every day some drop is lost. And it slowly becomes a certainty for us that we too will have to die, that, "I too will die." Then a fear takes hold: "I will die." This fear grips us because we are looking at others. We live watching others, and that is our problem.

Last night I was telling some friends a story.

Once a Jewish *fakir* became very upset by his troubles...Who doesn't get upset? We are all bothered by our woes, and our greatest bother is seeing others happy. Seeing that others are happy, we continue becoming unhappy. There is more mathematics behind this, the same kind of mathematics I spoke about in reference to death. We see our misery and we see the faces of others. We don't see the misery in others; we see their smiling eyes, the smiles on their lips. If we look at ourselves, we will see, in spite of being troubled inside, we go on smiling outwardly. In fact, a smile is a way to hide the misery.

No one wants to show he is unhappy. If he cannot really be happy then at least he wants to show that he has become happy, because to show oneself as unhappy is a matter of great humiliation, loss and defeat. That's why we keep a smiling face outwardly, and inside, we remain as we are. On the inside, tears keep collecting; on the outside, we practice our smiles. Then, when someone looks at us from the outside, he finds us smiling; however, when that person looks within himself he finds misery there. And that becomes a problem for him. He thinks the whole world is happy, that he alone is unhappy.

The same thing happened with this *fakir*. One night, in his prayers to God, he said, "I am not asking you not to give me unhappiness—because if I deserve unhappiness then I should certainly get it—but at least I can pray to you not to give me so much suffering. I see people laughing in the world, and I am the only one crying. Everyone seems to be happy; I am the only one who is unhappy. Everyone appears cheerful; I am the only one who is sad, lost in darkness. After all, what wrong have I done to you? Please do me a favor—give me some other person's unhappiness in exchange for mine. Change my unhappiness for that of anyone else you like, and I will accept it."

That night, while he slept, he had a strange dream. He saw a huge mansion which had millions of hanging pegs. Millions of people were coming in and every one was carrying a bundle of unhappiness on his back. Seeing so many bundles of unhappiness, he got very scared, he grew puzzled. The bundles brought by other people were very similar to his own. The size and shape of everyone's bundle was exactly the same. He became very confused. He had always seen his neighbors smiling—and every morning when the *fakir* asked him how things were, he would say, "Everything is just fine"—and this same man was now carrying the same amount of unhappiness.

He saw politicians and their followers, *gurus* and their disciples—everyone coming with the same size load. The wise and the ignorant, the rich and the poor, the healthy and the sick—the load in everyone's bundle was the same. The *fakir* was dumbfounded. He was seeing the bundles for the first time; up to now he had only seen people's faces.

Suddenly a loud voice filled the room: "Hang up your bundles!" Everyone, including the *fakir*, did as commanded. Everyone hurried to get rid of his troubles; no one wanted to carry his miseries even a second longer—and if we were to find such opportunity, we would also hang them up right away.

And then another voice sounded, saying: "Now, each of you should pick up whichever bundle he pleases." We might suspect that the *fakir* quickly picked up someone else's bundle. No, he did not make such a mistake. In panic, he ran to pick up his own bundle before anyone else could reach it—otherwise, it could have become a problem for him, because all the bundles looked the same. He thought it was better to have his own bundle—at least the miseries in it were familiar. Who knows what kinds of miseries were contained in the other peoples' bundles? Familiar misery is still a lesser kind of misery—it is a known misery, a recognizable misery.

So, in a state of panic, he ran and retrieved his own bundle before anyone else could lay his hands on it. When he looked around, however, he found that everyone else had also run and picked up their own bundles; no one had selected a bundle that was not his own. He asked, "Why are you in such a hurry to collect your own bundles?"

"We became frightened. Up to now we'd believed that everyone else was happy, that only we were miserable," they replied.

In that mansion, whomsoever the *fakir* asked, the reply was that they'd always believed everyone else was happy. "We even believed that *you* were happy too. You also walked down the street with a smile on your face. We never imagined that you carried a bundle of miseries inside you too," they said. With curiosity, the *fakir* asked, "Why did you collect your own bundle? Why didn't you exchange it for another?" They said, "Today, each of us had prayed to God, saying we wanted to exchange our bundles of misery. But when we saw that everyone's miseries were just the same, we became scared; we had never imagined such a thing. So we figured it was better to pick up our own bundle—it is familiar and known. Why fall into new miseries? By and by, we get used to the old miseries too." That night, nobody picked up a bundle that belonged to someone else. The *fakir* woke up, thanked merciful God for letting him have his own miseries back. And decided never to make such a prayer again.

In fact, the arithmetic behind it is the same. When we look at other people's faces and at our own reality—that is where we commit a great error. And with regard to our perception of life and death the same kind of wrong arithmetic is at work. You have seen other people die, but you have never seen yourself dying. We see other people's deaths, but we never come to know if anything within these people survives. Since we become unconscious at the time, death remains a stranger to us. Hence it is important we enter death voluntarily. If a person sees death once he becomes free from it, he triumphs over death. In fact, it is meaningless to call him victorious because there is nothing to win—then death becomes false; then death simply doesn't exist.

If after adding two and two a person writes down five, and the next day he comes to know that two plus two equals four, would he say he'd triumphed over five and made it four? He would say, in fact, that there was no question of triumph—there *was* no five. Making it five was his error, it was his illusion—his calculation was wrong, the total was four; he understood it as five, that was his mistake. Once you see the mistake, the matter is over. Would that man then say, "How can I get rid of five? Now I see two and two are four, but before, I had added them up as five. How can I be free of five?" The man would not ask for such freedom, because as soon as one finds out that two plus two equal four, the matter is over. There is no five any more. Then what does one have to be free of?

One neither has to be free from death nor does one have to triumph over it. One needs to know death. The very *knowing* it becomes freedom, the knowing itself becomes the victory. That's why I stated earlier that knowing is power, that knowing is freedom, that knowing is victory. Knowing death causes it to dissolve; then suddenly, for the first time, we become connected with life.

That's why I told you that the first thing about meditation is that it is a voluntary entry into death. The second thing I would like to say is that one who enters into death willingly, finds, all of a sudden, entrance into life. Even though he goes in search of death, instead of meeting death he actually finds ultimate life. Even though, for the purpose of his search he enters the mansion of death, he actually ends up in the temple of life. And one who escapes from the mansion of death never reaches the temple of life.

May I point out to you that the walls of the

temple of life are engraved with the shadows of death? May I also point out to you that the maps of death are drawn on the walls of the temple of life, and since we run away from death we are also, in effect, running away from the temple of life! Only when we accept death will we be able to accept these walls. If ever we could enter death, we would reach the temple of life. The deity of life dwells within the walls of death; the images of death are engraved all over the temple of life. We have simply been running away at the very sight of them.

If you have ever been to Khajuraho, you must have noticed a strange thing—all around its walls scenes of sex have been sculpted. The images look naked and obscene. If, after seeing them, a man simply runs away, then he will not be able to reach the deity of the temple inside. Inside is the image of God, and outside are engravings, images, of sex, passion, and copulation. They must have been a wonderful people who built the temples of Khajuraho. They depicted a profound fact of life: they have conveyed that sex is there, on the outside wall, and if you are to run away from there, then you will never be able to attain to *brahmacharya,* to celibacy—because *brahmacharya* is inside. If you are ever able to get beyond these walls, then you will also attain to *brahmacharya. Samsara,* the mortal world, is displayed on the walls, and running away from it will never bring you to God, because the one who is sitting inside the walls of *samsara* is God himself.

I am telling you exactly the same thing. Somewhere, someplace, we should build a temple whose walls have death displayed on it and the deity of life would be sitting inside. This is how the truth is. However, since we keep escaping from death, we miss the divinity of life as well.

I say both things simultaneously: meditation is entering voluntarily into death, and the one who enters death voluntarily attains to life. That means: one who encounters death ultimately finds that death has disappeared and he is in life's embrace. This looks quite contrary—you go in search of death and come across life—but it is not.

For example, I am wearing clothes. Now if you come in search of *me*, first you will come across my clothes—although I am not the clothes. And if you become frightened of my clothes and run away, then you will never be able to know me. However, if you come closer and closer to me, without being frightened of my clothes, then beneath my clothes you will find my body. But the body too, in a deeper sense, is a garment, and if you were to run away from my body, then you would not find the one who is seated inside me. If you were not to become frightened of the body and continued your journey inside, knowing that the body is a garment too, then you would certainly come across that one who sits inside, that one everyone is desirous of meeting.

How interesting it is that the wall is made of the body and the divine is seated graciously inside. The wall is made of matter and inside is the divine, the consciousness seated in glory. These are contrary things indeed—the wall of matter and the divinity of life. If you understand rightly, the wall is made of death and the divine is made of life.

When an artist paints a picture he provides a dark background to bring out the white color. The white lines become clearly visible against the dark background. If one were to get scared of the black, he wouldn't be able to reach the white. But he doesn't know that it is the black that brings out the white.

Similarly, there are thorns around the blooming roses. If one becomes frightened of the thorns he won't be able to reach the roses; if he goes on escaping from the thorns he will be deprived of the flowers too. But one who accepts the thorns and approaches them without fear finds to his amazement that the thorns are simply meant to protect the flower; they merely serve the purpose of being the outer wall for the flower—the wall of protection. The flower is blooming in the middle of the thorns; the thorns are not the flower's enemy. The flowers are part of the thorns and the thorns are part of the flowers—both have emerged from the same life-giving force of the plant.

What we call life and what we call death—both are part of one greater life. I am breathing. A breath comes out; a breath goes in. The same breath that comes out goes back in after a while, and the breath that goes in comes out after a while. Breathing in is life, breathing out is death. But both are steps of one greater life—life and death, walking side by side. Birth is one step, death is another step. But if we could see, if we could penetrate inside, then we would attain the vision of the greater life.

These three days we shall do the meditation of entering into death. And I shall speak to you on many of its dimensions. Tonight we shall do the first day's meditation. Let me explain a few things about it to you.

You must have understood my point of view by now: we have to reach a point within, deep inside, where there is no possibility of dying. We have to drop the whole outer circumference, as happens in death. In death the body drops, feelings drop, thoughts drop, friendship drops, enmity drops—everything drops. The entire external world departs—only *we* remain, only the self remains, only the consciousness remains aloof.

In meditation too, we have to drop everything and die—leaving only the observer, the witness within. And this death will happen. Throughout these three days of meditation, if you will show the courage of dying and drop your self a phenomenon can occur which is called *samadhi*.

Samadhi, remember, is a wonderful word. The state of total meditation is called *samadhi* and a grave built after a person's death is also called a *samadhi*. Have you ever thought about this?— both are called *samadhi*. In fact, both have a common secret, a common meeting point.

Actually, for a person who attains to the state of *samadhi*, his body remains just like a grave— nothing else. Then he comes to realize that there is someone else within; outside there is only darkness.

Following a person's death we make a grave and call it a *samadhi*. But this *samadhi* is made by others. If we can make our own *samadhi* before others make it, then we have created the very phenomenon we are longing for. Others will have the occasion to make our grave for certain, but we may perhaps lose the opportunity of creating our own *samadhi*. If we can create our own *samadhi*, then, in that state, only the body will die and there will be no question of our consciousness dying. We have never died, nor can we ever die. No one has ever died, nor can anyone ever die. To know this, however, we will have to descend all the steps of death.

I would like to show you three steps we shall follow. And who knows? That phenomenon might occur on this very seashore and you may have your *samadhi*—not the *samadhi* others make, but the one you create of your own will.

There are three steps. The first step is to relax your body. You have to relax your body so much that you begin to feel as if your body is lying far away from you, as if you have nothing to do with it. You have to withdraw the whole energy from your body and take it inside. We have given the energy to our bodies—whatever amount of energy we pour into the body goes into it; whatever amount we withdraw gets pulled inward.

Have you ever noticed something when you get into a fight with somebody? Where does your body get the additional energy from? In that state of anger you can lift a rock so big that you couldn't even budge it when you were calm. Although it was your body did you ever wonder where the energy came from? *You* put the energy in—it was needed, you were in trouble; there was danger, the enemy was facing you. You knew your life could be in danger unless you picked up the rock, and you put all your energy into the body.

Once it happened: a man was paralyzed for two years and was bedridden. He could not get up; he could not move. The physicians gave up, declaring the paralysis would remain with him for the rest of his life. Then one night his house caught fire and everyone ran out. After coming out, they realized the head of their family was trapped inside—he could not even run; what would happen to him? Some people had brought torches with them, and they found that the old man was already out. They asked him if he had walked out of the house. The man said, "How could I have walked? How did it happen?" But he certainly *had* walked; there was no question.

The house was on fire; everybody was leaving it—and for a moment he forgot his paralysis; he put his entire energy back into the body. But when people saw him in the torchlight and asked how he had managed to come out, he exclaimed, "Oh, I am paralyzed!" and fell down. He lost the energy. Now it is beyond him to comprehend how this phenomenon occurred. Now everyone started explaining to him that he was not really paralyzed, that if he could walk that much he could walk the rest of his life. The man kept saying, "I could not lift my hand; I could not even lift my foot—then how did it happen?" He couldn't say; he did not even know who had brought him out.

No one had brought him out; he had come out on his own. He did not know, however, that in the face of danger his soul had poured all his energy into his body. And then, because of his feeling of being paralyzed, the soul drew its energy inside again and the man became paralyzed once more. Such an incident has occurred not with one or two people, on this earth hundreds of instances have happened where a man stricken with paralysis has come out of his condition, where he has forgotten his condition in the event of a fire or in the face of another dangerous situation.

What I am saying is that we have put energy into our body, but we have no idea how to withdraw it. At night we feel rested because the energy is drawn inside and the body lies in a relaxed state, and in the morning we are fresh again. But some people are not even able to draw their energy inwards at night. The energy still remains locked in the body and then it becomes difficult for them to sleep. Insomnia is an indication that the energy put into the body earlier cannot find the way to return to its source. In the first stage of this meditation the entire energy has to be withdrawn from the body.

Now, the interesting thing is that just by feeling it the energy returns. If, for a while, someone can feel that his energy is withdrawing inside and his body is relaxing, he will find that his body is continuing to relax and relax. The body will reach to a point where the person will not be able to lift his hand even if he wants to—everything will be relaxed. Thus, through feeling it, we can withdraw our energy from the body.

So the first thing is the returning of the vital energy, the *prana*, back to its source. That will

make the body lie still—just like a shell—and it
will be observed throughout that a distance has
been created between the shell and the kernel
within the coconut—that we have become separate and the body is lying outside us, just like a
shell, just like cast-off clothes.

Then the next thing is to relax your breath.
Deep inside the breath contains the vital energy,
the *prana*, and that's why a man dies when the
breath discontinues. Deep down, the breath
keeps us connected to the body. Breath is the
bridge between the soul and the body; that's
where the link is. Hence, we call breath *prana*.
As soon as the breathing stops, the *prana* leaves.
Several techniques are applied in this respect.

What happens when a person relaxes his
breath completely, allows it to be still and quiet?
Slowly, the breath comes to a point where a man
doesn't know whether he is breathing inside or
not. He often begins to wonder whether he is
alive or dead, whether the breath is happening
or not. The breathing becomes so quiet one
doesn't know if it is moving at all.

You don't have to control breathing. If you try
to do so, the breath will never be controlled—it
will try to force itself out, and if you control it
from outside, it will try to force itself in. Hence,
I say, you don't have to do anything from your
side, just let it be more and more relaxed—more
and more quiet. Slowly, at one point, the breath
comes to rest. Even if it comes to rest just for a
moment, then in that moment one can see an infinite distance between the soul and the body—
in that very moment the distance is seen. It's as
if lightning were to strike right now and I were

to see all your faces in one moment. Afterwards, the lightning might no longer be there, yet I have seen your faces.

When the breath pauses for a moment, exactly right in the middle, then in that moment a lightning strikes within one's entire being and it becomes apparent that the body is separate and that you are separate—then death has happened. So in the second stage you have to relax your breath.

In the third stage the mind is to be relaxed. Even if the breath is relaxed but the mind is not, the lightning will of course strike, but you won't be able to know what happened because the mind will remain occupied with its thoughts. If lightning should strike right now and I were to remain lost in my thoughts, I would only come to know of it after it had happened. In the meantime, however, the lightning has occurred and I have been lost in my thoughts. The lightning will strike, of course, as soon as the breath pauses, but it will only be noticed if thoughts have ceased; otherwise it won't be noticed and the opportunity will be lost. Hence, the third thing is to relax the mind.

We shall go through these three stages and then, in the fourth stage, we shall sit silently. If you wish, you may either lie down or sit. It will be easier lying down—this is such a beautiful beach; it can be put to good use. Everyone should make a space around himself and lie down. It is all right if someone wants to sit, but the person should not control himself if his body begins to fall—because the body may fall once it becomes completely relaxed, and then your controlling it will not allow the body to be totally relaxed.

So we shall follow these three stages and then in the fourth stage we shall remain in silence for ten minutes. These three days, during that silence, there will be an effort on your part to see death, to let it descend. I will give suggestions for you to feel that the body is relaxing, that the breath is relaxing, that the mind is relaxing— then I will remain quiet, the lights will be turned off, and, lying down quietly, you will remain for ten minutes. You will remain still, in silence, watching whatsoever is going on inside.

Make enough space around you so that in case the body drops, it won't fall on anyone. Those who wish to lie down should make a space around themselves. It would be better if you were to lie down on the sand quietly . . . Nobody should talk . . . no one should leave in the middle.

Yes, be seated . . . Be seated wherever you are or lie down . . . Close your eyes . . . Close your eyes and relax your body. Let it be loose. Then as I give suggestions, begin to feel with me. As you keep feeling, your body will become more and more relaxed—then the body will be lying down, totally relaxed, as if there is no life in it.

Begin to feel. The body is relaxing . . . Keep relaxing it . . . keep relaxing your body and feel that it is relaxing. The body is relaxing . . . feel it . . . relax every part of your body. And feel inside . . . the body is relaxing. Your energy is returning inside . . . the energy from your body is withdrawing, turning in . . . the energy is withdrawing. The body is relaxing . . . the body is re-

laxing . . . the body is relaxing . . . the body is relaxing . . . Let go completely, as if you are not
alive anymore . . . Let the body drop as it is . . .
Let it be totally loose . . . The body has become
relaxed . . . the body has become relaxed . . . the
body has become relaxed . . . Let go . . . let go.

The body has become relaxed. The body has
become totally relaxed, as if there is no life in it.
The entire energy of the body has reached inside
. . . The body has become relaxed . . . the body
has become relaxed . . . the body has become relaxed . . . the body has become relaxed . . . the
body has become relaxed . . . Let go, let go completely, as if the body is no longer there.

We have moved within. The body has become
relaxed . . . the body has become relaxed . . . the
body has become relaxed . . . The breath is quiet-
ing down . . . Relax your breathing also . . . relax
it completely . . . let it come and go on its own .
. . let it be loose . . . No need to stop it or slow
it down; just let it be relaxed. Let the breath
come in as much as it can . . . let it come out as
much as it can . . . The breathing is becoming relaxed . . . the breathing is becoming calm . . .

Feel it like this: the breathing is becoming calm
. . . the breathing is becoming calm and relaxed
. . . the breathing is relaxing . . . the breath is
calming down . . . The breath has calmed down
. . . the breath has calmed down . . . the breath
has calmed down . . . Now let the mind be
relaxed and feel that thoughts are calming down
. . . thoughts are calming down . . . the mind has
calmed . . . the mind has calmed . . .

SEEING LIFE
AS A DREAM

Morning
October 29, 1969

A few questions have been asked about last night's talk. One friend has asked, *One can die fully conscious, but how can one be in full consciousness at birth?*

Actually, death and birth are not two events, they are two ends of the same phenomenon — just like two sides of the same coin. If a man can have one side of a coin in his hand, the other side will be in his hand automatically. It's not possible to have one side of a coin in my hand and then wonder how to get the other side — the other side becomes available automatically.

Death and birth are two sides of the same phenomenon. If death occurs in a conscious state, then birth inevitably takes place in a conscious state. If death occurs in an unconscious state, then birth happens in a state of unconsciousness too. If a person dies fully conscious at the time of his death, he will be filled with consciousness at the moment of his next birth also.

Since we all die in a state of unconsciousness and are born in a state of unconsciousness, we remember nothing of our past lives. However, the memory of our past lives always remains present in some corner of our minds, and this memory can be revived if we so desire.

With birth we cannot do anything directly; whatsoever we can do is possible only in relation to death. Nothing can be done after death; whatsoever is to be done must be done before death. A person dying in an unconscious state cannot do anything until he is born again—there is no way; he will continue to remain unconscious. Hence, if you died before in an unconscious state, you will have to be born again in an unconscious state. Whatsoever is to be done must be done *before* death, because we have lots of opportunities before death, the opportunity of a whole lifetime. With this opportunity an effort can be made towards awakening. So, it will be a great mistake if someone keeps waiting until the moment of death to awaken. You can't awaken at the time of death. The *sadhana*, the journey towards awakening, will have to begin long before death; a preparation will have to be made for it. Without preparation one is sure to remain unconscious in death. Although, in a way, this unconscious state is for your own good if you are not yet ready to be born in a conscious state.

Around 1915, the ruler of Kashi had an abdominal operation. This was the first such operation ever performed in the world without the use of anesthesia. There were three British physicians who refused to perform the operation without giving anesthesia, saying it was impossible to have a man's stomach open for one-and-a-half to two hours during a major operation without making the patient unconscious. It was dangerous—the danger was that the patient might scream, move, jump or fall because of the unbearable pain; anything might happen. Hence the doctors were not ready.

But the ruler maintained there was no cause for concern as long as he remained in meditation and said he could easily remain in meditation for one-and-a-half to two hours. He was not willing to take the anesthetic; he said he wished to be operated upon in his conscious state. But the physicians were reluctant; they believed it was dangerous to have someone go through such pain in a conscious state. However, seeing no other alternative, the physicians first asked him, as an experiment, to go into meditation. Then they made a cut in his hand—there was not even a tremor. Only two hours later did he complain that his hand hurt; he did not feel anything for two hours. Subsequently, the operation was performed.

That was the first operation ever to be performed in the world where physicians worked on a patient's open stomach for an hour-and-a-half without giving anesthetic. And the ruler remained fully conscious throughout the operation. Deep meditation is required to be in such awareness. The meditation has to be so deep as to make one totally aware, without an iota of doubt, that the self and the body are separate.

Even the slightest identification with the body can be dangerous.

Death is the biggest surgical operation there is. No physician has ever performed an operation as big as this—because in death, there is a mechanism to transplant the entire vital energy, the *prana*, from one physical body into another physical body. No one has ever performed such a phenomenal operation, nor can it ever be done. We may sever one part of the body or another, or transplant one part or another, but in the case of death, the entire vital energy has to be taken from one body and entered into another.

Nature has kindly seen to it that we become fully unconscious at the occurrence of this phenomenon. It is for our own good; we might not be able to bear that much pain. It is possible that the reason why we become unconscious is because the pain of death is so unbearable. It is in our own interest that we become unconscious; nature does not allow us to remember passing through death.

In every life we repeat almost the same mistakes we have repeated in our past lives. If we could only recall what we did in our past lives, we might not fall into the same ditches again. And if we could only remember what we did throughout our previous lives, we could no longer remain the same as we are now. It is impossible we could remain the same, because time and time again we have amassed wealth and every time death has made all that wealth meaningless. If we could recall this, we might not carry, any longer, the same craze for money within us as we did before. We have fallen in love a thousand times, and time and time again it has ultimately proven to be meaningless. If we could recall this, our craze for falling in love with others and for having others fall in love with us would disappear. Thousands upon thousands of times we have been ambitious, egoistic; we have attained success, high position, and in the end all of it has turned out to be useless, all of it has turned to dust. If we could recall this, perhaps our ambition would lose its steam, and then we would not remain the same people we are now.

Since we do not remember our past lives, we keep moving in almost the same circle. Man does not realize that he has gone through the same circle many times before, and that he is going through it once again in the same hope he carried with him so often before. And then death ruins all hopes. And once again the cycle begins. And man moves in circles like an ox on a water-wheel.

One can save oneself from this harm, but it requires great awareness and continuous experimentation. On cannot start waiting for death all at once, because one cannot become suddenly aware during such a big operation, under such a great trauma. We will have to experiment slowly. We will have to experiment slowly with small miseries to see how we can be aware while going through them.

For example, you have a headache. At one and the same time you become aware and begin to feel that *you* have a headache—not that the head is in pain. So one will have to experiment on the little headache and learn to feel that, "The pain is in the head and *I* am aware of it."

When Swami Ram was in America people had great difficulty following him in the beginning. When the President of America paid him a visit, he was puzzled too. He asked, "What language is this?"—because Ram used to speak in the third person. He would not say, "I am hungry," he would say, "Ram is hungry." He would not say, "I have a headache," he would say, "Ram has a severe headache."

In the beginning people had great difficulty following him. For example, he once said, "Last night Ram was freezing." When asked who he was referring to, he replied that he was referring to "Ram". When he was asked, "Which Ram?" he said, pointing to himself, "This Ram—the poor guy was freezing cold last night. We kept laughing and asked, 'How's the cold Ram?' "

He would say, "Ram was walking on the street and some people began swearing at him. We had a belly laugh and said, 'How do you like the swearing, Ram? If you seek honor, you are bound to meet with insult.' " When people asked, "Who are you talking about? Which Ram?" he would point to himself.

You will have to start experimenting with minor kinds of miseries. You encounter them every day in life; they are present every day—not only miseries, you will have to include happiness in the experiment also, because it is more difficult to be aware in happiness than it is to be in misery. It is not so difficult to experience that your head and the pain in it are two separate things, but it is more difficult to experience that,

"The body is separate and the joy of being healthy is separate from me too—I am not even that." It is difficult to maintain this distance when we are happy because in happiness we like to be close to it. While in misery, we obviously want to feel separate, away from it. Should it become certain that the pain is separate from us, we want it to stay that way so we can be free of it.

You will have to experiment on how to remain aware in misery as well as in happiness. One who carries out such experiments often brings misery upon himself, of his own free will, in order to experience it. This is basically the secret of all asceticism: it is an experiment to undergo voluntary pain. For example, a man is on a fast. By remaining hungry he is trying to find out what effect hunger has on his consciousness. Ordinarily, a person who is on a fast hasn't the slightest notion of what he is doing—he only knows that he is hungry and looks forward to having his meal the next day.

The fundamental purpose of fasting is to experience that, "Hunger is there, but it is far away from me. The body is hungry, 'I' am not." So by inducing hunger voluntarily, one is trying to know, from within, if hunger is there. Ram is hungry—"I" am not hungry. I know hunger is there, and this has to become a continuous knowing until I reach a point where a distance occurs between me and the hunger—where "I" no longer remain hungry—even in hunger *I* no longer remain hungry. Only the body stays hungry and I know it. *I* simply remain a knower. Then the meaning of fasting becomes very profound; then it does not mean merely remaining hungry.

Normally, one who goes on a fast keeps repeating twenty-four hours a day that he is hungry, that he has not eaten any food that day. His mind continues to fantasize about the food he will eat the next day and plans for it. This kind of fasting is meaningless. Then it is merely abstaining from food. The distinction between abstaining from food and fasting, *upvasa*, is this: fasting means residing closer and closer. Closer to what? It means coming closer to the self by creating a distance from the body.

The word *upvasa* does not imply going without food. Upvasa means residing—closer and closer. Closer to what? It means closer to the self, residing closer to the self and further away from the body. Then it is also possible that a man may eat and yet remain in the state of fasting. If, while eating, he knows from within that eating is taking place elsewhere and the consciousness is totally separate from the act, then it is *upvasa*. And it is also possible that a man may not really be fasting even though he may have denied himself food; for he may be too conscious of being hungry, that he is dying of hunger. *Upvasa* is a psychological awareness of the separation of the self and the physical state of hunger.

Other pains of a similar type can also be created voluntarily, but creating such voluntary pain is a very deep experiment. A man may lie on thorns just to experience that the thorns only prick the body and not his self. Thus a misery can be invited in order to experience the disassociation of consciousness from the physical plane.

But there are already enough uninvited miseries in the world—no need to invite any more. Already much misery is available—one should start experimenting with it. Miseries come uninvited anyway. If, during the uninvited misery, one can maintain the awareness that "I am separate from my suffering" then the suffering becomes a *sadhana*, a spiritual discipline.

One will have to continue this *sadhana* even with happiness which has come on its own. In suffering, it is possible we may succeed in deceiving ourselves because one would like to believe that "I am not pain." But when it comes to happiness, a man wants to identify himself with it because he already believes that "I am happy." Hence the *sadhana* is even more difficult with happiness.

Nothing, in fact, is more painful than feeling that we are separate from our happiness. Actually, a man wants to drown himself completely in happiness and forget that he is separate from it. Happiness drowns us; misery disconnects us and sets us apart from the self. Somehow, we come to believe that our identification with suffering is only because we have no other choice, but we welcome happiness with our whole being.

Be aware in the pain which comes your way; be aware in the happiness which comes your way—and occasionally, just as an experiment, be aware in invited pain also, because in it, things are a little different. We can never fully identify ourselves with anything we invite upon ourselves. The very knowledge that it is an invited thing creates the distance. The guest who comes to your home does not belong there—he is a guest. Similarly, when we invite suffering as our guest, it is already something separate from us.

While walking barefoot a thorn gets into your foot. This is an accident and its pain will be overwhelming. This unfortunate accident is different from when you purposely take a thorn and press it against your foot—knowing every moment that you are piercing the foot with the thorn and watching the pain. I am not asking you to go ahead and torture yourself; as it is, there is enough suffering already—what I mean is: first be alert in going through both suffering and happiness; then later, one day, invite some misery and see how far away from it you can set your consciousness.

Remember, the experiment of inviting misery is of great signifigance, because everyone wants to invite happiness but no one wants to invite misery. And the interesting thing is that the misery we don't want comes on its own, and the happiness we seek never comes. Even when it comes by chance, it remains outside our door. The happiness we beckon to never comes, while the happiness we never ask for walks right in. When a person gathers enough strength to invite misery, it means he is so happy that he can invite suffering now. He is so blissful that now there is no difficulty for him to invite suffering. Now misery can be asked to come and stay.

But this is a very deep experiment. Until we are prepared to undertake such an experiment, we must try to become aware of whatever suffering comes our way on its own. If we go on becoming more and more aware each time we come across misery, we will gather enough capability to remain conscious even when death arrives. Then nature will allow us to stay awake in death too. Nature, as well, will figure that if the man can stay conscious in pain, he can also remain conscious in death. No one can stay conscious in death, all of a sudden, without having had a previous experience in kind.

A man named P. D. Ouspensky died some years ago. He was a great mathematician from Russia. He is the only person in this century who has done such extensive experiments in relation to death. Three months before his death, he became very ill. The physicians advised him to stay in bed, but in spite of this, he made such an incredible effort it is beyond imagination. He would not sleep at night; he traveled, walked, ran, was always on the move. The physicians were aghast; they said he needed complete rest. Ouspensky called all his close friends near him but did not say anything to them.

The friends who stayed with him for three months, until his death, have said that for the first time they saw, before their eyes, a man accepting death in a conscious state. They asked him why did he not follow the physicians' advice. Ouspensky replied, "I want to experience all kinds of pain, lest the pain of death be so great that I might become unconscious. I want to go through every pain before death; that can create such a stamina in me that I can be totally conscious when death come." So for three months he made an exemplary effort to go through all kinds of pain.

His friends have written that those who were hale and hearty would get tired, but not Ouspensky. The physicians insisted that he must have complete rest, otherwise it would cause him great harm—but to no avail. The night he died, Ouspensky kept walking back and forth in his room. The physicians who examined him declared that his legs had no more strength left to walk—and yet he kept walking the whole night.

He said, "I want to die walking, lest I might die sitting and become unconscious, or I might die sleeping and become unconscious." As he walked, he told his friends, "Just a little bit longer—ten more steps and all will be over. I am sinking, but I shall keep walking until I have taken the last step. I want to keep on doing something until the very end, otherwise death may catch me unawares. I may relax and go to sleep—I don't want this to happen at the moment of death."

Ouspensky died while taking his last step. Very few people on this earth have died walking like this. He fell down walking; that is, he fell only when his death occurred. Taking his last step, he said, "That's it; this is my last step. Now I am about to fall. But before departing let me tell you I dropped my body long ago. You will see my body being released now, but I have been seeing for a long time now that the body has dropped and still I exist. The links with the body have all been broken and yet, inside, I still exist. Now only the body will fall—there is no way for *me* to fall down."

At the time of his death, his friends saw a kind of light in his eyes. A peace, joy and radiance were visible—which shine through when one is standing on the threshold of the world beyond. But one needs to make preparations for this, a continuous preparation. If a person prepares himself fully, then death becomes a wonderful experience. There is no other phenomenon more valuable than this, because what is revealed at the time of death can never be known otherwise. Then death looks like a friend, for only at the occurrence of death can we experience that we are a "living organism"—not before that.

Remember, the darker the night, the brighter the stars. The flash of lightning stands out like a silver strand, the darker the clouds are. Similarly, when, in its full form, death surrounds us from all sides, at that moment the very center of life manifests in all its glory—never before that. Death surrounds us like darkness, and in the middle that very center of life—call it *atman*, the soul—shines in its full splendor; the surrounding darkness makes it luminous. But at that moment we become unconscious. At the very moment of death, which could otherwise become the moment to know our being, we become unconscious. Hence one will have to make preparations towards raising one's consciousness. Meditation is that preparation.

Meditation is an experiment in how one attains to a gradual, voluntary death. It is an experiment in how one moves within and then leaves the body. If one meditates throughout his life, he will attain to total meditation at the moment of death.

When death happens in full consciousness, the soul of the person takes its next birth in full consciousness. Then the very first day of his new life is not a day of ignorance but of full knowledge. Even in the mother's womb he remains fully conscious. Only one more birth is possible for one who has died in a conscious state. There is no other birth possible for him after that—because one who has experienced what birth is, what death is and what life is, attains liberation.

One who has taken birth in awareness, we have called him *avatara, teerthankara,* Buddha, Jesus, Krishna. And the thing that distinguishes them from the rest of us is awareness. They are awakened and we are asleep. Having taken conscious birth, this becomes their final journey on earth. They have something we don't have, which, painstakingly, they continue to bring to us. The difference between the awakened ones and us is simply this: their previous death and the birth thereafter happened in a state of awareness—hence they live their entire life in awareness.

People in Tibet do a little experiment called *Bardo.* It is a very valuable experiment, carried out only at the time of death. When someone is about to die, people who know gather around him and make him do *Bardo.* But only he who has meditated in his life can be made to go through *Bardo*—not otherwise. In the experiment of *Bardo,* as soon as a person dies, instructions are given from the outside that he should remain fully awake. He is told to keep watching whatever follows next, because in that state, many times things happen which the dying person can never understand. New phenomena are not so easy to follow right away.

If a person can stay consocus after death, for a while he will not know that he is dead. When people carry his dead body and start burning it at the cremation ground only then will he come to know for certain that he is dead—because nothing actually dies inside, just a distance is created. In life, this distance has never been experienced before. The experience is so novel it cannot be grasped through conventional definition. The person merely feels that something has separated. But something has died, and that he only understands when people all around him start weeping and crying, falling over his body in grief, getting ready to carry the body away for cremation.

There is a reason why the body is brought for cremation so soon. The reason for burning or cremating the body as soon as possible is to assure the soul that the body is dead, that it is burned to ashes. But this, a man can know only if he has died in awareness; a man dying in an unconscious state cannot know this. So in order for a man to see his body burning in *Bardo*, he is prompted, "Take a good look at your burning body. Don't run or move away from their sight in haste. When people bring your body for cremation, make sure you accompany them and be present there. Watch your body being cremated with perfect attention, so that next time you do not get attached to the physical body."

Once you see something burning to ashes, your attachment for it disappears. Others will, of course, see your body being cremated, but if you also see it, you will lose all your attachment for it. Normally, in nine hundred and ninety-nine cases out of a thousand, the man is unconscious at the time of death; he has no knowledge of it. On the one occasion when he is conscious, he moves away from watching his burning body; he escapes from the cremation ground. So in *Bardo* he is told, "Look, don't miss this opportunity. Watch your body being cremated; just watch it once and for all. Watch that which you have been identifying your self with all along being destroyed totally. Watch it being reduced to ashes for certain, so that you may remember in your next birth who you are."

As soon as a person dies he enters into a new world, one we know nothing about. That world can be scary and frightening to us because it is neither like nor unlike any of our experiences. In fact it has no connection with life on earth whatsoever. Facing this new world is more frightening than it would be if a man were to find himself in a strange country where everyone was a stranger to him, where he was unacquainted with their language, with their ways of living. He would obviously be very perturbed and confused.

The world we live in is a world of physical bodies. As we leave this world the incorporeal world begins—a world we have never experienced. It is even more frightening, because in our world, no matter how strange the place, how different its people and their ways of living, there is still a bond between us and them: it is a realm of human beings. Entering into the world of bodiless spirits can be an experience frightening beyond imagination.

Ordinarily, we pass through it in an unconscious state, and so we don't notice it. But one who goes through it in a conscious state gets into great difficulty. So in *Bardo* there is an attempt to explain to the person what kind of a world it will be, what will happen there, what kind of beings he will come across. Only those who have been through deep meditation can be taken through this experiment—not otherwise.

Lately, I have often felt that those friends who are practicing meditation can be taken into the *Bardo* experiment in some form or other. But this is possible only when they have gone through deep meditation; otherwise, they would not even be able to hear what is being said to them. They would not be able to hear what is being said at the moment of death, or follow what is being told to them. In order to follow what is being said, a very silent and empty mind is needed. As the consciousness begins to fade and disappear, and as all earthly ties start being severed, only a very silent mind can hear messages given from this world; they cannot be heard otherwise.

Remember, it can be done only in respect to death, if anything; nothing can be done with respect to birth. But whatsoever we do with death, it consequently affects our birth as well. We are born in the same state in which we die.

An awakened one exercises his choice in selecting the womb. This shows that he never chooses anything blindly, unconsciously. He chooses his parents just as a rich man chooses his house. A poor man cannot have a house of his choice. You need a certain capacity to choose. One needs a capability to buy a house. A poor man never chooses his house. One should say that actually the house chooses the poor man; a poor house chooses a poor man. A millionaire decides where he should reside, what the garden should look like, where the doors and windows should be fixed—the sunlight should enter from the east or west; how the ventilation should be, how spacious the house should be—he chooses everything.

An awakened one chooses a womb for himself; that is his choice. Individuals like Mahavira or Buddha are not born anywhere and everywhere. They take birth after considering all possibilities: how the body will be and from which parents it will be conceived; what the energy will be like, how powerful he will be; what kind of facilities will be available to him. They take birth after looking into all of this. They have a clear choice of what to choose, where to go; hence, from the very first day of their birth they live the life of their own choice.

The joy of living a life of one's own choice is altogether different because freedom begins with having a life of one's own choice. There cannot be the same kind of joy in a life which is given to you because then it becomes servitude. In such cases one is merely pushed into life and then whatever happens, happens — the person has no role to play in it.

If such an awakening becomes possible then the choice can definitely be made. If the very birth happens *out* of our choice, then we can live the rest of our lives *in* choice. Then we can live like a *jeevan-mukta*. One who dies in an awakened state is born in an awakened state and then he lives his life in a liberated state.

We often hear the word *jeevan-mukta*, although we may not know what the word means. *Jeevan-mukta* means: one who is born in an awakened state. Only such a person can be a *jeevan-mukta;* otherwise, he may work his whole life for liberation, yet he can attain freedom only in his next life — he will not be free in this life. In order to be a *jeevan-mukta* in this life a man must have the freedom to choose from the very first day of his birth. And this is possible only if one has attained to full consciousness in the dying moment of one's previous life.

But at this point that is not the question. Life is here, death has not arrived yet. It is sure to come; there is nothing more certain than death. There can be doubt regarding other things, but about death nothing whatsoever is in doubt. There are people who have doubts about God, there are others who have doubts about the soul, but you may never have come across a man who has doubts about death. It is inevitable — it is sure to come; it is already on its way. It is approaching closer and closer every moment. We can utilize the moments which are available before death for our awakening. Meditation is a technique to that effect. My effort in these three days will be to help you understand that meditation is the technique for that very awakening.

A friend has asked: *What is the relation between meditation and* Jati-smaran, *past life remembering?*

Jati-smaran means: a method of recalling past lives. It is a way to remember our previous existences. It is a form of meditation. It is a specific application of meditation. For example, one might ask, "What is a river, and what is a canal?" Our answer would be that the canal is a specific application of the river itself — well planned, but controlled and systematic. The river is chaotic, unrestrained; it too will reach somewhere, but its destination is not certain. The destination of the canal is assured.

Meditation is like a big river — it will reach to the ocean; it is sure to reach. Meditation will surely bring you to God. There are, however, other intermediary applications of meditation also. Like small tributaries these can be directed into canals of meditation. *Jati-smaran* is one such auxiliary method of meditation. We can channelize the power of meditation towards our past lives also; meditation simply means the focusing of attention. There can be applications where one's attention is focused on a given object, and one such application is *jati-smaran* — focusing on the dormant memories of past lives.

Remember, memories are never erased; a memory either remains latent or it arises. But the latent memory appears to be erased. If I ask you what you did on January 1, 1950, you will not be able to answer — which does not mean that you might not have done anything on that day. But suddenly the day of January 1, 1950 feels like a total blank. It could not have been blank; as it passed, it was filled with activity. But today it feels like a blank. Similarly, today will become blank tomorrow as well. Ten years from now there will be no trace left of today.

So it is not that January 1, 1950 did not exist, or that you did not exist on that day — what is implied is that since you are unable to recall that day, how can you believe it ever existed? But it did exist and there is a way to know about it. Meditation can be focused in that direction as well. As soon as the light of meditation falls on that day, to your surprise you will see that it looks more alive than it ever was before.

For example, a person enters a dark room and moves around with a flashlight. When he turns the light to the left, the right side becomes dark — but nothing disappears on the right side. When he moves the light to the right, the right side becomes alive again, but the left side remains hidden in the dark.

Meditation has a focus, and if one wants to channel it in a particular direction then it has to be used like a flashlight. If, however, one wants to turn it towards the divine, then meditation has to be applied like a lamp. Please understand this carefully.

The lamp has no focus of its own; it is unfocused. A lamp merely burns and its light spreads all around. A lamp has no interest in lighting up one direction or the other; whatsoever falls within the radius of light is lit up. But the form of a flashlight is like a focused lamp.

In a flashlight we keep all the light and shine it in one direction. So it is possible that under a burning lamp things may become visible, but hazy, and in order to see them clearly we concentrate the light on one place — it becomes a flashlight; then the thing becomes clearly visible, however, the remaining objects are lost to view. In fact, if a man wants to see an object clearly he will have to focus his total meditation in one direction only and turn the rest of the area into darkness.

One who wants to know the truth of life directly will develop his meditation like a lamp — that will be his sole purpose. And, in fact, the lamp's only objective is to see itself; if it can shine this much it is enough — that's the end of it. But if some special application of the lamp has to be made — such as remembering past lives — then meditation will have to be channeled in one direction.

I will share with you two or three clues as to how meditation can be channelized in that direction. I won't give you all the clues because, most likely, hardly any of you have any intent of doing so, and those who have can see me personally. So I will mention two or three clues which, of course, won't really enable you to experiment with remembering past lives, but will give you just an idea. I won't discuss the whole thing because it's not advisable for everyone to experiment with this idea. Also, this experiment can often put you in danger.

Let me tell you of an incident so that what I am saying becomes clear to you. For about two or three years, in respect to meditation, a lady professor stayed in touch with me. She was very insistent on experimenting with *jati-smaran*, on learning about her past life. I helped her with the experiment; however, I also advised her that it would be better if she didn't do the experiment until her meditation was fully developed, otherwise it could be dangerous.

As it is, a single life's memories are difficult to bear — should the memories of the past three or four lives break the barrier and flood in, a person can go mad. That's why nature has planned it so we go on forgetting the past. Nature has given us a greater ability to forget more than you can remember, so that your mind does not have a greater burden than it can carry. A heavy burden can be borne only after the capacity of your mind has increased, and trouble begins when the weight of these memories falls on you before this capacity has been raised. But she remained persistent. She paid no heed to my advice and went into the experiment.

When the flood of her past life's memory finally burst upon her, she came running to me around two o'clock in the morning. She was a real mess; she was in great distress. She said, "Somehow this has got to stop. I don't ever want to look at that side of things." But it is not so easy to stop the tide of memory once it has broken loose. It is very difficult to shut the door once it crashes down — the door does not simply open, it breaks open. It took about fifteen days — only then did the wave of memories stop. What was the problem?

This lady used to claim that she was very pious, a woman of impeccable character. When she encountered the memory of her past life, when she was a prostitute, and the scenes of her prostitution began to emerge, her whole being was shaken. Her whole morality of this life was disturbed.

In this sort of revelation, it is not as if the visions belong to someone else — the same woman who claimed to be chaste now saw herself as a prostitute. It often happens that someone who was a prostitute in a past life becomes deeply virtuous in the next; it is a reaction to the suffering of the past life. It is the memory of the pain and the hurt of the previous life that turns her into a chaste woman.

It often happens that people who were scoundrels in past lives become holy men in this life. Hence there is quite a deep relationship between scoundrels and holy men. Such a reaction often takes place, and the reason is, what we come to know hurts us and so we swing to the opposite extreme.

The pendulum of our minds keeps moving in the opposite direction. No sooner does the pendulum reach the left than it moves back to the right. It barely touches the right when it swings back to the left. When you see the pendulum of a clock moving towards the left, be assured it is gathering energy to move back to the right — it will go as far to the right as it has gone to the left. Hence, in life it often happens that a virtuous person becomes a sinner, and a sinner becomes virtuous.

This is very common; this sort of oscillation occurs in everyone's life. Do not think, therefore, that it is a general rule that one who has become a holy man in this life must have been a holy man in his past life also. It is not necessarily so. What *is* necessarily so is the exact reverse of it — he is laden with the pain of what he went through in his past life and has turned to the opposite.

I have heard . . .

A holy man and a prostitute once lived opposite each other. Both died on the same day. The soul of the prostitute was to be taken to heaven, and that of the holy man, however, to hell. The envoys who had come to take them away were very puzzled. They kept asking each other, "What went wrong? Is this a mistake? Why are we to take the holy man to hell? Wasn't he a holy man?"

The wisest among them said, "He was a holy man all right, but he envied the prostitute. He always brooded over the parties at her place and the pleasures that went on there. The notes of music which came drifting to his house would jolt him to his very core. No admirer of the prostitute, sitting in front of her, was ever moved as much as he — listening to the sounds coming from her residence, the sounds of the small dancing bells she wore on her ankles. His whole attention always remained focused on her place. Even while worshipping God, his ears were tuned to the sounds which came from her house.

"And the prostitute? While she languished in the pit of misery, she always wondered what unknown bliss the holy man was in. Whenever she saw him carrying flowers for morning worship, she wondered, 'When will I be worthy to take flowers of worship to the temple? I am so impure that I can hardly even gather enough courage to enter the temple.' The holy man was never as lost in the incense smoke, in the shining lamps, in the sounds of worship as the prostitute was. The prostitute always longed for the life of the holy man, and the holy man always craved for the pleasures of the prostitute."

Their interests and attitudes, so totally opposite each other's, so totally different from each other's, had completely changed. This often happens — and there are laws at work behind these happenings.

So when the memory of her past life came back to this lady professor, she was very hurt. She felt hurt because her ego was shattered. What she learned about her past life shook her, and now she wanted to forget it. I had warned her in the first place not to recall her past life without sufficient preparation.

Since you have asked, I shall tell you a few basic things so that you can understand the meaning of *jati-smaran*. But they won't help you to experiment with it. Those who wish to experiment will have to look into it separately.

The first thing is that if the purpose of *jati-smaran* is simply to know one's past life, then one needs to turn one's mind away from the future. Our mind is future-oriented, not past-oriented. Ordinarily, our mind is centered in the future; it moves toward the future. The stream of our thoughts is future-oriented, and it is in life's interests that the mind be future-oriented, not past-oriented. Why be concerned with the past? It is gone, it is finished — so we are interested in that which is about to come. That's why we keep asking astrologers what is in store for us in the future. We are interested in finding out what is going to happen in the future. One who wants

to remember the past has to give up, absolutely,
any interest in the future. Because once the
flashlight of the mind is focused on the future;
once the stream of thoughts has begun to move
towards the future, then it cannot be turned
back towards the past.

So the first thing one needs to do is to break
oneself completely away from the future for a
few months, for a certain specific period of time.
One should decide that he will not think of the
future for the next six months. If a thought of the
future does occur, he will simply salute it and let
it go; he will not become identified with and carried away by any feeling of future. So the first
thing is that, for six months, he will allow that
there is no future and will flow towards the past.
And so, as soon as future is dropped, the current
of thoughts turns towards the past.

First you will have to go back in this life; it is
not possible to return to a past life all at once.
And there are techniques for going back in this
life. For example, as I said earlier, you don't remember now what you did on January 1, 1950.
There is a technique to find out. If you go into
the meditation which I have suggested, after ten
minutes — when the meditation has gone
deeper: the body is relaxed, the breathing is relaxed, the mind has become quiet — then let
only one thing remain in your mind: "What took
place on January 1, 1950?" Let your entire mind
focus on it. If that remains the only note echoing
in your mind, in a few days you will all of a sudden find a curtain is raised: the first of January
appears and you begin to relive each and every
event of that day from dawn to dusk. And you

will see the first of January in far more detail than you may have seen it, in actuality, on that very day — because on that day, you may not have been this aware. So, first, you will need to experiment by regressing in this life.

It is very easy to regress to the age of five; it becomes very difficult to go beyond that age. And so, ordinarily, we cannot recall what happened before the age of five; that is the farthest back we can go. A few people might remember up to the third year, but beyond that it becomes extremely difficult — as if a barrier comes across the entrance and everything becomes blocked. A person who becomes capable of recalling will be able to fully awaken the memory of any day up to the age of five. The memory starts to be completely revived.

Then one should test it. For example, note down the events of today on a piece of paper and lock it away. Two years later recall this day: open the note and compare your memory with it. You will be amazed to find that you have been able to recall more than what was noted on the paper. The events are certain to return to your memory.

Buddha has called this *alaya-vigyan*. There exists a corner in our minds which Buddha has named *alaya-vigyan*. *Alaya-vigyan* means: the storehouse of consciousness. As we store all our junk in the basement of a house, similarly, there is a storehouse of consciousness that collects memories. Birth after birth, everything is stored in it. Nothing is ever removed from there, because a man never knows when he might need those things. The physical body changes, but, in our ongoing existence, that storehouse continues, remains with us. One never knows when it might be needed. And whatsoever we have done in our lives, whatsoever we have experienced, known, lived — everything is stored there.

One who can remember up to the age of five can go beyond that age — it is not very difficult. The nature of the experiment will be the same. Beyond the age of five there is yet another door which will lead you to the point of your birth, to when you appeared on earth. Then one comes across another difficulty, because the memories of one's stay in the mother's womb never disappear either. One can penetrate these memories too, reaching to the point of conception, to the moment when the genes of the mother and father unite and the soul enters. A man can enter into his past lives only after having reached this point; he cannot move into them directly. One has to undertake this much of the return journey, only then is it possible to move into one's past life as well.

After having entered the past life, the first memory to come up will be of the last event that took place in that life. Remember, however, that this will cause some difficulty and will make little sense. It is as if we run a film from the end or read a novel backwards — we feel lost. And so, entering into one's past life for the first time will be quite confusing because the sequence of events will be in the reverse order.

As you go back into your past life, you will come across death first, then old age, youth, childhood, and then birth. It will be in reverse order, and in that order it will be very difficult to figure out what is what. So when the memory surfaces for the first time, you feel tremendously restless and troubled, because it is difficult to make sense; it is as if you are looking at a film or reading a novel from the end. Perhaps you will only make heads or tails of an event after rearranging the order several times. So the greatest effort involved in going back to the memories of one's past life is seeing, in reverse order, events which ordinarily take place in the right order. But, after all, what is the right or reverse order? It is just a question of how we entered the world and how we departed from it.

We sow a seed in the beginning, and the flower appears in the end. However, if one were to take a reverse look at this phenomenon, the flower would come first, followed in sequence by the bud, the plant, the leaves, the saplings and in the end the seed. Since we have no previous knowledge of this reverse order, it takes a lot of time to rearrange memories coherently and to figure out the nature of events clearly. The strangest thing is that death will come first, followed by old age, illness, and then youth; things will occur in the reverse order. Or, if you were married and then divorced, while going down memory lane the divorce will come first, followed by the love and then the marriage.

It will be extremely difficult to follow events in this regressive fashion, because normally we understand things in a one-dimensional way. Our minds are one-dimensional. To look at things in opposite order is very difficult — we are not used to such an experience; we are accustomed

to moving in a linear direction. With effort, however, one can understand the events of a past life
by following, in sequence, the reverse order.
Surely, it will be an incredible experience.

Going through memories in this reverse order
will be a very amazing experience, because seeing the divorce first and then the love and then
the marriage, will make it instantly clear that the
divorce was inevitable — the divorce was inher-
ent in the kind of love that happened; the divorce was the only ultimate possible outcome of
the kind of marriage that took place. But at the
time of that past life marriage we hadn't the
faintest idea it would eventually end in divorce.
And indeed, the divorce was the result of that
marriage. If we could see this whole thing in its
entirety, then falling in love today would become a totally different thing — because now we
could see the divorce in it beforehand, now we
could see the enmity around the corner even before making the friendship.

The memory of the past life will completely
turn this life upside-down, because now you
won't be able to live the way you lived in your
past life. In your previous life you felt — and the
same feeling exists even now — that success and
great happiness were to be found by making a
fortune. What you will see first in your previous
life is your state of unhappiness *before* seeing
how you made the fortune. This will clearly
show that instead of being a source of happiness, making the fortune led, in fact, to unhappiness — and friendship led to enmity, what was
thought to be love turned into hatred, and what
was considered a union resulted in separation.

Then, for the first time, you will see things in their right perspective, with their total import. And this implication will change your life, will change the way you are living now completely — it will be an entirely different situation.

I have heard that a man went to a monk and said, "I would be much obliged if you would accept me as your disciple." The monk refused. The man asked why he would not make him his disciple. The monk replied, "In my previous birth I had disciples who later turned into enemies. I have seen the whole thing and now I know that to make disciples means to make enemies, to make friends means to sow the seeds of enmity. Now I don't want to make any enemies, so I don't make any friends. I have known that to be alone is enough. Drawing someone close to you is, in a way, pushing the person away from you."

Buddha has said that the meeting with the beloved brings joy and the parting of the unbeloved also brings joy, that the parting of the beloved brings sorrow and the meeting with the unbeloved brings sorrow as well. This is how it was perceived; this is how it was understood. However, later we come to understand that the one we feel is our beloved can become the unbeloved, and the one we considered the unbeloved can become a beloved. And so, with the recollection of past memories, the existing situations will change radically; they will be seen in an entirely different perspective.

Such recollections are possible, though neither necessary nor inevitable, and sometimes, in meditation, these memories may strike

unexpectedly as well. If the memories of past
lives ever do come all of a sudden — without
being involved in any experiment, but simply
keeping up with one's meditation — don't take
much interest in them. Just look at them; be a
witness to them — because ordinarily, the mind
is incapable of bearing such vast turbulence all at
once. Attempting to cope with it, there is a distinct possibility of going mad.

Once a girl was brought to me. She was about
eleven years old. Unexpectedly, she had remembered three of her past lives. She had not ex-
perimented with anything; but often, for some
reason mistakes do happen all of a sudden. This
was an error on the part of nature, not its grace
upon her; in some way nature had erred in her
case. It is the same as if someone had three eyes,
or four arms — this is an error. Four arms would
be much weaker than two arms; four arms
couldn't work as effectively as two arms could —
four arms would make the body weaker, not
stronger.

So the girl, eleven years old, remembered
three past lives, and many inquiries were made
into this case. In her previous life she had lived
about eighty miles from my present residence,
and in that life she died at the age of sixty. The
people she lived with then are now the residents
of my hometown, and she could recognize all of
them. Even in a crowd of thousands, she could
recognize her past relatives — her own brother,
her daughters; and her grandchildren — from
the daughters, from the sons-in-law. She could
recognize her distant relatives and tell many
things about them even they had forgotten.

Her elder brother is still alive. On his head there is a scar from a small injury. I asked the girl if she knew anything about that scar. The girl laughed and said, "Even my brother doesn't know about it. Let him tell you how and when he got that injury." The brother could not recall when the injury occurred; he had no idea at all, he said.

The girl said, "On the day of his wedding, my brother fell while he was mounting the marriage horse. He was ten years old then." The elderly people in the town supported her story, admitting that the brother had, indeed, fallen from the horse. And the man himself had no recollection of this event. Then, as well, the girl displayed a treasure she had buried in the house she had lived in during her previous life.

In her last birth she died at the age of sixty, and previous to that birth she had been born in a village somewhere in Assam. Then she had died at the age of seven. She could not give the village name, nor her address, but she could speak as much of the Assamese language as a seven-year-old child could. Also, she could dance and sing like a seven-year-old girl could. Many inquiries were made, but her family from that life could not be traced.

The girl has a past-life experience of sixty-seven years plus eleven years of this life. You can see in her eyes the resemblance to a seventy-five to seventy-eight-year-old woman, although she is actually eleven years old. She cannot play with children of her own age because she feels too old. Within her, she carries the memory of seventy-eight years; she sees herself as a seventy-eight-year-old woman. She cannot go to school because, although she is eleven, she can easily look upon her teacher as her son. So, even though her body is eleven years old, her mind and personality are those of a seventy-eight-year-old woman. She cannot play and frolic like a child; she is only interested in the kinds of serious things old women talk about. She is in agony; she is filled with tension. Her body and mind are not in harmony. She is in a very sad and painful state.

I advised her parents to bring the girl to me and to let me help her forget the memories of her past lives. Just as there is a method to revive memories, there is also a way to forget them. But her parents were enjoying the whole affair! Crowds of people came to see the girl; they began to worship her. The parents were not interested in having her forget the past. I warned them the girl would go mad, but they turned a deaf ear. Today she is on the verge of insanity, because she cannot bear the weight of so many memories. Another problem is, how to get her married? She finds it difficult to conceive of marriage when, in fact, she feels like an old woman of seventy-eight. There is no harmony of any kind within her; her body is young but the mind is old. It is a very difficult situation.

But this was an accident. You can also break open the passage with an experiment. But it is not necessary to go in that direction; however, those who still wish to pursue it, can experiment. But it is not necessary to go in that direction; however, those who still wish to pursue it, can experiment. But before moving into the experiment it is essential they go through deep meditation so their minds can become so silent and strong that when the flood of memories breaks upon them, they can accept it as a witnessing. When a man grows into being a witness, past lives appear to be no more than dreams to him. Then he is not tormented by the memories; now they mean nothing more than dreams.

When one succeeds in recalling past lives and they begin to appear like dreams, immediately one's present life begin to look like a dream too. Those who have called this world *maya* have not done so just to propound a doctrine of philosophy. *Jati-smaran* — recalling past lives — is at the base of it. Whosoever has remembered his past lives, for him the whole affair has suddenly turned into a dream, an illusion. Where are his friends of past lives? Where are his relatives, his wife and children, the houses he lived in? Where is that world? Where is everything he took to be so real? Where are those worries that gave him sleepless nights? Where are those pains and sufferings that seemed so insurmountable, that he carried like a dead weight on his back? And what became of the happiness he longed for? What happened to everything he so toiled and suffered for? If you ever remember your past life, and if you lived for seventy years then — whatever you might have seen in those seventy years, would that look like a dream or a reality? Indeed, it would look like a dream which had come and withered away.

I have heard . . .

Once a king's only son lay on his deathbed. For eight days he was in a coma — he couldn't be saved nor would death claim him. On the one hand the king prayed for his life, while on the other hand, aware of so much pain and suffering all around, he felt the futility of life at the same time. The king could not sleep for eight nights, but then, around four o'clock one morning, sleep overtook him and he began to dream.

We generally dream of those things which we have not fulfilled in life, and so the king, sitting by his only son, his dying son, dreamed that he had twelve strong and handsome sons. He saw himself as the emperor of a large kingdom, as the ruler of the whole earth, with large and beautiful palaces. And he saw himself as extremely happy. As he was dreaming all this . . .

Time runs faster in a dream; in a dream timing is totally different from our day-to-day time. In a moment a dream can cover a span of many years, and after waking up you will find it difficult to figure out how so many years were covered in a dream that lasted just a few moments! Time actually moves very fast in a dream; many years can be spanned in one moment.

So, just as the king was dreaming about his twelve sons and their beautiful wives, about his palaces and the great kingdom, the ill, twelve-year-old prince died. The queen screamed, and the king's sleep came to an abrupt end.

He awoke with a shock. Worriedly, the queen asked, "Why do you look so frightened? Why are there no tears in your eyes? Why don't you say something?" The king said, "No, I am not frightened, I am confused. I am in a great quandary. I am wondering who I should cry for? Should I cry for the twelve sons I had a moment ago, or should I cry for this son I have just lost? The thing that's bothering me is, who has died? And the strange thing is that when I was with those twelve sons, I had no knowledge of this son. He was nowhere at all; there was no trace of him, or of you. Now that I am out of the dream, this palace is here, you are here, my son is here — but those palaces and those sons have disappeared. Which is true? Is this true, or was that true? I cannot figure it out."

Once you remember your past lives, you will find it difficult to figure out whether what you are seeing in this life is true or not. You will realize you have seen the same stuff many times before and none of it has endured forever — everything is lost. Then the question will arise: "Is what I am seeing now just as true as what I saw before? Because this will run its course too and fade away like all other previous dreams."

When we watch a movie it appears to be real. After the film has ended, it takes us a few moments to come back to our reality, to acknowledge that what we saw in the theater was merely an illusion. In fact, many people who ordinarily are incapable of giving vent to their feelings are moved to tears in a movie. They feel greatly relieved, because otherwise, they would have had to find some other pretext for releasing their feelings. They let themselves cry or laugh in the theater. When we come out of the movie, the first thing that occurs to us is how deeply we let ourselves become identified with the happenings on the screen. If the same movie is seen every day the illusion gradually begins to clear. But then we also forget what happened to us

during the last movie, and once again, when we
go to a new film, we start believing in its events.

If we could regain the memories of our past
lives, our present birth would also begin to look
like a dream. How many times before have these
winds blown! How many times before have
these clouds moved in the sky! They all appeared and then they vanished, and so will the
ones here now — they are *already* in the process
of disappearing! If we can come to realize this,
we will experience what is known as *maya*.
Along with this we will also experience that all
happenings, all events are quite unreal — they
are never identical, but they are transient. One
dream comes, is followed by another dream, and
is followed by yet another dream. The pilgrim
starts from one moment and enters into the next
one. Moment after moment, the moments keep
disappearing, but the pilgrim continues moving
on.

So two experiences occur simultaneously: one,
the objective world is an illusion, *maya* — only
the observer is real; second, what appears is
false — only the seer, only the witness of it is
true. Appearances change every day — they
have always changed — only the witness, the
observer is the same as before, changeless. And
remember, as long as appearances seem real,
your attention will not focus on the onlooker, on
the witness. Only when appearances turn out to
be unreal does one become aware of the witness.

Hence, I say, remembering past lives is useful,
but only after you have gone deeper into meditation. Go deep into meditation so you may attain
the ability to see life as a dream. Becoming a

mahatma, a holy man, is as much of a dream as becoming a thief — you can have good dreams and you can have bad dreams. And the interesting thing is that the dream of being a thief is likely to dissolve soon, whereas the dream of being a *mahatma* takes a little longer to disappear because it seems so very enjoyable. And so the dream of being a *mahatma* is more dangerous than the dream of being a thief. We want to prolong our enjoyable dreams, while the painful ones dissolve by themselves. That's why it so often happens that a sinner succeeds in attaining to God while a holy man does not.

I have told you a few things about remembering your past lives, but you will have to go into meditation for this. Let us start to move within from this very day onward; only then can we be prepared for what follows next. Without this preparation, it is difficult to enter into past lives.

For example, there is a big house with underground cellars. If a man, standing outside the house, wants to enter the cellars, he will first have to step inside the house, because the way to the cellar is from inside the house. Our past lives are like cellars. Once upon a time we lived there, and then we abandoned them — now we are living somewhere else. Nevertheless, we are standing outside the house at this point. In order to uncover the memories of past lives, we shall have to enter the house. There is nothing difficult, bothersome or dangerous about it.

Another friend has asked, *My friend, who is a yogi, claims he was a sparrow in his past life. Is this possible?*

It is possible that in the course of his evolution a man may have once been an animal, but he cannot be born as an animal again. In the process of evolution one cannot fall back; retrogression is impossible. It is possible to move ahead from the previous form of birth, but it is not possible, from an advanced form of birth, to fall back. There is no going back in this world; there is no chance. There are only two ways — either we move ahead or stay where we are; we cannot go back.

It is just as when a child passes first grade he moves on to the second grade — but if he fails he remains in the first grade. There is no way, however, to pull him below first grade. Similarly, if he fails in the second grade we can leave him there, but in no way can we bring him back to the first grade. We may either remain in one species for a very long time or move forward into the next species, but we cannot go back to a species lower than where we are.

It is indeed possible for someone to have previously been an animal or a bird; he must have been. But how long he remained in those species is a different matter. If we delve into our past lives, we will be able to recall the species we have passed through so far. We may have been an animal, a bird, a little sparrow . . . lower and lower. Once, we must have been at such a point of inertness where it is difficult to locate any sign of consciousness.

Mountains are alive as well; however, they contain almost no consciousness. They contain ninety-nine percent inertness and one percent consciousness. As life evolves, consciousness keeps on growing and inertness keeps on decreasing. God is one hundred percent consciousness. The difference between God and matter is of percentage. The difference between God and matter is of quantity, not of quality. That's why matter can ultimately become God.

It is neither strange nor difficult to accept that a man may have been an animal in his past life. What is really amazing is that in spite of being human we behave like animals! It is not at all surprising that in some past life we have all been animals, but even as humans our consciousness can be so low that we may appear like humans only on the physical level. If we look into our tendencies, it seems that although we are no longer animals we have not yet become human beings either; it seems we are stuck somewhere in between. As soon as an opportunity arises, we don't lose much time in reverting to the animal level once again.

For example, you are walking along the road like a gentleman and some fellow comes and punches you, swears at you. Instantly, the gentleman in you gives way and you find yourself expressing the same animal in you that you must have been in some past life. Scratch the surface a little and the beast emerges from within — and it comes out so violently that one wonders if the person was ever a human being at all.

Our state of being now contains all we have ever been before. There is layer upon layer of all the states we have been through in the past. If we dig inside a little, we can reach to the inner layers of our being — we can even reach the

state when we were a rock; that too constitutes a
layer inside. Deep down inside we are still rocks;
that's why when someone pushes us to that
layer we behave like a rock, we can act like a
rock. We can also behave like animals — in fact,
we do. What lies ahead of us are merely our
potentialities — they are not layers. Hence, at
times, although we take a jump and touch these
potentialities, we drop back to earth again.

We can be gods some day, but at present
we're not. We have the potential to become divine; however, what we are now consists of
what we have been in the past.

So there are these two things: if we dig within,
we come across our various past states of being;
and if we are thrown forward in the chain of
births, we experience the states which lie ahead
of us. However, just as when someone takes a
jump — for a second he goes off the ground and
into the air, but the very next moment he is back
on the ground — at times we jump out of our
animal state and become human beings, but
then we revert to the same state again. If you ob-
serve carefully, you will find that in a twenty-
four-hour period, only once in a while, at certain
moments, are we truly human beings. And we
all know this only too well.

You must have observed beggars. They always come to beg in the morning. They never
come in the evening, because by evening the
possibility of someone remaining a human being
is virtually non-existent. In the morning, when a
man gets up — refreshed by a good night's rest,
fresh and cheerful — the beggar hopes he will be
a little humane. He does not expect any charity

in the evening because he knows what the man has gone through the whole day — the office, the marketplace, the riots and protests, the newspapers and the politicians — all must have created a mess for him. Everything must have aggravated and activated the animal layers inside him. By evening the man is tired; he has turned into a beast. That's why you see beasts in nightclubs, displaying beastly tendencies. Man, tired of being a human the whole day, craves for alcohol, for noise, for gambling, for dancing, for striptease — he wants to be among other beasts. The nightclubs cater to the animal in man. This is the reason why mornings are the best for prayer, why the evening is ill-suited for it. In all the temples the bells toll in the morning; at night the doors open to the nightclubs, the casinos, the bars. Prostitutes are unable to invite anyone in the morning, they invite their customers only at night.

After a hard day's work, man turns into an animal; hence the world of night is different from the world of the day. The mosque gives the call to prayer in the morning, and the temple rings its bells in the morning. There is some hope that the man, up and refreshed in the morning, will turn towards God; there is less hope for this to happen from a man who is tired in the evening.

For the same reason, there is much hope that children will turn towards God, but there is less hope for old people — they are in the twilight of their lives; life must have taken everything away from them by now. So, one should start on the journey as soon as possible, as early in the morning as possible. The evening is sure to descend — but, before it descends, if we have set out on the journey in the morning, it is possible that, in the evening, we may find ourselves in the temple of the divine as well.

So our friend is right in asking whether it is possible that a man may have been an animal or a bird in his past life. What we need to be aware of, though, is not to continue to be a bird or a beast in this life.

Before we move into the meditation, let us understand a few things. First of all, you have to let yourself go completely. If you hold yourself back even a tiny bit, it will become a hurdle in meditation. Let yourself go as if you are dead, as if you have really died. Death has to be accepted as if it has already arrived, as if all else has died and we are sinking deeper and deeper within. Now only that which always survives will survive. We will drop everything else which can die. That's why I have said that this is an experiment with death.

There are three parts to this experiment. The first is: relaxation of the body; second: relaxation of breathing; third: relaxation of thought. Body, breathing and thought — all these have to be slowly let go of.

Please sit at a distance from each other. It is possible that somebody may fall, so keep a little distance between yourselves. Move a little back or come a little forward, but just see to it that you don't sit too close to each other; otherwise the whole time you will be busy saving yourself from falling over somebody.

When the body becomes loose, it may fall forwards or backwards; one never knows. You can be sure of it only as long as you have a hold over it. Once you give up your hold on the body, it automatically drops. Once you loosen your grip from within, who will hold the body? — it is bound to fall. And if you remain preoccupied with preventing it from falling, you will stay where you are — you won't be able to move into meditation. So, when your body is about to fall, consider it a blessing. Let go of it at once. Don't hold it back, because if you do you will keep yourself from moving inward. And don't be upset if someone falls on you; let it be so. If someone's head lies in your lap for a while, let it be so; don't be bothered by it.

Now close your eyes. Close them gently. Relax your body. Let it be completely loose, as if there is no life in it. Draw all the energy from your body; take it inside. As the energy moves within, the body will become loose.

Now I will begin my suggestions that the body is becoming loose, that we are becoming silent . . . Feel the body becoming loose. Let go. Move within just as a person moves inside his house. Move inside, enter within. The body is relaxing . . . let go completely . . . let it be lifeless, as if it is dead. The body is relaxing, the body has relaxed, the body has completely relaxed . . .

I take it that you have totally relaxed your body, that you have given up your hold over it . . . If the body falls, so be it; if it bends forward, let it bend. Let whatever has to happen, happen — you relax. See that you are not holding anything back. Take a look inside to be sure that you are not holding your body back . . . You ought to be able to say, "I am not holding back anything. I have let myself go completely."

The body is relaxed, the body is loose. The breath is calming down, the breath is slowing down. Feel it . . . the breathing has slowed down . . . let it go completely. Let your breathing go too, just give up your hold on it completely. The breath is slowing down, the breath is calming down . . . The breathing has calmed down, the breathing has slowed down . . .

The breathing has calmed down . . . thoughts are calming down too. Feel it . . . Thoughts are becoming silent . . . let go . . . You have let the body go, you have let the breathing go, now let thoughts go as well. Move away . . . Move within totally, move away from thoughts also.

Everything has become silent, as if everything outside is dead. Everything is dead . . . Everything has become silent . . . Only consciousness is left within . . . a burning lamp of consciousness — the rest is all dead. Let go . . . let go completely — as if you are no more. Let go totally . . . as if your body is dead, as if your body is no more. Your breathing is still, your thoughts are still — as if death has occurred. And move within, move totally within. Let go . . . let everything go. Let go totally, don't keep anything. You are dead.

Feel as if everything is dead, as if all is dead — only a burning lamp is left inside; the rest is all dead. Everything else is dead, erased. Be lost in emptiness for ten minutes. Be a witness. Keep watching this death. Everything else around you has disappeared. The body is also left, left far behind, far away — we are just watching it. Keep watching, remain a witness. For ten minutes keep looking within.

Keep looking inside . . . everything else will be dead outside. Let go . . . be totally dead. Keep watching, remain a witness . . . Let everything go as if you are dead and the body on the outside is dead. The body is still, thoughts are still, only the lamp of consciousness is left watching, only the seer is left, only the witness is left. Let go . . . let go . . . let go totally . . .

Whatever is happening, let it happen . . . Let go completely, just keep watching inside and let the rest go. Give up your hold completely . . .

The mind has become silent and empty, the mind has become totally empty . . . The mind has become empty, the mind has become totally empty . . . If you are still holding back a little, let that go also, let go totally, disappear — as if you are no more. The mind has become empty . . . the mind has become silent and empty . . . the mind has become totally empty . . .

Keep looking inside, keep looking inside with awareness — everything has become silent. The body is left behind, left far away; the mind is left far away, only a lamp is burning, a lamp of consciousness, only the light is left burning . . .

Now, slowly, take a few breaths. Keep watching your breath . . . With each breath the silence will go deeper. Take a few breaths slowly and keep looking within; remain a witness to the breathing also. The mind will become even more silent . . . Take a few breaths slowly, then gently open your eyes. If anyone has fallen, take a deep breath first and then get up slowly. Don't rush if you are unable to rise . . . Don't rush if you find it difficult to open your eyes . . . First take a deep breath, then open your eyes slowly . . . rise very softly. Don't do anything with a sudden movement—neither rising nor opening your eyes . . .

Our morning session of meditation is now over.

THE WHOLE UNIVERSE IS A TEMPLE

Evening
October 29, 1969

A friend has asked: *You have shown us the method of negation for realizing the truth or the divine being — the method of excluding everything else in order to know the self. Is it possible to achieve the same result by doing the opposite? Can we not try to see God in everything? Can we not feel him in all?*

It will be helpful to understand this.

One who cannot realize God within himself can never realize him in all. One who has not yet recognized God within himself can never recognize him in others. The self means that which is nearest to you; then anyone who is at a little distance from you will have to be considered as being farther away. And if you cannot see God in yourself, which is nearest you, you cannot possibly see him in those far from you. First you will have to know God in yourself; first the knower will have to know the divine — that is the nearest door.

But remember, it is very interesting that the individual who enters his self, suddenly finds the entrance to all. The door to one's self is the door to all. No sooner does a man enter his self, than he finds he has entered all, because although we are outwardly different, inwardly we are not.

Outwardly, all leaves are different from each other. But if a person could penetrate just one leaf, he would reach to the source of the tree where all the leaves are in unison. Seen individually, each leaf is different — but once you have known a leaf in its interiority, you will have reached to the source from which all leaves emanate and into which all leaves dissolve. One who enters himself, simultaneously enters all.

The distinction between "I" and "you" remains only so long as we have not entered within ourselves. The day we enter our "I," the "I" disappears and so does the "you" — what remains then is all.

Actually, "all" does not mean the sum of "I" and "you." All means where I and you have both disappeared, and what subsequently remains is all. If "I" has not yet dissolved, then one can certainly add "I's" and "you's," but the sum will not equal truth. Even if one adds all the leaves, a tree does not come into being — even though it has had all the leaves added to it. A tree is more than the sum of all the leaves. In fact, it has nothing to do with addition; it is erroneous to add. Adding one leaf to another, we assume each one is separate. A tree is not made of separate leaves at all.

So, as soon as we enter the "I," it ceases to exist. The first thing that disappears when we enter within is the sense of being a separate entity. And when that I-ness disappears, you-ness and the other-ness both disappear. Then what remains is all.

It's not even right to call it all, because "all" also has the connotation of the same old "I." Hence, those who know would not even call it all; they would ask, "the sum of what? What are we adding?" Furthermore, they would declare that only one remains. Although they would perhaps even hesitate to say that, because the assertion of one gives the impression that there are two — it gives the idea that, alone, one has no meaning without the corresponding notion of two. One exists only in the context of two. Therefore, those who have a deeper understanding do not even say that one remains, they say *advaita,* non-duality, remains.

Now this is very interesting. These people say that "Two are not left." They are not saying "One remains," they are saying "Two are not left." *Advaita* means there are not two.

One might ask, "Why do you talk in such roundabout ways? Simply say there is only one!" The danger in saying "one" is that it gives rise to the idea of "two." And when we say there are not two, it follows that there are not three either; it implies that there is neither one, nor many, nor all. Actually, this division resulted from the perception based on the existence of "I." So with the cessation of "I," that which is whole, the indivisible, remains.

But to realize this, can we do what our friend is suggesting — can we not visualize God in everyone? To do so would be nothing more than fantasizing and fantasizing is not tantamount to perceiving the truth.

Long ago some people brought a holy man to me. They told me this man saw God everywhere, that for the last thirty years he had been seeing God in everything — in flowers, plants, rocks, in everything. I asked the man if he had been seeing God in everything through practice—because if that were so then his visions were false. He couldn't follow me. I asked him again, "Did you ever fantasize about or desire to see God in everything?" He replied, "Yes indeed. Thirty years ago I started this *sadhana* in which I would attempt to see God in rocks, plants, mountains, in everything. And I began to see God everywhere." I asked him to stay with me for three days and, during that period, to stop seeing God everywhere.

He agreed. But the very next day he told me, "You have done me great harm. Only twelve hours have passed since I gave up my usual practice and I have already begun to see a rock as a rock and a mountain as a mountain. You have snatched my God away from me! What sort of a person are you?"

I said, "If God can be lost by not practicing for just twelve hours, then what you saw was not God — it was merely a consequence of your regular exercise." It is similar to when a person repeats something incessantly and creates an illusion. No, God has not to be seen in a rock; rather, one needs to reach a state in which there is nothing left to be seen in a rock *except* God. These are two different things.

Through your efforts to see him there, you will begin to see God in a rock, but that God will be no more than a mental projection. That will be a God superimposed by you on the rock; it will be the work of your imagination. That God will be purely your creation; he will be a complete figment of your imagination. Such a God is nothing more than your dream — a dream which you have consolidated by reinforcing it again and again. There is no problem seeing God like this, but it is living in an illusion, it is not entering truth.

One day, of course, it happens that the individual himself disappears and, consequently, he sees nothing but God. Then one doesn't feel that God is in the rock, then the feeling is "Where is the rock? Only God is!" Do you follow the distinction I am making? Then one doesn't feel that God exists in the plant or that he exists in the rock; that the plant exists and, in the plant, so does God — no, nothing of the kind. What one comes to feel is "Where is the plant? Where is the rock? Where is the mountain?" Because, all around, whatever is seen, whatever exists is only God. Then seeing God does not depend upon your exercise, it depends upon your experience.

The greatest danger in the realm of *sadhana*, of spiritual practice, is the danger of imagination. We can fantasize truths which must, otherwise, become our own experience. There is a difference between experiencing and fantasizing. A person who has been hungry the whole day eats at night in his dream and feels greatly satisfied. Perhaps he does not find as much joy in eating when he is awake as he does when he is dreaming — in the dream he can eat any dish he wants. Nevertheless, his stomach still remains empty in the morning, and the food he has consumed in his dream gives him no nourishment. If a man decides to stay alive on the food he eats in dreams, then he is sure to die sooner or later. No matter how satisfying the food eaten in the dream may be, in reality it is not food.

It can neither become part of your blood, nor your flesh, nor your bones or marrow. A dream can only cause deception.

Not only are meals made of dreams, God is also made of dreams. And so is *moksha*, liberation, made of dreams. There is a silence made of dreams, and there are truths made of dreams. The greatest capacity of the human mind is the capacity to deceive itself. However, by falling into this kind of deception, no one can attain joy and liberation.

So I am not asking you to start seeing God in everything. I am only asking you to start looking within and seeing what is there. When, to see what is there, you begin to look inside, the first person to disappear will be you — *you* will cease to exist inside. You will find, for the first time, that your *I* was an illusion, and that it has disappeared, vanished. As soon as you take a look inside, first the "I", the ego, goes. In fact, the sense that "I am" only persists until we have looked inside ourselves. And the reason we don't look inside is perhaps because of the fear that, if we did, we might be lost.

You may have seen a man holding a burning torch and swinging it round and round until it forms a circle of fire. In reality there is no such circle, it is just that when the torch is swinging round with great speed, it gives the appearance of a circle from a distance. If you see it close up, you will find that it is just a fast-moving torch, that the circle of fire is false. similarly, if we go within and look carefully, we will find that the "I" is absolutely false. Just as the fast-moving torch gives the illusion of a circle of fire, the fast-moving consciousness gives the illusion of "I". This is a scientific truth and it needs to be understood.

You may not have noticed, but all life's illusions are caused by things revolving at great speed. The wall looks very solid; the rock under your feet feels clearly solid, but according to scientists there is nothing like a solid rock. It is now a well-known fact that the closer scientists observed matter, the more it disappeared. As long as the scientist was distant from matter, he believed in it. Mostly it was the scientist who used to declare that matter alone is truth, but now that very scientist is saying there is nothing like matter. Scientists say that the fast movement of particles of electricity creates the illusion of density. Density, as such, exists nowhere.

For example, when an electric fan moves with speed, we cannot see the three moving blades; one cannot actually count how many there are. If it moves even faster, it will appear as if a piece of circular metal is moving. It can be moved so fast that even if you sat on top of it, you wouldn't feel the gap between the blades; you would feel as if you were sitting on top of solid metal.

The particles in matter are moving with similar speed — and the particles are not matter, they are fast-moving electric energy. Matter appears dense because of fast-moving particles of electricity. The whole of matter is a product of fast-moving energy — even though it appears to exist, it is actually nonexistent. Similarly, the energy of consciousness is moving so fast that, because of it, the illusion of "I" is created.

There are two kinds of illusions in this world: one, the illusion of matter; second, the illusion of "I", the ego. Both are basically false, but only by coming closer to them does one become aware they don't exist. As science draws closer to matter, matter disappears; as religion draws nearer "I", the "I" disappears. Religion has discovered that the "I" is nonexistent, and science has discovered that matter is nonexistent. The closer we come, the more we become disillusioned.

That's why I say: go within; look closely — is there any "I" inside? I am not asking you to believe that you are not the "I". If you do, it will turn into a false belief. If you take my word for it and think, "*I* am not; the ego is false. *I* am *atman*, *I* am *Brahman*; the ego is false," you will throw yourself into confusion. If this merely becomes a repetitive thing, then you will only be repeating the false. I am not asking you for this sort of repetition. I am saying: go within, look, recognize who you are. One who looks within and recognizes himself discovers that "I am not." Then who *is* within? If I am not, then someone else must be there. Just because "I am not", doesn't mean no one is there, because even to recognize the illusion, *someone* has to be there.

If I am not, then who is there? The experience of what remains after the disappearance of "I" is the experience of God. The experience becomes at once expansive — dropping "I", "you" also drops, "he" also drops, and only an ocean of consciousness remains. In that state you will see that only God is. Then it may seem erroneous to say that God is, because it sounds redundant.

It is redundant to say "God is", because God is the other name of "that which is". Is-ness *is* God — hence to say "God is" is a tautology; it isn't correct. What does it mean to say "God is"? We identify something as "is" which can also become "is not". We say "the table is", because it is quite possible the table may not exist tomorrow, or that the table did not exist yesterday. Something which did not exist before may become nonexistent again; then what is the sense in saying "it is"? God is not something which did not exist before, nor is it possible that he will never be again; therefore, to say "God is" is meaningless. He *is*. In fact, another name for God is "that which is". God means existence.

In my view, if we impose our God on "that which is," we are pushing ourselves into falsehood and deception. And remember, the Gods we have created are made differently; each has his respective trademark. A Hindu has made his own God, a Mohammedan has his own. The Christian, the Jain, the Buddhist — each has his own God. All have coined their own respective words; all have created their own respective

Gods. A whole great God-manufacturing industry abounds! In their respective homes people
manufacture their God; they produce their own
God. And then these God-manufacturers fight
among themselves in the marketplace the same
way the people who manufacture goods at home
do. Everyone's God is different from the other's.

Actually, as long as "I am", whatsoever I
create will be different from yours. As long as "I
am", my religion, my God will be different from
other people's because they will be the creation
of "I", of the ego. Since we consider ourselves
separate entities, whatever we create will have a
separate character. If, to create religion, the appropriate freedom could be granted, there
would be as many religions in the world as there
are people — not less than that. It is because of
the lack of the right kind of freedom that there
are so few religions in the world.

A Hindu father takes certain care to make his
son a Hindu before he becomes independent. A
Mohammedan father makes his son a Mohammedan before he becomes intelligent, because
once intelligence is attained, a person won't
want to become either a Hindu or a Mohammedan. And so there is the need to fill a child with
all these stupidities before he achieves intelligence.

All parents are anxious to teach their children
religion right from childhood, because once a
child grows up he will start to think and to cause
trouble. He will raise all sorts of questions —
and not finding any satisfactory answers, will
do things difficult for the parents to face. This is

why parents are keen to teach their children religion right from infancy — when the child is unaware of many things, when he is vulnerable to learning any kind of stupidity. This is how people become Mohammedans, Hindus, Jains, Buddhists, Christians — whatsoever you teach them to become.

And so, those we call religious people are often found to be unintelligent. They lack intelligence, because what we call religion is something which has poisoned us before intelligence has arisen — and even afterwards it continues its inner hold. No wonder Hindus and Mohammedans fight with each other in the name of God, in the name of their temples and their mosques.

Does God come in many varieties? Is the God Hindus worship of one kind, and the God the Mohammedans worship of another? Is that why Hindus feel their God is desecrated if an idol is destroyed. Or Mohammedans feel their God is dishonored if a mosque is destroyed or burned?

Actually, God is "that which is". He exists as much in a mosque as he does in a temple. He exists as much in a slaughterhouse as he does in a place of worship. He exists as much in a tavern as he does in a mosque. He is as present in a thief as he is in a holy man — not one iota less; that can never be. Who else is dwelling in a thief if not the divine? He is as present in Rama as he is in Ravana — he is not one iota less in Ravana. He exists as much within a Hindu as he does within a Mohammedan.

But the problem is: if we come to believe that

the same divinity exists in everyone, our God-manufacturing industry will suffer heavily. So in order to prevent this from happening, we keep on imposing our respective Gods. If a Hindu looks at a flower he will project his own God on it, see his God in it, whereas a Mohammedan will project, visualize his God. They can even pick a fight over this, although perhaps such a Hindu-Mohammedan conflict is a little far-fetched.

Their establishments are at a little distance from each other — but there are even quarrels between the closely related "divinity shops". For example, there is quite a distance between Benares and Mecca, but there is not much distance in Benares between the temples of Rama and Krishna. And yet the same degree of trouble exists there.

I have heard about a great saint . . . I am calling him great because people used to call him great, and I am calling him a saint only because people used to call him a saint.

He was a devotee of Rama. Once he was taken to the temple of Krishna. When he saw the idol of Krishna holding a flute in his hands, he refused to bow down to the image. Standing before the image, he said, "If thou wouldst take up the bow and arrow, only then could I bow down to thee, for then thou wouldst be my Lord." How strange! We place conditions on God also — how and in which manner or position he should present himself. We prescribe the setting; we make our requirements — only then are we prepared to worship.

It is so strange we determine what our God should be like. But that's how it has been all along. What, up to now, we have been identifying as "God", is a product based on our own specifications. As long as this manmade God is standing in the way, we will not be able to know that God who is not determined by us. We will never be able to know the one who determines us. And so we need to get rid of the manmade God if we wish to know the God which is. But that's tough; it's difficult even for the most kind-hearted person. Even for someone we otherwise consider a man of understanding, it's hard to get rid of this manmade God. He, as well, clings firmly to the basic foolishness as much as a stupid man does. A stupid man can be forgiven, but it is difficult to forgive a man of understanding.

Khan Abdul Gaffar Khan arrived in India recently. He is preaching Hindu-Mohammedan unity all over the country, but he himself is a staunch Mohammedan; about this, there is not the slightest doubt. It doesn't bother him that he prays in the mosque like a loyal Mohammedan, yet he is going about preaching Hindu-Mohammedan unity. Gandhi was a staunch Hindu, and he also used to preach Hindu-Mohammedan unity. As the *guru*, so is the disciple: the *guru* was a confirmed Hindu; the disciple is a confirmed Mohammedan. And so long as there are confirmed Hindus and confirmed Mohammedans in the world, how can such unity come about? They need to relax a little, only then unity is possible. These zealous Hindus and Mohammedans are at the root of all the trouble between the two religions, although the roots of these troubles are not really visible. Those who preach Hindu-Mohammedan unity do not have the vaguest idea how to bring it about.

As long as God is different things to different people, as long as there are different places of worship for different people, as long as prayers are different and scriptures are different — *Koran* being father for some and *Gita* being mother for others — the vexing troubles between religions will never come to an end. We cling to the *Koran* and the *Gita*. We say, "Read the *Koran* and teach people to drop enmity and to become one. Read the *Gita* and teach people to drop enmity and to become one." We don't realize, however, that the very words of *Koran* and *Gita* are the root cause of all the trouble.

If a cow's tail gets cut off, a Hindu-Mohammedan riot will break out, and we will blame ruffians for causing the fight. And the funny thing is that no hoodlum has ever preached that the cow is our sacred mother. This is actually taught by our *mahatmas*, our holy men, who put the onus for creating riots on "hoodlums". Because when the tail does get cut off, then for the *mahatmas'* purpose, it is not the tail of the cow, it is the tail of the holy mother! When they bring this to people's attention, the riots, in which the hoodlums get involved and are later blamed for starting, begin.

So the people we call *mahatmas* are in fact at the root of all such troubles. Were they to step aside, the hoodlums would be harmless, they would have no power to fight. They get strength from the *mahatmas*. But the *mahatmas* remain so well hidden underground, that we never ever realize they could be at the root of the problem.

What is the root of the problem, really? The root cause of all the trouble is your God — the God manufactured in your homes. Try to save yourselves from the Gods you create in your respective homes. You cannot manufacture God in your homes; the existence of such a God will be pure deception.

I am not asking you to project God. After all, in the name of God, what will you project? A devotee of Krishna will say he sees God hiding behind a bush holding a flute in his hand, while a devotee of Rama will see God holding a bow and arrow. Everyone will see God differently. This kind of seeing is nothing but projecting our desires and concepts. God is not like this. We cannot find him by projecting our desires and our concepts — to find him we will have to disappear altogether. *We* will have to disappear — along with all our concepts and all our projections. Both things cannot go hand in hand. As long as you exist as an ego, the experience of God is absolutely impossible. You as an ego will have to go; only then is it possible to experience him. I cannot enter the door of the divine as long as my "I", my ego, exists.

I have heard a story that a man renounced everything and reached the door of the divine. He had renounced wealth, wife, house, children, society, everything, and having renounced all, he approached the door of the divine. But the guard stopped him and said, "You cannot enter yet. First go and leave everything behind."

"But I have left everything," pleaded the man.

"You have obviously brought your 'I' along with you. We are not intersted in the rest; we are only concerned with your 'I'. We don't care about whatever you say you have left behind, we are concerned with your 'I'," The guard explained. "Go, drop it, and then come back."

The man said, "I have nothing. My bag is empty — it contains no money, no wife, no children. I possess nothing."

"Your 'I' is still in the bag — go and drop it. These doors are closed to those who bring their 'I' along; for them the doors have always been closed," said the guard.

But how to we drop the "I"? The "I" will never drop by our attempts to do so. How can "I" drop the very "I" itself? This is impossible. It will be like someone trying to lift himself up by his shoelaces. How do I drop the "I"? Even after dropping everything, "I" will still remain. At the most one might say, "I have dropped the ego," and yet this shows he is still carrying his "I". One becomes egoistic even about dropping the ego. Then what should a man do? It's quite a difficult situation.

I say to you: there is nothing difficult about it — because I don't ask you to drop anything. In fact, I don't ask you to *do* anything. The "I", the ego, becomes stronger because of all the doing. I am merely asking you to go within and look for the "I". If you find it, then there is no way to drop it. If it always exists there, what is there left to be dropped? And if you don't find it, then too, there is no way to drop it. How can you drop something which doesn't exist?

So go within and see if the "I" is there or not. I am simply saying that one who looks inside himself begins to laugh uproariously, because he cannot find his "I" anywhere within himself. Then what does remain? What remains then is God. That which remains with the disappearance of the "I" — could *that* ever be separate from you? When the "I" itself ceases to exist, who is going to create the separation? It is the "I" alone which separates me from you and you from me.

Here is the wall of this house. Under the illusion that they divide space into two, walls stand — although space never becomes divided in half; space is indivisible. No matter how thick a wall you erect, the space inside the house and the space outside are not two different things; they are one. No matter how tall you raise the wall, the space inside and outside the house is never divided. The man living inside the house, however, feels that he has divided the space into two — one space inside his house and another outside it. But if the wall were to fall, how would the man differentiate the space within the house from the space without? How would he figure it out? Then, only space would remain.

In the same way, we have divided consciousness into fragments by raising the walls of "I". When this wall of "I" falls, then it is not that I will begin to see God in you. No, then I won't be seeing *you*, I'll only be seeing God. Please understand this subtle distinction carefully.

It will be wrong to say I would begin to see God in you — I won't be seeing *you* any more, I will only be seeing the divine. It's not that I would see God in a tree — I would no longer see a tree, only the divine. When somebody says God exists in each and every atom he is absolutely wrong, because he is seeing both the atom and God. Both cannot be seen simultaneously. The truth of the matter is that each and every atom *is* God, not that God exists in each and every atom. It is not that some God is sitting enclosed inside an atom — whatever is, is God.

God is the name given out of love to "that which is". "That which is", is truth — in love we call it God. But it makes no difference by which name we call it. I do not ask, therefore, that you begin to see God in everyone, I am saying: start looking inside. As soon as you look within, *you* will disappear. And with your disappearance what you'll see is God.

Another friend has asked: *If meditation leads to samadhi and samadhi leads to God, then what need is there to go to the temples? Shouldn't we do away with them?*

It is useless to go to temples, but it is equally useless to do away with them. Why should one bother to do away with something in which God doesn't exist anyway? Let temples be where they are. What question is there of getting rid of them? But every so often this trouble comes up.

For example, Mohammed said that God is not to be found in idols, so the Mohammedans thought it meant idols should be destroyed. And then a very funny thing started happening in the world: there were already people crazy about making idols; now another bunch of crazy people cropped up to destroy the idols. Now the idol-makers are zealously busy making idols, while the idol-destroyers are occupied day and night figuring out ways to destroy the idols. Someone should ask when Mohammed said that God is to be found in destroying idols? God may not be present in an idol, but who said God is present in destroying idols? And if God is present in destroying idols, then what's the problem with God being present *in* the idol? God can be present in the idol too. And if he is not present in the idol, how can he be present in its destruction?

I am not saying we should do away with temples. What I am saying is that we must realize the truth that God is everywhere. Once we have realized this truth, everything becomes his temple — then it's difficult to distinguish between a temple and a non-temple. Then wherever we stand, that will be his temple; whatever we look at, that will be his temple; wherever we sit, that will be his temple. Then there will no longer be any sacred places of pilgrimage — the entire world will be a holy place. Then it will be meaningless to create separate idols, because then whatever is will be his image.

I am not advocating that you should get involved in doing away with temples, or that you should dissuade people from going to temples. I have never said that God is not present in the temple. What I am simply saying is that one who sees God only in a temple and nowhere else, has no knowledge whatsoever of God.

One who has realized God will feel God's presence everywhere — in a temple as well as in a place which is not a temple. Then how will he distinguish what is a temple and what is not a temple? We identify a temple as a place which has God's presence in it, but if one feels his presence everywhere then every place is his temple. Then there will no longer be any need to build separate temples, or, by the same token, to do away with temples either.

I have observed that instead of making sense out of what I am saying, people very often make the mistake of understanding something totally opposite to what I may have said. People become interested more in what is to be done away with, what is to be destroyed, what is to be eliminated — they don't try to understand what is. Such mistakes happen continuously.

One of the fundamental errors committed by man is that he hears something totally different from what is communicated to him. Now, some of you may take me as an enemy of temples, but you will rarely find a person more in love with temples than me. Why do I mention this? For the simple reason that I would like the whole earth to be seen as a temple; my concern is that everything be turned into a temple. But after listening to me, someone may come to understand that things would be better if we did away with temples. No purpose will be served by getting rid of these temples. Things will only work out well when the whole of life is made into a temple.

Those who see God in temples and those who destroy temples — both are wrong. One who only sees God in the temple is mistaken. His mistake is: who else does he see outside the temple? Obviously, his mistake is that he does not see God except in the temple. Your temple is

very puny; God is very vast — you cannot con-
fine God to your puny little temples. The other
person's error is: he wants to get into doing
away with temples, into destroying them — only
then, he thinks, can he see God. Your temples
are too small to serve as dwelling places of God
or to prevent anyone from seeing God. Remember, your temples are so ridiculously small they
cannot become God's residence, nor can they
become his prison, which, when destroyed,
would supposedly make him free. You need to
understand exactly what I am saying.

What I am saying is: only when we have entered meditation do we ever enter a temple.
Meditation is the only temple with no walls;
meditation is the only temple where, as soon as
you enter, you *really* enter a temple. And one
who begins to live in meditation begins living in
the temple twenty-four hours a day.

What's the point in a man visiting the temple
if he does not live in meditation? What's the
sense in his going to someplace we generally
identify as a "temple"? It's not so easy that,
while sitting in your shop, you may suddenly
find your way to the temple. Of course, it's easy
to carry your body to the temple; the body is
such a poor thing you can bring it along with
you anywhere you like. The mind is not that
simple. A shopkeeper counting money in his
shop can in fact get up suddenly, if he wants to,
and bring his body to the temple. Just because
his body is in the temple, the man may foolishly
think that *he* is in the temple. However, if he
ever peeked into his mind a little, he would find,

to his astonishment, that he was still sitting in his shop counting money.

I have heard . . .

A man was terribly harassed by his wife . . . All men are, but he was harassed a little too much. He was a religious man, but the wife was not at all religious. Ordinarily the opposite is the case — the wife is religious, the husband is not — but then, everything is possible! My understanding is that only one of the two can become religious. Both husband and wife can never become religious together; one will always be opposite the other. In this case the husband had become religious first, while the wife did not care to; however, every day the husband tried to make her religious.

A religious person carries a fundamental weakness: he wants to make others like himself. This is very dangerous; this is being violent. It is ugly to try to make others like oneself. It is enough to state our point of view to others, but to get on their case and force them to believe what we believe amounts to what we might call a kind of "spiritual violence".

All *gurus* indulge in this kind of activity. You can rarely find a person more violent than a *guru*. With his hands around the disciple's neck, a *guru* attempts to dictate what clothes to wear, how to keep his hair, what to eat, what to drink, when to sleep, when to get up — this, that, and all kinds of things are thrust upon him. With impositions like these, the *gurus* just about kill people.

So the husband was very keen to make his wife religious. Actually, people find great pleasure in making other people religious. To become religious, as such, is a matter of great revolution, but people find tremendous satisfaction in pestering others to become religious, because, in doing so, they have already assumed they are religious people. But the wife would not listen to her husband. In despair, the husband approached his *guru* and begged him to come to his house and persuade his wife.

Early one morning, at about five o'clock, the *guru* arrived. The husband was already in the room of worship. The wife was sweeping the courtyard. The *guru* stopped her right then and there and said, "I have heard from your husband that you are not a religious person. You never worship God, you never pray, you never enter the temple your husband has made in your house. Look at your husband — it is five o'clock and already he is in the temple."

The wife replied, "I don't recall my husband ever going to the temple."

The husband, sitting in his temple, overheard what his wife said and grew red with rage. A religious person gets angry very easily, and this is true, beyond one's imaginings, about one who is sitting in a temple. Heaven knows whether people sit in the temple to hide the flames of their anger or for something else. If one person becomes religious, he creates hell for the rest of the household.

The husband was totally outraged. He was halfway through his prayers when he overheard his wife. He couldn't believe his ears; what she said was total rubbish. Here he is, sitting in the temple, and she is telling his *guru* she doesn't know if he ever goes in there! He hurried to finish his prayer so he could come out and repair such a lie.

The *guru* began scolding the wife, "What are you talking about?" Your husband goes to the temple regularly." Hearing this, the husband began reciting his prayer even more loudly. The *guru* said, "See how vigorously he is praying!"

Laughing, the wife said, "I can hardly believe you are taken in by this loud recitation too! Of course he is chanting the Lord's name loudly, but as far as I can see he is not in the temple, he is at the shoemaker's, haggling over the price."

Now this was too much! The husband could hold himself back no longer. He dropped his worship and came running out of the temple. "What are all these lies? Didn't you see I was praying in the temple?" he shouted.

The wife said, "Look within yourself a little more closely. Were you really praying? Were you not bargaining with the shoemaker? And didn't you get into a fight with him?" The husband was taken aback, because what she was saying was true.

"But how did you know this?" he asked.

"Last night, before going to bed, you told me the first thing you would do this morning was go and buy a pair of shoes you badly needed. You also said you felt the shoemaker was asking too much for the shoes. It's my experience that the last thought before going to bed at night becomes the first thought the next morning. So I merely guessed you must be at the shoestore," the wife answered.

The husband said, "There is nothing left for me to say, because you are right. I was indeed at the shoemaker's and we fought over the price of the shoes. And the more heated the argument became, the louder I repeated the Lord's name. I may have been chanting God's name outwardly, but inside I was involved in a fight with the shoemaker. You are right; perhaps I have never really been in the temple."

Entering a temple is not so easy — it is not that you can enter any place and say that you are in a temple. Your body may have entered the temple, but what about your mind? How can you trust where your mind will be the next moment? And once your mind has entered the temple, why bother if the body is in the temple or not? The mind which has found the entrance into the temple suddenly discovers that it is surrounded on all sides by the vast temple, that now it is impossible to step out of the temple. Wherever you go, you will still be within his temple. You may go to the moon . . . Recently Armstrong landed on it. Does that mean he left God's temple? There is no way you can step out of God's temple. Do you imagine there is any place left where one can be outside his temple?

So those who think the temple they have made is the only temple of God, and that no temple of God exists outside of it, they are wrong. And those who think that this temple should be destroyed because God is not present here — they are equally wrong as well.

Why blame the poor temples? If we could step

out of our illusion that God exists only in temples, our temples could become very beautiful, very loving, very blissful. A village, in fact, looks incomplete without a temple. It can be a very joyful thing to have a temple. But a Hindu temple can never be a source of joy, nor, for that matter, can a Mohammedan or a Christian temple be a source of joy. Only God's temple can be a source of joy.

But Hindu, Mohammedan and Christian politics are so deep that they never allow a temple to represent the divine being. That's the reason Hindu shrines and Mohammedan mosques look so ugly. An honest man hesitates to even look on them. They have turned into the hotbeds of scoundrels; all kinds of mischief is planned there. And those who plan this mischief do not necessarily know what they are doing. It is my understanding that no one plans mischief with much understanding; mischief is always planned in unawareness. And the whole earth is caught up in this mess.

If temples ever do disappear from the face of the earth, it will not be because of the atheists, but because of the so-called theists. Temples are already disappearing; they have almost disappeared. If we want to save temples on this earth, first we will have to see the vast temple around us — existence itself. Then the smaller temples will automatically be saved; then they will survive as symbols of the divine presence. It's as if I gave you a handkerchief as a gift . . . The gift may be worth a few *paise*, but you preserve it safely in a treasure chest.

Once I visited a village. People came to see me

off at the railway station and someone put a garland around my neck. I took it off and handed it to a girl standing nearby. I visited the same village after six years, and the same girl came up to me and said, "I have saved the garland you gave me last time. Although the flowers have faded and people say there is no fragrance left in them, yet they are as fresh and fragrant as they were the first day. After all, *you* gave them to me."

I visited her house and she brought out a lovely wooden box in which the garland was carefully placed. The flowers had withered and were all dry; they had lost their fragrance. Anyone seeing it might have asked, "Why have you left this rubbish in such a beautiful box? What's the need? The box is valuable and the rubbish is worthless." The girl could throw the box away but not the rubbish. She could see something else in the rubbish — for her it was a symbol; it contained someone's loving memory. It might be rubbish to the rest of the world, but not to her.

If the temples, the mosques, the churches could just remain the reminders of man's longing to ascend toward God . . . And this is the truth. Take a look at the rising steeple of a church, the rising minaret of a mosque, the sky-high dome of a temple. They are nothing but symbols of man's desire to rise, symbols of his journey in search of God. They are symbols of the fact that man is not happy with only a house, he wants to build a temple as well. Man is not happy only being on the earth, he wants to ascend towards the sky as well.

Have you ever noticed the earthen lamps burning in the temples? Have you ever wondered why these lamps, containing *ghee*, containing purified butter, are kept burning in the temple? Have you ever realized that these lamps are the only things on earth whose flame never goes downwards? — it always moves upwards. Even if you turn the lamp upside down, the flame still moves upwards. The flame, which always moves upwards, is a symbol of human aspirations. We may be living on the earth, but we would also like to make our abode in the sky. We may remain tied to the earth below, but we also long to move freely in the open skies.

And have you ever noticed how fast a flame rises and disappears? Also, have you ever observed that once the flame has risen and disappeared, you can never find a trace of it? This is symbolic too — of the fact that the one who ascends, disappears. The earthen lamp is solid matter, while the flame is very fluid — no sooner does it rise than it disappears. So the flame of the lamp contains the message. It is a symbol of the fact that whosoever rises above the gross will disappear.

It is purely out of love that a man chooses to burn *ghee* in his lamp. Although there is nothing wrong in using kerosene oil in a lamp — God is not going to prevent you from doing so — we feel that only one who has become pure like *ghee* can move upwards. The flame of a kerosene lamp will move upwards too — kerosene is no less than *ghee* — but *ghee* is a symbol of our feeling that one who has become pure will be able to rise higher.

Temples, mosques, and churches are also symbols of a similar type. They can be very lovely. They are beautiful symbols — incredible illustrations created by man. But they have become ugly because so much nonsense has entered them. Now a temple no longer remains a temple — it has become the temple of the Hindus. And not only of the Hindus but of the *Vaishnavas*. And not only of the *Vaishnavas* but the temple of such and such a person. And so, with such continuous disintegration, all temples have turned into hotbeds of politics. They nurture the groupism and bigotry that lead everyone to disaster. By and by, they have all turned into establishments which continue to exploit and maintain their vested interests.

I am not asking you to do away with temples, I am asking you to get rid of all that is worthless and has become part of the temples. Their vested interests have to be destroyed. Temples have to be saved from turning into establishments; they have to be saved from groupism and bigotry. A temple is a very beautiful place if it remains just a reminder of God, if it remains his symbol, if it reflects a phenomenon rising towards the sky.

What I am saying is that as long as temples remain the mainspring of politics, they will continue to cause misfortune. And, indeed, now the temples are nothing but the mainsprings of politics. When a temple is built for the Hindus, it automatically becomes a hotbed of politics, because politics means groupism. And religion is something which has absolutely nothing to do with groupism. Religion means a *sadhana*, an individual commitment to spirituality, and politics means groupism. Always be aware that religion can be related to a *sadhana*, but it can have no relation to groupism. Politics survives on groupism, groupism survives on hatred, and hatred survives on blood — and the whole mischief goes on . . .

As a symbol of God the temple has become impure. That impurity has to be removed; then it will be a symbol of great beauty. If a village has a temple which belongs neither to the Hindus nor to the Mohammedans nor to the Christians, the village will look beautiful. The temple will become an adornment of the village. The temple will become a reminder of the infinite. Then those who enter the temple will not feel that, by doing so, they have come near God, that outside they were away from him, people will simply feel that the temple is a place which makes it easy to enter within themselves; that the temple is only meant to be a place where one experiences beauty, peace and solitude. Then the temple will simply be an appropriate place for meditation. And meditation is the path leading to God.

Everyone cannot find it easy to make his house so peaceful it can be used for meditation, but together a whole village can certainly build such a peaceful house. Everyone cannot afford to hire a tutor for his children and provide them with a separate school building, garden and playground. If each and every person started doing this, it would create a problem — only a limited number of children would get educated — so we build a school in the village and provide all that is necessary for the children of the entire village. Similarly, each village should have a place for *sadhana*, for meditation. That is all a temple and a mosque mean, nothing more. At present, they are no longer places for *sadhana*, they have become centers for spreading trouble and mischief.

So we don't need to do away with the temples. We must, however, take care that a temple does not continue to be a center for causing trouble. We must also take care that the temple returns to the hands of religion, and does not remain in the hands of Hindus or Mohammedans.

If the children of a town can go as freely to the mosque as they can to the temple, as freely to the church as they can to the temple of Shiva, then such a town is truly a religious town. Then the people of this town are good people. Then the parents of this town are not the enemies of their children. One can see that the parents of this town love their children, and are laying a foundation so that their children do not fight amongst themselves. The parents of this town would tell their children, "A mosque is your house as much as a temple is. Go wherever you find peace. Sit there, seek God there. All houses are God's, but to have a glimpse of him is what matters. And for this, go within yourself. Or go wherever you feel." The day this will become a reality, the right kind of temple will be created in the world. We have not been able to build it as yet.

I am not among those who wish to get rid of temples. On the contrary, I am saying that our temples have already been destroyed by the very people who claim to be their guardians. But when we will be able to see this is hard to say. And then people misunderstand; they get the idea that I am among the destroyers of temples. What would I gain by destroying a temple? Whatsoever is unlike a temple, which has gathered around the temple, must, of course, be eliminated. It is quite all right to involve oneself in an effort to do so.

One last question, and we will begin our meditation. One friend has asked after the morning discussion: *Do souls sometimes wander after leaving the body?*

Some souls do find it difficult to take on a new body right after death. There is a reason for this, and perhaps you may not have thought that this could be the reason. All souls, if divided, would fall into three categories. One is the lowest — people with the most inferior type of consciousness; another is of the very highest kind, very superior, the purest kind of consciousness; and the third consists of people in between — a combination of something of both.

Let's take the example of a *damroo*, a small drum. It is broad at the ends and thin in the center. Were we to reverse it so that it was broad in the center and narrow at the ends, we would understand the situation of disembodied souls. At the narrow ends there are very few souls. The most lowly souls find it as difficult to take a new body as the superior ones do. Those in between do not face the slightest delay — they attain a new body as soon as they leave the previous one. The reason is that for the mediocre souls, the middle ones, a suitable womb is always available.

As soon as a person dies, the soul sees hundreds of people, hundreds of couples, copulating — and whichever couple it becomes attracted to, it enters the womb. Many superior souls, however, cannot enter ordinary wombs; they require extraordinary wombs. The superior soul requires the union of a couple with an exceptionally high level of consciousness so that the highest degree of possibilities becomes available for their birth. And so, a superior soul has to wait for the right womb. Similarly, inferior souls have to wait also, because they cannot easily find a couple either, they cannot easily find a womb of an inferior type. Thus, both the highest and the lowest types are not easily born, while the mediocre types have no difficulty. There are wombs continuously available to receive them — the mediocre soul is immediately attracted to any one of them.

I talked about *Bardo* in the morning. In this method the dying man is told, "You will see hundreds of couples copulating. Don't be in a hurry. Think a little, take a little time, remain there for a while before you enter a womb. Don't immediately enter whichever womb attracts you." It is as if a person goes downtown and buys whatsoever catches his fancy in a showroom. Whichever shop comes into view first, he is pulled to it; he enters the shop immediately.

So in the *Bardo* method the dying man is warned, "Beware! Don't rush, don't hurry, keep searching; give it thought, take everything into consideration." This is told to him because, continuously, hundreds of people are copulating. The person clearly sees hundreds of couples making love, and among them he is only attracted to that couple capable of giving him a suitable womb.

Both superior and inferior souls have to wait until they find a suitable womb. The inferior souls do not easily find a womb of such an inferior character that, through it, they can attain their possibilities. As well, superior souls do not readily find a womb of a superior character. The inferior souls, stranded without bodies, are what we call evil spirits, and the superior souls waiting to take birth, we call them *devatas*, gods. Superior souls waiting for the right womb are gods. Ghosts and evil spirits are the lowest kind of souls — stranded because of their inferior quality. For the ordinary soul a womb is always available. No sooner does death occur than the soul instantly enters a womb.

The same friend has also asked: *Can these souls, who are awaiting to be born, enter into someone's body and harass that person?*

This, too, is possible — because the inferior souls, those who have not yet found a body, remain very tormented; while, without bodies, the superior souls are happy. You should keep this distinction in mind. Higher souls always look upon the body as a kind of bondage of one sort or another. They wish to remain so light they even prefer not to carry the weight of a body. And, ultimately, they want to be free from the body, because they find even the body is nothing but a prison. Eventually, they feel the body makes them do certain things which are not worth doing. And so these souls are not very attracted to the body. The inferior souls cannot live for a moment without a body; their interest, their happiness is tethered to the body.

Certain pleasures can be attained without being in a body. For example, there is the soul of a thinker. Now, one can have the pleasure of thinking without being in a body, because thought has nothing to do with the body. So if the soul of a thinker begins to wander and does not attain a body, it never shows any hurry to be in the body again because it can enjoy the pleasure of thinking even in the state it is in. But, let's say someone enjoys food with a passion. That pleasure is not possible without being in a body, so in such a case, the soul becomes tremendously restless to find a way to enter a body. And if it fails to find a suitable womb, then it can enter a body which has a weak soul. A weak soul means one which is not the master of its body. And this happens when the weak soul is in a state of fear.

Remember, fear has a very deep meaning. Fear means that which causes you to shrink. When you are in fear you shrink; when you are happy you expand. When a person is in a state of fear his soul shrinks, and consequently, a large space is left vacant in his body for another soul to enter and occupy. Not only one, many souls can enter and occupy that space at once. So when a man is in a state of fear, a soul can enter his body. And the only reason a soul would do that is because all its cravings are tethered to the body; it attempts to satisfy its cravings by entering someone's body. This is totally possible. Complete facts are available to support it; it is totally based on reality.

What this means is that a fearful person is always in danger; he is always in a shrunken state. He lives, as it were, in one room of his house, while the rest of the rooms remain vacant and can be occupied by other guests.

Occasionally, higher souls also enter a human body, but they do so for very different reasons. There are some acts of compassion which cannot be carried out without being in a body. Say, for example, that a house catches fire and no one steps forward to save it from burning down. The crowd stands there, powerless; no one dares enter the burning house. Suddenly a man steps forward, puts out the fire and manages to save somebody trapped inside. Later on, when everything is over, the man himself wonders how he did it. He feels quite sure he moved and acted under the influence of some unknown power — that it was not his doing, that someone else did it. In such instances, where man is unable to muster the courage for some good cause, some higher soul can enter a human body and accomplish the task. But these are rare happenings.

Since it is difficult for superior souls to find suitable wombs, they sometimes have to wait for hundreds of years before their next birth. And surprisingly enough, these souls appear on the earth almost at the same time. For example, Buddha and Mahavira were both born in India 2,500 years ago. Both were born in Bihar and, during the same period, six other enlightened beings were present in the same state, in Bihar. Their names are not known to us because they did not initiate any disciples, because they had no followings — that is the only reason — but they were of the same caliber as Buddha and Mahavira. And they conducted a very daring experiment: none of them initiated any followers. One of these people was Prabuddha Katyayana, another was Ajit Keshkambal, and yet another was Sanjay Vilethi Putra. Then there was Makhali Gosal, and there were others. In that period of time, eight people of the same genius and the same potential were born simultaneously, in that very state of Bihar. With all the world available, these eight souls waited for a long time to be born in that small area of Bihar. And when the opportunity came, it came all at once.

Often it happens, as well as for evil souls, that a chain of births comes to pass for the good. At the same time as Buddha and Mahavira, Socrates was born in Greece, followed after a time by Plato and Aristotle. At about the same time, in China, Confucius, Lao Tzu, Chuang Tzu and Mencius, Meng Tzu, were born. Some incredible people took birth all at once in different parts of the world at approximately the same time. The whole world was filled with some fascinating people. It seems as if the souls of all these people were waiting for some time. Then an opportunity came their way; wombs became available to them.

When, by chance, wombs do become available, many wombs become available all at once. It is just like the blooming of a flower. When the season arrives, you find one flower has blossomed, and then you see the second flower, and then the third. The flowers were just waiting to bloom. Dawn arrives, and it is just a question of the sun rising above the horizon and the flowers begin to bloom. The buds burst open and the flower blooms. The flowers were waiting the entire night, and as the sun arose, they bloomed.

Exactly the same thing happens with inferior souls. When a suitable environment develops on earth, they take birth in a chain. For example, in our time, people like Hitler, Stalin and Mao were all born during the same period. Such horrible people must have waited for thousands of years to take birth; they can't find wombs that easily. Stalin alone killed about six million people in the Soviet Union, and Hitler killed about ten million people all by himself.

The death contraptions devised by Hitler were unique in the history of mankind. He carried out mass murder in a way no one had ever done before; before him, Tamerlaine and Genghis Khan seem novices. Hitler devised gas chambers for mass murder. He found it too cumbersome and costly to kill people one by one and then dispose of their bodies, so he devised ingenious methods of mass murder. There are other means of mass murder too — for example, as happened in the recent communal riots at Ahmedabad, or at other places — but these are all very expensive methods.

Also, it is such an effort to kill people one by one — and it takes a lot of time as well. Killing people one by one doesn't work: you kill one here, and another is born somewhere else. So

Hitler would have five thousand people put in a gas chamber together, and with the flick of a button these five thousand people were virtually turned into vapor; they would simply evaporate. The chamber would be empty; no sign of them would be left. Not a drop of blood was spilled, not a single grave was dug. It was all very neat.

No one can accuse Hitler of bloodshed. If God is still dispensing justice by the old standards, he will find Hitler totally innocent. He did not spill a drop of blood; he pierced no breast with his sword, he simply devised an ingenious method of killing, a means beyond description. He placed people in a gas chamber, switched on a high-voltage button and the people simply evaporated. Not a sign was left to prove they had ever existed. Hitler, for the first time, got rid of people as one boils water and turns it into vapor. He turned ten million people into gas!

It is very difficult for a soul like Hitler's to find a new body quickly. And it is good it is so difficult, otherwise the earth would be in great trouble. Hitler will have to wait for a very long time, because it is extremely difficult for a conception of such a low quality to take place again.

What does it mean to be born through an inferior conception? It means that generations of the parents' ancestors have a long chain of evil deeds to their credit. In a single lifetime one cannot accumulate enough evil to account for the conception of a person like Hitler. To produce a son like Hitler, how much evil, how many murders can one man commit in one lifetime? For a son like Hitler to choose his parents, a long chain of evil deeds is required, deeds performed by the parents for hundreds, thousands, millions of years. This means that if a person were to work in a slaughterhouse continuously for thousands of years, only then could his genes, his breed, become capable of attracting a soul like Hitler's.

The same holds true for a good soul. For an average, ordinary soul there is no difficulty taking birth; there are wombs all over ready to receive such souls. And besides, its demands are very ordinary. There are the same cravings: eating, drinking, making money, enjoying sex, seeking honor and position — such ordinary longings. Everyone longs for these things, and so the soul has no problem finding a womb. All parents can give any soul the opportunity to achieve all this ordinary stuff. However, if, in a human body, a soul wants to live a life so pure that he will even hesitate to press the earth with his feet, he will live in such total love that he won't want anyone to be troubled by his love or his love to become a burden on anyone, then we will have to wait a long time for such souls to take birth.

Now let's get ready for the evening meditation.

Let me first make a few things clear. I have observed that you sit very close to each other, and this doesn't allow you to sit without worrying you might fall on somebody else. This situation won't allow you to go deep. So the first thing you need to do is: be at a distance from each other. Those who feel like lying down, may do so. Even later, during the meditation, if you feel your body is going to fall on the ground, then don't hold yourself back. Let go completely; allow the body to drop.

Now, turn off the lights.

The first thing: close your eyes. Relax your body . . . Relax your body totally, as if there is no body left any more. Feel that all the energy of your body is moving in . . . Feel that you are moving inside the body . . . You have to withdraw all your energy inside.

For three minutes I will give suggestions that your body is relaxing, and you have to feel it. You have to keep feeling your body and relaxing it. Slowly you will feel that you have lost your hold over the body — then if the body begins to fall, let it fall; don't hold it. If it falls forward, let it fall; if it falls backwards, let it fall. From your side, don't maintain any hold on the body. Let your hold over the body go. This is the first stage.

Now I will give suggestions for three minutes. Similarly, I will give suggestions for your breathing, and then for your thoughts. At the end, for ten minutes, we will be lost in silence.

Your body is relaxing. Feel it: your body is relaxing . . . your body is relaxing . . . your body is relaxing . . . Let go, as if the body is no more. Give up your hold . . . Your body is relaxing . . . Drop all control over the body, as if your body is dead.

You have moved inside; the energy has been sucked inside — now the body is left behind like a shell. The body is relaxing . . . the body is totally relaxed . . . Let go . . . You will feel that it has gone, gone, gone. Let it fall if it will. The body is relaxed, as if you are dead now, as if the body is no more, as if the body has disappeared. . .

Relax your breathing also. Your breathing is relaxing . . . Feel that your breathing is relaxing . . . your breathing has totally relaxed . . . Let go . . . Let the body go; let the breathing go too . . . Your breathing has relaxed.

Your thoughts are also becoming silent . . . Thoughts are becoming silent . . . Feel your thoughts becoming totally silent . . . Feel inside, thoughts are calming down . . . The body is relaxed, the breathing is relaxed, thoughts are silent . . .

Everything is silent within you . . . We are sinking into this silence; we are sinking, we are falling deeper and deeper as one falls into a well, keeps on falling deeper and deeper . . . just like this, we are falling deeper and deeper into emptiness, into *shunya*. Let go, let go your hold completely . . . Keep drowning in emptiness, keep drowning . . . Inside, only consciousness will remain, burning like a flame, watching, just a witness.

Just remain a witness. Keep watching inside . . . Outside everything is dead; the body has become totally inert . . . Breathing has slowed down, thoughts have slowed down; inside, we are falling into silence . . . Keep watching, keep watching, watching continuously — a much deeper silence, a much more profound silence will grow. In that watching state, "I" will also disappear — only a shining light, a burning flame will remain.

Now I will be still for ten minutes, and you

keep on disappearing within, deeper and deeper . . . Give up your hold, let go. Just keep watching. For ten minutes, just be an onlooker, be a witness.

Everything is silent . . . Look within, keep looking within . . . Inside, let there be just watching. The mind is becoming more and more silent . . . At a distance you will see your body lying — as if it is someone else's body . . . You will move away from the body, as if you have left the body . . . It seems someone else is breathing . . .

Go even further within, go deeper inside . . . Keep watching, keep looking inside, and the mind will totally sink into nothingness . . . Go deeper, go deeper down within . . . keep watching . . . the mind has become totally silent.

The body is left behind, the body is as if dead . . . We have moved away from the body . . . Let go, let go totally; do not hold back at all, as if you are dead inside . . . The mind is becoming even more silent . . . The body is lying far away; we have moved far away from the body . . . The mind has become totally silent . . .

Look inside. The "I" has disappeared totally, only consciousness is left, only knowing is left. Everything else has disappeared . . .

Slowly, take a few deep breaths. The mind is now totally silent. Watch each and every breath, and you will feel the mind becoming even more silent. Your breathing will also seem separate from you, far away from you. Breathe softly and slowly . . . Watch how far away the breath is . . . watch how distant it is from you.

Slowly, take a few deep breaths . . . Then

open your eyes slowly. There is no need to hurry to get up. If you are unable to open your eyes, there is no need to hurry. Open your eyes slowly and softly, and then look outside for a moment. . .

Our evening meditation is now over.

RETURNING TO THE SOURCE

Morning
October 30, 1969

A friend has asked: *According to what you have said, one can triumph over death through meditation or sadhana. But then, doesn't the same state exist when we are in sleep? And if it does, then why can't death be conquered through sleep?*

The first thing that needs to be understood is that triumph over death does not mean there is something like death to conquer. To triumph over death simply means you will come to know there is no death. To know that death is not, is to conquer it. There is nothing like death to be conquered. As soon as one knows there is no death, our ongoing and losing battle with death ceases. Some enemies exist, and there are others that, in reality, do not exist but only seem to exist. Death is one of those enemies with no real existence; it only seems to exist.

And so, do not take the triumph to mean that somewhere death exists and that we shall conquer it. This would be like a man going crazy fighting with his shadow, until someone points out to him, "Look closely, the shadow has no substance. It is merely an appearance." If the man looked at the shadow and realized what he was doing, he would laugh at himself; only then could he know he has conquered the shadow. Conquering the shadow simply means there was not even the tiniest shadow to be fought with; anyone attempting to do so would go crazy. One who fights with death will lose; one who knows death will triumph over it.

This also means that if death is not, then, in reality, we never ever die — whether we are aware of it or not. The world does not consist of those people who die and those who do not die — no, it's not like that. In this world no one ever dies. There are two kinds of people, however: those who know this as a fact, and those who don't — this is the only difference.

In sleep we reach the same place we do in meditation. The only difference is that in sleep we are unconscious, while in meditation we are fully conscious. If someone were to become fully aware, even in his sleep, he would have the same experience as in meditation.

For example, if we were to put a person under anesthetic, and in his unconscious state bring him on a stretcher to a garden where flowers are in full bloom, where fragrance is in the air, where the sun is shining and the birds are singing, the man would be completely unaware of all this. After we brought him back and he was out of the anesthesia, if we asked him how he liked the garden, he would not be able to tell us anything. Then, if you were to take him to the same garden when he was fully conscious, he would experience everything present there when he had been brought in before. In both cases, although the man was brought to the same place, he was unaware of the beautiful surroundings in the first instance, while in the second instance he would be fully aware of the flowers, the fragrance, the song of the birds, the rising sun. So, although you will undoubtedly reach as far in an unconscious state as you will reach in a conscious state, to reach some place in an unconscious state is as good as not reaching there at all.

In sleep, we reach the same paradise we reach in meditation, but we are unaware of it. Each night we travel to this paradise, and then we come back — unaware. Although the fresh breeze and the lovely fragrance of the place touch us, and the songs of the birds ring in our ears, we are never aware of it. And yet, in spite of returning from this paradise totally unaware of it, one might say, "I feel very good this morning. I feel very peaceful. I slept well last night."

What do you feel so good about? Having slept well, what good happened? It cannot be only because you slept — surely you must have been somewhere; something must have happened to you. But in the morning you have no knowledge of it, except for a vague idea of feeling good. One who has had a deep sleep at night gets up refreshed in the morning. This shows the person has reached a rejuvenating source in sleep — but in an unconscious state.

One who is unable to sleep well at night finds

himself more tired in the morning than he was the previous evening. And if a person does not sleep well for a few days it becomes difficult for him to survive, because his connection with the source of life is broken. He is unable to reach the place it is essential he should.

The worst punishment in the world is not death — as a punishment death is easy; it occurs in a few moments. The worst punishment ever devised on earth is not letting a person go to sleep. Even to this day, there are countries like China and Russia where prisoners are made to go without sleep. The torture a prisoner goes through, if he is not allowed to sleep for fifteen days, is beyond our imagination — he almost goes mad. He begins to divulge all the information he otherwise would not have let the enemy know. He begins to blabber, totally unaware of its implications.

In China, systematic methods have been devised. For six months prisoners are not allowed to sleep. Consequently, they become totally insane. They completely forget who they are, what their names are, what their religion is, which town or city they come from, what their country is — they forget everything. Lack of sleep throws their consciousness into complete disorder, into chaos. In that condition they can be made to learn anything.

When the American soldiers captured in Korea returned from the prison camps of Russia and China, denial of sleep had left them in such terrible shape that when they came out they were openly antagonistic to America and in favor of communism. First these soldiers were

not allowed to sleep, and when their conscious-
nesses became disordered, they were indoctri-
nated into communism. Once their identities
were thrown into chaos, through repeated suggestions they were told they were communists.
And so, before their release, they were completely brainwashed. Looking at these soldiers,
American psychologists were dumbfounded.

If a person is denied sleep, he becomes cut off
from the very source of life. Atheism will continue to grow in the world in the same ratio as
sleep continues to get lighter. In countries where
people have lighter sleep, atheism will be more
on the increase there. And in countries where
people have deeper sleep, the more theism will
be on the increase. But this theism and atheism
are a totally strange thing for man, because they
grow out of an unconscious state. A person who
has a deep sleep spends the next day in peace,
while the one who does not have a deep sleep
remains restless and troubled the following day.
How in the world can a restless and troubled
mind be receptive to God? A mind which is disturbed, dissatisfied, tense and angry, refuses to
accept God, denies his existence.

Science is not at the bottom of the increasing
atheism in the West; the disorderly, chaotic condition of sleep is at the root of it. In New York, at
least thirty percent of the people cannot sleep
without tranquilizers. Psychologists believe that
if this condition prevails for the next hundred
years, not a single person will be able to sleep
without medication.

People have completely lost sleep. If a man
who has lost sleep were to ask you how you go

to sleep, and your answer were, "All I do is put my head on the pillow and fall asleep," he will not believe you. He will find this impossible and suspect there must be some trick he doesn't know to it — because he lays his head on the pillow too, and nothing happens.

God forbid, but a time may come, after a thousand or two thousand years, when everyone will have lost natural sleep, and people will refuse to believe that a thousand or two thousand years before their time, people simply rested their heads on their pillows and fell asleep. They will take this as fiction, a mythical story from the *Puranas*. They will not believe it to be true. They will say, "This is not possible, because if that isn't true about us, how can it be true about anyone else?"

I am drawing your attention to all of this because three or four thousand years ago people would close their eyes and go into meditation as easily as you go to sleep today. Two thousand years from now it will be difficult to sleep in New York — it is difficult even today. It is becoming difficult to sleep in Bombay, and soon it will become difficult in Dwarka as well — it is just a matter of time. Today it is hard to believe there was a time when a man could close his eyes and go into meditation — because now, when you sit with your eyes closed, you reach nowhere; inside, thoughts keep hovering around and you remain where you are.

In the past, meditation was as easy for those who were close to nature as sleep is for those who live close to nature. First meditation disappeared; now sleep is on its way out. Those

things are first lost which are conscious; after
that, those things are lost which are unconscious. With the disappearance of meditation the
world has almost become irreligious, and when
sleep disappears the world will become totally irreligious. There is no hope for religion in a sleepless world.

You will not believe how closely, how deeply,
we are connected to sleep. How a person will
live his life depends totally on how he sleeps. If
he does not sleep well, his entire life will be a
chaos: all his relationships will become entangled, everything will become poisonous, filled
with rage. If, on the contrary, a person sleeps
deeply, there will be freshness in his life —
peace and joy will continuously flow in his life.
Underlying his relationships, his love, everything else, there will be serenity. But if he loses
sleep, all his relationships will go haywire. He
will have a messed-up life with his family, his
wife, his son, his mother, his father, his teacher,
his students — all of them. Sleep brings us to a
point in our unconscious where are are im-
mersed in God — although not for too long.
Even the healthiest person only reaches to his
deeper level for ten minutes of his nightly eight
hours' sleep. For these ten minutes he is so completely lost, drowned in sleep, that not even a
dream exists.

Sleep is not total as long as one is dreaming —
one keeps moving between the states of sleep
and wakefulness. Dreaming is a state in which
one is half-asleep and half-awake. To be in a
dream means, even though your eyes are closed,
you are not asleep; external influences are still

affecting you. The people you met during the day, you are still with them at night in your dreams. Dreams occupy the middle state between sleep and wakefulness. And there are many people who have lost sleep — they merely remain in the dreaming state, without ever reaching the state of sleep. And that you don't remember in the morning that you dreamt all night is beside the point. Much research on sleep is being carried out in America. Some ten big laboratories have been experimenting on thousands of people for about eight to ten years.

Americans are showing interest in meditation because they have lost sleep. They think that perhaps meditation may bring their sleep back, that it may bring some peace into their lives. That's why they look upon meditation as nothing more than a tranquilizer. When Vivekananda first introduced meditation in America, a physician came to him and said, "I enjoyed your meditation immensely. It is absolutely a non-medicinal tranquilizer. It's not a medicine and yet it puts one to sleep — it's great." Yogis are not the reason their influence is growing so much in America — the lack of sleep is the real cause. Their sleep is in a mess, and consequently, life in America is filled with heaviness, depression, tension. And so, in America, we see the growing need for tranquilizers — somehow, to bring sleep to people.

Every year, millions of dollars are being spent on tranquilizers in America. Ten big laboratories are conducting research on thousands of people who are being paid to undergo nights of rather uncomfortable, painful sleep. All kinds of electrodes and thousands of wires are attached to people's bodies, and they are examined from all angles to find out what is happening inside them.

One incredible discovery these experiments have revealed is that man dreams almost the whole night. Waking up, some people said they didn't dream, while some said they did. But in fact, all of them dreamt. The only difference was that those with better memories remembered dreaming, while those with weaker memories could not recall dreaming. It was found, however, that a completely healthy person was able to slip into a deep, dreamless sleep for ten minutes.

Dreams can be scanned through machines. Nerves in the brain remain active during our dreaming state, but as the dream stops, the nerves cease to be active as well, and the machine indicates a gap has occurred. The gap shows that, at that time, the man was neither dreaming nor thinking — he was lost somewhere.

It is interesting that the machines keep recording movement inside the man while he is in the dreaming state, but as soon as he falls into dreamless sleep, the machine shows a gap. They don't know where the man disappeared in that gap. So, dreamless sleep means the man has reached a place beyond the machine's range. It is in this gap that man enters the divine.

The machine is unable to detect this space in between, this gap. The machine records the internal activity as long as the man is dreaming — then comes the gap and the man disappears somewhere. And then, after ten minutes, the machine starts recording again. It is difficult to say where the man was during that ten-minute interval. American psychologists are very intrigued by this gap; hence they consider sleep the biggest mystery. The fact is that next to God, sleep is the only mystery. There is no other mystery.

You sleep every day, yet you have no idea what sleep is. A man sleeps all through his life, and yet nothing changes — he knows nothing about sleep. The reason you don't know anything about sleep is that when sleep is there, you are not. Remember, you *are* only as long as sleep is not. And so, you come to know only as much as the machine knows. Just as in the face of the gap the machine stops and is unable to reach where the man has been transported, you cannot reach there either — because you are no more than a machine as well.

Since you do not come across that gap either, sleep remains a mystery; it remains beyond your reach. This is so because a man falls into wakeless sleep only when he ceases to exist in his "I-am-ness". And therefore, as the ego keeps growing, sleep becomes less and less. An egoistic person loses his capacity to sleep because his ego, the "I", keeps asserting itself twenty-four hours a day. It is the "I" that wakes up, the same "I" that walks on the street. The "I" remains so present the entire twenty-four hours that at the moment of falling asleep, when the time approaches to drop the "I", one is unable to get rid of it. Obviously, it becomes difficult to fall asleep. As long as the "I" exists, sleep is impossible. And, as I told you yesterday, as long as the "I" exists, entering into God is impossible.

Entering into sleep and entering into God are exactly one and the same thing; the only difference is that through sleep one enters into God in an unconscious state, while through meditation one enters into God in a conscious state. But this is a very big difference. You may enter God through sleep for thousands of lives, yet you will never come to know God. But if, even for a moment, you enter meditation you will have reached the same place you have reached in deep sleep for thousands and millions of lives — although always in an unconscious state — and it will transform your life totally.

The interesting thing is that once a person enters meditation, enters that emptiness where deep sleep takes him, he never remains unconscious — even when he is asleep. When Krishna says in the *Gita* that the yogi stays awake when everyone else is asleep, he does not mean the yogi never sleeps at all. In fact, no one sleeps as beautifully as a yogi does. But even in his deepest sleep, that element in him which has entered into meditation remains awake. And, every night, the yogi enters sleep in this awakened state. Then, for him, meditation and sleep become one and the same thing — no difference between the two remains. Then he always enters sleep in full consciousness. Once a person moves within himself through meditation, he can never be in an unconscious state in his sleep.

Ananda lived with Buddha for many years. For years he slept near Buddha. One morning he asked Buddha, "For years I have been watching you sleep. Not once do you ever change sides; you sleep the whole night in the same position. Your limbs stay where they were when you laid down at night; there is not the slightest movement. Many times I have gotten up at night to check whether you have moved. I have stayed up nights watching you — your hands, your feet, rest in the same position; you never ever change sides. Do you keep some kind of a record of your sleep the whole night?"

"I don't need to keep any record," Buddha replied. "I sleep in a conscious state, so I find no need to change sides. I can if I want to. Turning from one side to another is not a requirement of sleep, it's a requirement of your restless mind." A restless mind cannot even rest in one place for a single night, let alone during the day. Even sleeping at night, the whole time the body shows its restlessness.

If you watch a person asleep at night, you will see he is continuously restless the whole time. You will find him moving his hands in much the same way he does when he is awake during the day. In his dream at night, you will find him running and panting in much the same way it happens with someone during the day — he feels out of breath, tired. At night, in dreams, he fights in much the same way he fights during the day. He is as angry at night as he is during the day. He is filled with passion during the day; at night as well. There is no fundamental difference between the day and the night of such a person, except that at night he lies down exhausted, unconscious; everything else continues to function as usual. So Buddha said, "I can change sides if I want to, but there is no need."

But we don't realize . . . A man sitting in a chair keeps jiggling his legs. Ask him: "Why are your legs jiggling like that? It's understandable if they move when you walk, but why are they moving when you are sitting in a chair?" No sooner do you say this than the man will stop immediately. Then he won't even move for a second, but he will have no explanation as to why he was doing it. It shows how the restlessness within causes agitation in the entire body. Inside is the restless mind; it cannot be still, in one position, even for a moment. It will keep the whole body fidgeting — the legs will move, the head will shake; even sitting, the body will change sides.

That's why, even for ten minutes, you find it so difficult to sit still in meditation. And from a thousand different spots the body urges you to twitch and turn. We do not notice this until we sit with awareness in meditation. We realize then what sort of a body this is; it doesn't want to remain still in one position even for a second. The confusion, the tension, and the excitement of the mind stir up the entire body.

For about ten minutes everything disappears in wakeless sleep — although these ten minutes are available only to one who is completely healthy and peaceful, not to everyone. Others get this kind of sleep anywhere from one to five minutes; most people get only two, or one minute of deep sleep. The little juice we receive in that one minute of reaching to the source of life, we apply to making our next twenty-four hours work. Whatever little amount of oil the lamp receives in that short period, we utilize it to carry on our lives for a full twenty-four hours. The lamp of one's life burns on whatsoever amount of oil it receives then. This is the reason the lamp burns so slow — not enough oil is collected to make the lamp of life burn brightly, so it can become a flaming torch.

Meditation brings you slowly to the source of life. Then it is not that you keep taking a handful of nourishment out of it, you are simply *in* the source itself. Then it is not that you refill your lamp with more oil — then the entire ocean of oil becomes available to you. Then you begin to live in that very ocean. With that kind of living, sleep disappears — not in the sense that one doesn't sleep any more, but in the sense that even when one is asleep, someone within remains wide awake. Then dreams exist no more. A yogi stays awake, he sleeps, but he never dreams — his dreams disappear totally. And when dreams disappear, thoughts disappear. What we know as thoughts in the wakeful state are called dreams in the sleeping state. There is only a slight difference between thoughts and dreams: thoughts are slightly more civilized dreams, while dreams are a little primitive in nature. Of the two, one is the original thought.

In fact, children, or the aboriginal tribes, can think only in pictures, not in words. Man's first thoughts are always in pictures. For example, when a child is hungry he does not think in words, "I am hungry." A child can visualize the mother's breast; he can imagine himself sucking the breast. He can be filled with the desire to go to the breast, but he cannot form the words. The word formation starts much later; pictures appear first.

When we don't know a particular language, we use pictures to express ourselves as well. If you happen to go to a foreign country and you don't know the language, and you want to drink water, you can cup your palms to your mouth and the stranger will understand that you are thirsty — because when words are not at hand, the need for pictures arises. And the interesting thing is that languages of words are different in different places, but the language of pictures is universal—because every man's picture language is the same.

We have invented different words, but pictures are not our invention. Pictures are the universal language of the human mind. A painting, therefore, is understood anywhere in the world. There is no need to change your language to understand a sculpture at Khajuraho or a painting by Leonardo. A sculpture at Khajuraho will be as understood by a Chinaman, a Frenchman and a German, as it is by you. And if you visit the museum of the Louvre in France, you will have no difficulty in following the paintings either. You may not understand the titles, because they are in French, but you will have no problem following the painting. The language of pictures is everyone's language.

The language of words is handy during the day, but it is not useful at night. We again become primitive at night. We disappear in sleep as we are. We lose our degrees, our university educations, everything. We are transported to a point where the original man once stood. That's why pictures emerge at night in sleep, and words appear during the day. If we want to make love during the day, we can think in terms of words, but at night there is no way to express love except through images.

Thoughts do not seem as alive as dreams. In dreams the whole image appears before you. That's why we enjoy watching a movie based on a novel more than reading the novel itself. The only reason for this is that the novel is in the language of words while the movie is in the language of images. In the same manner, you feel greater joy being here and listening to me live. You would not feel the same joy listening to this talk on a tape, because here the image is present, on tape there are only words. The language of images is nearer to us, more natural. At night words turn into pictures; that's all the difference there is.

The day dreams disappear, thoughts disappear too; the day thoughts disappear, dreams disappear as well. If the day is empty of thoughts, the night will be empty of dreams. And remember, dreams don't allow you to sleep, and thoughts don't allow you to awaken. Make sure you understand both things: dreams do not let you sleep, and thoughts do not let you awaken. If dreams disappear, sleep will be total; if thoughts disappear, awakening will be total. If the awakening is total and the sleep is total, then not much difference exists between the two. The only difference is in keeping the eyes open or closed, and in the body being at work or at rest.

One who is totally awakened sleeps totally, but in both states his consciousness remains exactly the same. Consciousness is one, unchangeable; only the body changes. Awake, the body is at work; asleep, the body is at rest.

The friend who has asked why God is not attained in sleep . . . My answer is: he can be attained if you can remain awake even in your sleep. And so, my method of meditation is a sleeping method — sleeping in awareness, entering into sleep with awareness. That's why I ask you to relax your body, to relax your breathing, to calm down your thoughts. All this is a preparation for sleep. Therefore, it so often happens that some friends go to sleep during meditation — obviously; this is a preparation for sleep. And, while preparing for it, they don't know when they go to sleep. That's why I repeat the third suggestion: stay awake inside, remain conscious within; let the body be totally relaxed, let the breathing be totally relaxed, more relaxed than it normally is while sleeping. But stay awake within. Within, let your awareness burn like a lamp so you don't fall asleep.

The initial conditions of meditation and sleep are the same, but there is a difference in the final condition. The first condition is that the body should be relaxed. If you suffer from insomnia, the first thing a doctor will teach you is relaxation. He will ask you to do the same thing I am asking: relax your body, don't let any tension remain in your body; let your body be totally loose, just like a fluff of cotton. Have you ever noticed how a dog or a cat sleeps? They sleep as if they are not. Have you ever noticed a baby sleeping? There is no tension anywhere — its arms and legs remain unbelievably loose. Watch a youth and an old man — you will find everything tense in them. So the doctor would ask you to relax totally.

The same condition applies to sleep: the breathing should be relaxed, deep and slow. You must have noticed that jogging, the breathing becomes faster. Similarly, when the body exerts itself at work, the breathing becomes faster and the blood circulation increases. For sleeping, the blood circulation should slow down — the situation should be just the opposite to jogging — and then the breathing will relax. So the second condition is: relax your breathing.

When thoughts run faster, the blood has to circulate rapidly in the brain — and when this happens, sleep becomes impossible. The condition of sleep requires a slower flow of blood to the brain. That's why we use pillows — to reduce the flow of blood to the brain. Without a pillow, the head lies at the same level as the body, and consequently, the blood flows at the same rate from head to toe. When the head is raised, the blood has difficulty moving upwards; its flow is reduced in the brain and moves throughout the rest of the body. And so, the greater the difficulty one has in falling asleep, the more pillows he will need to shove under his head to raise it. As the flow of blood is reduced, the brain relaxes and one finds it easy to fall asleep.

With fast-moving thoughts, the blood has to run faster too — because, for its movement, a thought has to rely on blood as the vehicle. The veins in the brain begin to work faster. You must have noticed that when a person is angry his veins swell. This is so because the veins have to make more space to let extra blood run through them. When the head cools down, the blood pressure also decreases.

In anger, the face and the eyes turn red. This is due to the extra blood that runs through the veins. In that state, thoughts move so fast that the blood has to flow faster. And breathing also becomes faster. When sex takes hold of the mind, the breathing becomes very heavy and the blood flows faster — because thoughts move so rapidly, the mind begins to function so fast, that all the veins in the brain start rushing with blood at great speed.

So the conditions for meditation are primarily the same as those applicable to sleep: relax your body, relax your breathing, let go of thoughts. And so, for sleep as well as for meditation, the initial conditions are equally true. The difference is in the final condition. In the former you remain deep in sleep; in meditation you remain fully awake — that's all.

So this friend is right in asking the question. There *is* a deep relationship between sleep and meditation, between *samadhi* and *sushupti*, deep sleep. However, there is one very significant difference between the two: the difference between a conscious and an unconscious state. Sleep is unawareness, meditation is awakening.

Another friend has asked: *What is the difference between what you call meditation, and auto-hypnosis?*

The difference is the same as that which exists between sleep and meditation. This also needs to be understood.

Sleep is that which comes naturally, while the sleep induced through effort is self-hypnosis. This is the only difference. The word "hypnos" also means sleep. Hypnosis means *tandra*, sleepiness. One is the kind of sleep which comes on its own, the other kind is cultivated, induced. If someone has difficulty sleeping, then he will have to do something about it. If a man lies down and begins to think continuously that he is falling asleep, and should this thought enter his being and take hold of his mind, the body will begin to respond accordingly too. The body will begin to relax, the breathing will begin to slow down, the mind will begin to quiet down.

If an environment for sleep is created within the body, the body will start functioning accordingly. The body is not concerned with facts, the body is very obedient. If you feel hungry every day at eleven o'clock, and if your clock stopped at eleven o'clock the previous night, one look at the clock and your stomach would say, "Time to eat" — even though it might be only eight o'clock in the morning. It is not eleven o'clock yet — there are still three more hours before eleven — but if the clock shows eleven o'clock, the stomach will complain of hunger because the stomach works mechanically. If you are used to going to bed at midnight, and if by chance your clock is two hours ahead, you will begin to feel drowsy as soon as the clock strikes twelve — even though it may be only ten o'clock. The body will immediately say, "It is twelve o'clock. Time to go to bed!"

The body is very obedient. The healthier the body, the more obedient it is. A healthy body means an obedient body. A sick body is one which has stopped obeying: you feel sleepy and the body refuses to sleep; you feel hungry and the body doesn't want to eat. A body which stops obeying is an ill body, and the body which is obedient is a healthy body — because the body follows us like a shadow. Difficulty arises when the body stops being obedient. So hypnosis simply means that the body has to be ordered, that it has to be made to follow commands.

Most of our illnesses are just pseudo. Almost fifty percent of our ailments are false. The reason behind the growing illness in the world is not that there is an increase in disease, it is because man's pretense is on the increase. Make sure you understand this well. With increased knowledge and better economic conditions there should be a decline in the number of diseases. But that has not happened, because man's capacity to lie has kept on growing. Man not only lies to others, he lies to himself too. He creates new diseases as well.

For example, if a man has suffered heavily in business and is on the verge of bankruptcy, he may not want to accept that he is bankrupt and so he is afraid to go into the marketplace; he knows he will have to face his creditors. All of a sudden he finds he has been overpowered by an illness that has made him bedridden. This is an illness created by his mind. It has a double advantage. Now he can tell others his illness

prevents him from attending to his business —
he has already convinced himself about this and
now he can convince others as well — and now
this illness is incurable. In the first place, it is not
an illness at all, and the more treatment he is
given, the sicker he will become.

If medicine fails to cure you, know well your
illness is not curable through medication — the
cause of the illness lies somewhere else; it has
nothing to do with medication. You may curse
the medicine and call the doctors stupid for not
finding the right treatment for you; you may try
ayurvedic medicine or naturopathic treatment;
you may turn to allopathy or homeopathy — nothing will work. No doctor can be of any use to
you, simply because a doctor can only treat an
authentic illness — he has no control over something pseudo. And the interesting thing is that
you keep busy creating illnesses like that, and
you want them to remain.

More than fifty percent of female sicknesses
are false. Women have learned a formula from
childhood: they get love only when they are
sick, otherwise not. Whenever the wife is ill, the
husband takes off work, pulls up a chair and sits
by her bedside. He may curse himself for doing
so, but he does it. So whenever a woman wants
attention from her man, she promptly falls ill.
That's why we find women sick almost all the
time. They know that by being ill they can hold
sway over the entire household.

An ill person becomes a dictator, a tyrant. If
the person says, "Turn off the radio!" it is
promptly turned off. If the person says, "Put off
the lights and go to sleep", or "Everyone stays

home; no one is to go out", the members of the household do as he says. The more there is a dictatorial tendency in a person, the more he will get sick — because who wants to hurt the feelings of someone ill? But this is dangerous. This way, we actually contribute to his sickness. It is good if a husband sits beside his wife when she is well; it is understandable. But for heaven's sake he should not stop going to the office when she is sick and thus contribute to her sickness. It's too costly a bargain.

A mother should not pay too much attention when her child gets sick; otherwise, whenever the child wants attention, he will fall ill. When a child gets ill, be less worried about him so that no association between illness and love becomes established in his mind. The child should not get the impression that whenever he is ill the mother will pat his head and tell him stories. Instead, the mother should pamper the child when he is happy, so that love becomes associated with joy and happiness.

We have associated love with misery, and that is very dangerous — because it means that whenever one needs love, he will invite misery so love can follow. And so whosoever longs for love will fall sick, because he knows sickness brings love. But love is never to be found through sickness. Remember, illness brings pity, not love, and to be an object of pity is insulting, very degrading. Love is a totally different thing. But we have no awareness of love.

What I am saying is that the body follows our suggestions — if we want to be ill, the poor body gets ill. Hypnosis is useful in curing such illnesses. What this means is that for a fake illness, fake medicine will work — not real medicine. If we can make ourselves believe we are ill, we can also make ourselves believe we are not ill and rid ourselves of the illness. To this end, hypnosis is of great value. Today, there is hardly a hospital in a developed country without a hypnotist on its staff. In the West, the physician is accompanied by the hypnotist, because there are a number of illnesses for which a doctor is totally useless, for which only a hypnotist is of use. He puts the patient under hypnosis and then gives suggestions that he is feeling well.

Do you know that only three percent of all snakes are poisonous? But generally, a man dies from any snake bite if he believes a snake bite can kill a man. And if he were to be fully convinced that a snake had actually bitten him, he would die. He would die not because of the snake bite, but because of the belief that a snake had bitten him.

I have heard . . .

Once it happened that a man stayed overnight in an inn. He ate dinner at night and left early the next morning. A year later he returned to the same inn. The innkeeper was shocked to see him. "Are you all right?" he asked the traveler.

"I am all right. Why, what's the matter?"

"We were quite frightened," said the innkeeper. "You see, the last night you stayed here, a snake fell into the pot and was cooked with the food served to you. Four other people who ate the food died soon after. We couldn't figure out what happened to you because you left quite early. We were so worried about you."

When the traveler heard this, he said, "What? A snake in my food?" and dropped dead. A year later! He died of fear.

For such ailments, hypnosis is very useful. Hypnosis only means that the falsehood we have created around ourselves can be neutralized by another falsehood. Remember, if an imaginary thorn has pricked your foot, don't try to remove it with the help of a real thorn; it would be dangerous. First of all, the imaginary one will never be removed, and furthermore, the real one will hurt your foot. A false thorn has to be pulled out with the help of a false thorn.

So, what is the relation between meditation and hypnosis? Only this: hypnosis is required to pull out the false thorns stuck in your body.

An example of hypnosis is when I tell you to feel that the body is relaxing. This is hypnosis. Actually you yourself have assumed that the body cannot relax. In order to nullify this assumption, hypnosis is necessary — otherwise not. Were it not for your false assumption, feeling, just once, that the body is relaxed, it will relax. The suggestions I give you are not really to relax your bodies, but to take away your belief that the body can never relax. This cannot be done without creating a counter-belief in you that the body is relaxing. Your false concept will be neutralized by *this* false concept, and when your body relaxes, you will know it is relaxed. Relaxation is a very natural quality of the body, but you have filled yourselves with so much tension that now you have to do something to get rid of it.

This is as far as hypnosis goes. When you begin to feel the body is relaxing, the breathing is relaxing, the mind is calming down — this is hypnosis. But only up to this point. What follows afterwards is meditation — up to this point there is no meditation. Meditation begins after this, when you are in the state of awareness. When you become aware within, when you begin to witness that the body is relaxed, that the breathing is relaxed, that thoughts have either ceased or are still moving — when you begin to watch, just watch — this watching, this state of witnessing is meditation. Whatever is before that is only hypnosis.

So hypnosis means a cultivated sleep. When we are not sleepy, we induce sleep; we make an effort, we invite sleep. Sleep can also be invited if we prepare for it and move into a state of let-go. But meditation and hypnosis are not one and the same thing. Please understand this. As long as you are feeling according to my suggestions, that is hypnosis. Once you feel my suggestions stopping and awareness beginning, that is the start of meditation. Meditation begins with the advent of the state of witnessing.

Hypnosis is needed because you have gotten yourselves into a reverse kind of hypnosis. In scientific terms, this is not hypnosis, it is *de*hypnosis. We are already hypnotized, although we are not aware how we became hypnotized and what kind of tricks we have used to create this hypnosis. We have lived the major part of our lives under the influence of hypnosis. And when we want to be hypnotized, we don't realize what we are doing. We live throughout our lives like this. If this becomes clear, the hypnotic spell will break — and once this hypnosis breaks, entering within will become possible, because hypnosis, basically, is a world of non-reality.

For example, a man is learning to ride a bicycle. To practice, he starts out on a wide road. The road is sixty feet wide, and there is a milestone on the edge. Even if the man decided to ride blindfolded on that wide road, there is very little chance of his hitting the milestone. But the man doesn't yet know how to ride a bicycle.

He never looks at the road; his eyes spot the milestone first and the fear that he might hit the milestone grips him. That's it. As soon as this fear of hitting the stone grips him, he is hypnotized. To say he becomes hypnotized means he no longer sees the road, he begins to see the stone alone. He becomes afraid, and the handle of his bicycle starts turning toward the stone. The more the handle turns, the more afraid he gets. The handle, of course, will turn where his attention is, and his attention is on the stone because he is afraid to hit it. So the road disappears from his vision and only the stone remains. Hypnotized by the stone, he is pulled towards it. The more pulled he is, the more he is scared; the more he is scared, the more he is pulled. Finally he hits the milestone.

Watching this, any sensible person might wonder how, on such a wide road, the man hit the milestone? How come he couldn't keep himself away from it? Obviously, he was hypnotized. He concentrated on the stone in order to save himself from landing on top of it, and this made him see nothing but the stone. When his mind became fixed on the stone, his hands automatically turned the bicycle in that direction, because the body follows your attention. The more scared he grew, the more he had to concentrate on the stone. He became hypnotized by the stone; his fear drew him toward the stone, and he finally crashed into it.

In life, we often make those very mistakes we would rather avoid. We become hypnotized by them. A man, for example, is afraid he may lose his peace of mind and get angry. In this situation, he will find himself getting angry twenty-four times in twenty-four hours. The more afraid he is of getting angry, the more he will be hypnotized by anger. Then he will look for excuses to be angry the whole twenty-four hours.

Another man who is afraid to look at beautiful women because they might excite him sexually, will see beautiful women the whole twenty-four hours. By and by, even ugly women will appear beautiful to him; even men will begin to look like women to him. If, from behind, he sees a *sadhu* with long hair, he will make sure which it is, a man or a woman. Eventually women in pictures and on posters will begin to attract him, to hypnotize him. He will hide pictures of nude women in the *Gita* and the *Koran*, and will look at them without even wondering how he can be so hypnotized by mere lines and colors. He has always wanted to save himself from women and now he is afraid of them; now he sees women everywhere. Whether he goes to a temple or to a mosque, or anywhere else, he sees nothing but women. This is hypnosis too.

A society which is against sex eventually becomes sexual. A society which is anti-sex, which denounces sex — its whole mind will become sexual, because it will be hypnotized by the very thing it criticizes; all its attention will be concentrated on it. The more a society talks of celibacy, the more dirty-minded and lecherous will the people be who are born into it. The reason is that too much talk of celibacy focuses the mind on sexuality. All this is hypnosis — created by us — and we are living in it. The whole world is entangled in this hypnosis. And it is difficult to break, because the hypnosis grows right along with whatsoever attempts we make to break it.

In this fashion, God knows how many kinds of hypnoses we have already created, and are still continuing to create for ourselves. And then we live with them. They need to be broken so we can wake up. But to cut through this false web, we need to discover false means.

In a way, all *sadhana*, all spiritual practice, is meant to remove the falsehood from around us. And so, all *sadhana* is false. Methods devised all over the world to help us reach God are false, because we have never been away from him. Only in thought have we been away from him.

It is just as if a man were to sleep in Dwarka and dream that he is in Calcutta. Now, in his dream, he begins to worry: his wife is ill and here he is in Calcutta; he must get back to Dwarka. He goes around asking people, checking the railway timetable, inquiring about plane flights, to get back to Dwarka as soon as he can. But any suggestion he might take on how to reach Dwarka will be wrong, will get him into trouble, because he is not in Calcutta in the first place. He never went to Calcutta — it was only a dream, a hypnosis. Whatever way someone might show him for returning to Dwarka will only put him into trouble.

No path has any meaning; all paths are false. Even if the man returns to Dwarka, the route he would take would be false. He cannot find the right way back because there can never be one: he never went to Calcutta in the first place. What does it mean for him to find a way back? The train he will ride to Dwarka will be as false as Calcutta was. If he goes to Howrah Station, buys a ticket and catches a train to Dwarka — all of this will be false. All the stations he will pass on his way back will be false. Then he would arrive in Dwarka and wake up happy. But he would be surprised to find that he had never gone anywhere, that he had been in his bed all along. Then how did he come back? His going was false and so was his return.

No one has ever gone outside God. One cannot, because, all over, only he is — there is no way one can step out of him. And so, all going is false, all returning is false. However, since we have already left on an imaginary journey, we will have to return; there is no other way. We will have to find the means to return. But once you have returned, you will find that all methods were false, all *sadhana* was false. The *sadhana* was necessary to bring us back from the dream. Once we have understood this, perhaps nothing will have to be done then, and you will suddenly find that you have returned. But this is difficult to understand because you are already in Calcutta. You may say, "What you are saying is right but I am already in Calcutta. Show me the way back!"

Another friend has asked: *Have you found God?*

This is just the kind of question the traveler to Calcutta would ask. I would like to ask this friend, "Did you ever lose God?" — because, if I say I have found God, it means I had assumed him lost. He is already found. Even when we feel we have lost him, he is still with us. It is simply that we are under hypnosis and therefore feel we have lost him. So, if a man says, "Yes, I have found God", he is mistaken. He still doesn't understand that he had never lost him in the first place. Therefore, those who come to know God will never say they have found God. They will say, "He was never lost."

The day Buddha became enlightened, people gathered around him and asked, "What have you attained?" Buddha replied, "I have attained nothing. I have simply come to see that which I had never lost. I have found what I already had."

So, in sympathy, the people of the village said, "Too bad. You labored in vain."

"Yes," said Buddha, "in that sense it is true I labored in vain. But now there is no need for me to labor any more — this much advantage I have gained. Now I won't go out seeking, now I won't wander to attain anything, now I won't set out on any journey — that is my gain. Now

I know that I am where I already was."

We only go away in our dreams. We never actually reach the places we feel we have. Hence, in a sense, all religions are false; all *sadhanas*, all yogas are false. They are false in the sense that they are all methods of returning. And yet, they are very useful.

A village *shaman* who shakes off snake poison with the help of *mantras* is very useful for those who are bitten by a snake — even if they are bitten by a false snake. Otherwise, without him, people would die of the bite from a snake which was not there.

Such a man once lived in my neighborhood. He is now dead. People came to him from far and wide to draw snake venom out. He was a very clever man; he had tamed a few snakes. When a person bitten by a snake came to him he would use his *shaman* skills and ask what kind of snake it was, where it had bitten, whether the snake was dead or alive. After obtaining all the information, he would apply his trick and call the snake. He had everything worked out — which snake was to be set loose, on which signal, et cetera. Within an hour or so, a snake that matched the description would come through the door, hissing. The whole thing would create a sensation; the bitten man would feel dumbfounded.

Someone bitten by a snake can rarely see or figure anything out right — What bit him? What did it look like? Where was it? — he is so overwhelmed by being bitten the snake disappears in the meantime. If the snake had been killed, the *shaman* would call its soul to accompany his snake. Then he would scold and rebuke the snake for biting this man. The snake would then hit its head on the ground and beg forgiveness. In the meantime the poison in the man would start wearing off. Then the snake would be told to draw out the poison. The snake would promptly go up to the man who had been bitten and put its mouth to the wound, and the man would recover.

Unfortunately, it once happened a snake bit this man's son. He got into trouble because none of his treatments worked. He came running to me and said, "Please help. I am in trouble. Please tell me what I should do? A snake has bitten my son and he knows about my pet snakes. I am so unfortunate, please tell me what shall I do? I am helpless. My son won't survive!"

I was surprised. I asked, "But what about your treatment? People come to you from afar for this cure!"

"That's all fine," he said, "but even *I* would be in trouble if a snake were to bite me; I wouldn't even be able to save myself. I know the tricks of the trade; I wouldn't trust anybody to treat me the way I do." The boy died. He could not save his son.

False means are needed to remove the falsehood. And they have their own meaningfulness. They are meaningful because we have gone into falsehoods. So never bother to ask; in the beginning it is indeed hypnosis. The initial stages are of hypnosis, of sleep; only the final stage is of meditation — and that is the precious one. Before you can attain to that stage, this background is quite necessary — necessary so you can come out of the falsehood you have strayed into.

Never ask, "Have you or have you not found God?" This is all wrong. Who is going to find? What is going to be found? That which is, is. The day you come to know this, you will see that you have never lost anything, nor have you ever gone anywhere; nothing has ever been destroyed, nothing has ever died. What is, is. That day, all journeys, all going anywhere, will stop.

And now this question: *What is the meaning of liberation from the cycle of birth and death?*

Liberation from the cycle of birth and death does not mean that you will not be born here again. It means that now there is neither "coming" nor "going" — nowhere, not on any plane. Then you remain rooted where you are. The day this happens, the springs of joy burst forth on all sides. We cannot experience joy being in an imaginary place, we can only find joy being where we really are. We can only be happy being what we are, we can never be happy being what we are not. So moving through the cycle of birth and death means we are wandering through illusory places — we are lost somewhere we have never ever been. We are wandering through some place where we are never ever supposed to be, while the place where we actually are, we have lost sight of it. So freedom from birth and death means coming back to where we are, coming back home.

Moving into God means being exactly what we actually are. It is not as if someday you will come across God standing somewhere and you will salute him and say, "Thank heaven I met you!" There is no such God as this, and if you happen to come across one, now well it is all hypnosis. Such a God will be your own creation, and meeting him will be as false as losing him was. This is not the way you will ever find God.

Our language often proves misleading, because the expression "to find God" or "to attain God" gives the impression one will be able to see God face-to-face. Such words are very erroneous. Listening to them one gets the idea that somebody will reveal himself, that one will have an eye-to-eye contact with him, that one will be able to embrace him. This is all wrong. If you ever do come across such a God, beware! Such a God will be totally a creation of your mind — it will be hypnosis.

We have to get out of all hypnosis and retrace our steps back to the point where there is no sleep, no hypnosis, where we are fully aware, rooted in our own beings. The experience one will have then will be the experience of the unity of life; it will be the experience of existence being one, indivisible. The name of that experience is God.

Now let us prepare for the morning meditation.

FIND YOUR OWN WAY

Evening
October 30, 1969

A friend has asked: *You mentioned once that there is no other truth greater than death. You have also said somewhere that there is nothing like death. Which of the two statements is true?*

Both are true. When I say there is no other truth greater than death, I am drawing your attention to the fact that the phenomenon of death is an enormous reality in this life — in what we call "life" and understand as "life"; in terms of one's personality, which consists of what I describe as "I". This personality will die; what we call "life" will die too. Death is inevitable. Certainly, you will die and I will die, and this life will also be destroyed, turned into dust, erased.

When I say there is no other greater truth than death, I want to remind you of the fact that we are all going to die. And when I say that death is totally false, I want to remind you that within this "I", within "you", there is someone else who will never die. And there is also a life that is different from what you believe to be life, a life without death. Both these things are true; they are simultaneously true. If you take only one of them to be true, you will not be able to comprehend the whole truth.

If someone says that the shadow is a reality, that darkness is a reality, he is right. Darkness exists and so does the shadow. And if someone else says there is no darkness, he is right too. What he is saying is that darkness does not have a positive existence. If I ask you to bring me a couple of bags of darkness, you won't be able to. A room is filled with darkness, and if you are asked to throw the darkness out, you won't be able to. Or, if I say, "If darkness is in there, then please bring it out," you will be unable to. Why? It is because darkness has a negative existence; darkness is merely the absence of light.

Although darkness exists, nevertheless it is only the absence of light. And so if someone were to say there is no darkness, he is right. There is the presence of light and there is the absence of light, but there is nothing like darkness as such. That's why we can do whatsoever we want with light, but with darkness we can do nothing. If you want to remove darkness, you will have to bring in light; if you want to bring in darkness, you will have to put out the light. With darkness, nothing can be done directly.

You are jogging along the road. Your shadow appears behind you; it also runs with you. Everyone can see the shadow; no one can deny it. And yet it can be said that there is no shadow because it has no entity of its own. The shadow exists because your body obstructs the sunlight. When the light is covered by your body, a shadow is formed; when the sun comes above your head, no shadow is formed because the sunrays are not obstructed. If we were to make a human figure of glass, no shadow would ever appear because the rays would pass through the glass.

When light is hindered, a shadow is formed; a shadow is merely an absence of light. So if a person says the shadow exists, he is not wrong. But this is a half-truth. He should further add that the shadow does not exist. Then the truth becomes complete. This means a shadow is something which exists and yet does not exist. But with our way of thinking, we cannot see anything unless it is divided into two independent parts.

Once a man was tried for murder. He had killed a man, and those who had seen the crime being committed had come forward as witnesses. One witness said, "The crime was committed in the open and there were stars shining in the sky. I saw the stars as well as the murder." He was followed by another eyewitness who said, "The crime was committed inside the house, near the door, close to a wall. There are bloodstains on the wall, and since I was standing beside the wall, my clothes were also stained with blood. This murder took place inside the house."

The judge was puzzled. How could both be telling the truth? Obviously, one of them was lying. The murderer began to laugh. The judge asked what was so funny. The man said, "Let me tell you that both of them are right. The house was incomplete; the roof had not yet been laid — the stars could be seen above. The murder took place under the open sky, but close to the door, close to the wall which bears the bloodstains. The house was almost ready; the walls had been raised, only the roofing was not yet done. So both are right."

Life is so complicated that even the things we find contradictory in it turn out to be right. Life is highly complex. Life is not the way we think it is — it contains many contradictions; it is very vast.

In one sense, death *is* the greatest truth — because the way we are living will come to an end; we will die the way we are, and the framework we have created will also be destroyed. Those we see as constituting our whole world — wife, husband, son, father, friend — they will all die. And yet death is a falsehood, because there is someone who dwells inside the son who is not the son and who will never die. There is someone who dwells inside the father who is not the father and who will never die. The father, of course, will die, but there is someone within him besides — different from the father, separate, more than any relative — who will never die. The body will die but there is someone within the body who never dies. Both these things are simultaneously true. And so, both these things need to be kept in mind to understand the nature of death.

Another friend has asked: *The things we want to destroy — such as the chains of blind faith or superstition — find even more confirmation in your talks. It seems, according to what you are saying, that there is life after death, that there are gods and there are ghosts, that there is transmigration of the soul. In that case, it would be difficult to get rid of superstitions. Won't they become even stronger?*

Two things need to be understood here. One is: if something is accepted as a superstition without researching and investigating it properly, then that is tantamount to creating an even greater superstition; it shows a highly superstitious mind. One man believes there are ghosts and evil spirits and you call him superstitious; you believe there are none and that makes you feel that you are very knowledgeable. But the question is: what is superstition? If someone believes there are ghosts and evil spirits without any investigation, that is superstition; and if someone else believes there are no such things, without investigation, then that is superstition too. Superstition means believing something without knowing it to be true. Just because someone holds beliefs contrary to yours does not mean he is superstitious.

A believer in God can be as gullible as a nonbeliever. We must understand the definition of superstition. It means: to believe in something blindly without verification. The Russians are superstitious atheists; the Indians are superstitious theists — both suffer from blind faith. The Russians have never cared to discover there is no God and then believed it to be so, nor have the Indians tried to ascertain that God is before believing it to be so. So do not be mistaken in thinking that theists alone are superstitious, atheists have their own superstitions too. And the strange thing is that there is also a *scientific* superstition. It sounds contradictory. How can there be a scientific superstition?

If you have studied geometry, you must have come across Euclid's definition where he says a line has length but no breadth. Now, what can be more superstitious than this? There has never been a line with no breadth. Children are taught that a point has neither length nor breadth, and even the greatest scientist works on the assumption that a point has no length or breadth. Can a point exist without length and breadth?

We are all used to the digits one through nine. One may well ask: is this any less than superstition? Why nine digits? No scientist can explain why nine digits. Why not seven? What's wrong with seven? Why not three? There are mathematicians — Liebnitz was one of them — who got along with three digits. He said: one, two, three is followed by ten, eleven, twelve, thirteen; then twenty, twenty-one, twenty-two, twenty-three. His numbering system was such; he got along very well with it, and he challenged those who disagreed with him to prove him wrong. He questioned the need for nine digits.

Later on, Einstein said that even three digits are also unnecessary, that one can even get along with two; it will be difficult with only one digit, but one can manage with two. That there should be nine digits in mathematics is a scientific superstition. But the mathematician is not ready to give up either. He says, "How can you work with less than nine digits?" So this is just a belief too; it has no more significance than that.

From a scientific point of view we believe thousands of things to be right, but they are actually superstitions. Scientists are also superstitious, and in this age, religious superstitions are fading, while scientific superstitions are growing. The difference between the two is simply that if you ask a religious person how he came to know about God he will say it is written in the *Gita*, and if you ask him how he came to know there are nine digits in arithmetic, he will say it is written in such-and-such a mathematician's book.

What is the difference between the two? One kind of answer is found in the *Gita*, in the *Koran*; another kind of answer is found in a book of mathematics. What is the difference? This shows we have to understand what is really meant by superstition. Superstition means: that which we believe in without having knowledge of it. We accept many things and we reject many things without knowing anything about them — this is superstitious too.

Suppose a man in a village is possessed by a ghost. Educated people will say it is superstition. Let us assume the uneducated people are superstitious; we have already branded them as superstitious because, being uneducated, these simple people are unable to offer any argument in favor of their belief. So all the educated people of the village maintain that the story of this man being possessed by an evil spirit is fake, but they don't know that at a university like Harvard, in America, there is a department conducting research into ghosts and spirits. The department has even circulated photographs of them. They have no idea that, currently, some highly recognized scientists are deeply involved in research into ghosts and spirits, and have attained so many results, that sooner or later they will come to see that it was they, the educated men, who were superstitious, and that those they called superstitious, may not have known anything about what they believed in, although what they were saying was right.

If you read Ryon or Oliver Lodge, you will be amazed. Oliver Lodge was a Nobel prize-winning scientist. Throughout his life he was involved in investigating ghosts and spirits. Before his death, he left a document in which he said, "All the truths of science I have discovered are not half as true as ghosts and spirits. But we have no knowledge of them because the superstitious educated do not care to find out about the discoveries happening in the world."

If one man says he can read another's mind, we will call it superstition. In Russia, where there are what we may call "rigorous" scientists, there is a man by the name of Fiodev. He is a great Russian scientist. Sitting in Moscow, he has communicated his thoughts, without any visible means, to the mind of a person sitting a thousand miles away in Tiflis. This was examined scientifically and found to be correct. Scientists are engaged in this kind of research because sooner or later it will be useful in space travel. In the event of a mechanical failure in a spaceship, which is always possible, through these means scientists can establish contact with the travelers. Otherwise the spaceship may be lost forever. It is out of this concern that Russian scientists are conducting intensive research into telepathy and have achieved some astounding results.

Fiodev carried out his research with the help of a friend. A thousand miles away in Tiflis, his friend hid himself behind a bush in a garden with a wireless set in his hand. And he and Fiodev stayed in touch with each other. After a while he informed Fiodev that a man had arrived and sat on bench number ten. He asked Fiodev to send this man a message to go to sleep within three minutes. The man was wide awake; he was smoking and humming away to himself. Fiodev began sending him suggestions — the same as I do — that "You are relaxing. You are relaxing." From a distance of a thousand miles, for three minutes Fiodev suggested intensely, "Go to sleep. Go to sleep," and, concentrating on bench number ten, he continued suggesting the same thought, "Go to sleep. Go to sleep." In exactly three minutes the man sitting on the bench was asleep, the cigarette fallen from his hands.

But this could have been a coincidence. Perhaps the man sitting on the bench was tired, and so he had fallen asleep. And so, the friend told Fiodev that the man had indeed fallen asleep, but that it could be a coincidence, so he asked Fiodev to wake him up in exactly seven minutes. Fiodev kept suggesting to that man to wake up, and in seven minutes precisely the man opened his eyes and got up. The man on the bench was a total stranger; he had no idea what was happening, and Fiodev's friend approached him and asked if he'd felt anything unusual.

The man said, "Yes, I certainly did. I was very puzzled. I came here to wait for somebody, and suddenly I felt that my body was about to fall asleep. I lost control and went to sleep. And then, I felt strongly as if someone was telling me 'Get up. Get up. Get up in seven minutes!' I can't figure any of this out." The man had no idea what had happened.

Communication of thought without any medium has become a scientific truth, but an educated man would call it superstition. It is possible that a sick man in one town can be cured from a faraway town; it's not too difficult. It's also possible that a snakebite can be healed from a distance of thousands of miles; there's not much difficulty to it. But there are many different kinds of superstitions. And remember, the superstition of an educated man is always more dangerous than that of an uneducated man, because the educated man does not consider his superstition to be superstition. For him it is a result arrived at after great deliberation.

Now this friend says we have to break the chains of superstition. First make sure there are any chains, otherwise you may break somebody's arms and legs in the process. Chains can only be broken if there are any. What if there are none? You must also make sure that what you believe is a chain that needs to be broken does not happen to be an ornament you may have to remake. All these things require very careful consideration.

I am absolutely against superstition; all kinds

of superstitions must be destroyed — but this does not mean that I am superstitious about this destruction. It does not mean one should go about destroying them without a clear under-standing of them, that without due considera-tion one should simply be bent upon breaking them. Then such arbitrary destruction will also become superstition.

Every age has its own superstitions. Re-member, superstitions have their fashion too. In every age superstitions take on a new form. Man drops old superstitions and takes on new ones, but he never gets rid of them forever; he alters them and he changes them. But we never realize this.

For example, once upon a time there was a superstition that the man who applied *tilak*, the forehead mark, was considered religious. What has applying *tilak* to do with being religious? But that's the way it was understood. And someone who didn't apply the *tilak* was looked down upon as irreligious. This old superstition is no longer in vogue. Now we have new supersti-tions, equally as foolish. If a man wears a tie he is considered distinguished, otherwise he is con-sidered ordinary — it is the same thing; there is no difference at all. The tie has replaced the *tilak*, while the man has remained the same. Where is there any difference?

The tie is no better than the *tilak*. Perhaps it's even worse, because at least there was a mean-ing to applying the *tilak*. The tie has absolutely no meaning in this country, although it may have a meaning in some other country. A tie is useful in cold countries where it helps protect the throat against cold. In those countries, a man who cannot afford to cover his throat against the cold must obviously be a poor man. A man of means is able to cover his throat with the help of a necktie; however, when somebody puts a tie around his neck in a hot country such as this, then it seems a little scary — one wonders whether such a man is affluent or insane!

To be affluent does not mean one has to suffer from heat or wear this noose around his neck. A tie means a noose; a tie means a knot. Using it in a cold country makes sense, but in a hot country it is totally meaningless. And yet, a man who has an idea of dignity — the magistrate, the attorney, the politician — is out there with this noose around his neck! And these very people denounce the *tilak* wearers as superstitious! One can well ask them, "Isn't wearing a necktie a superstition too? Which scientific system are you applying, that you have tied this tie around your neck?" But since the tie is a superstition of this age it is acceptable, and since the *tilak* is a superstition of the past, it is unacceptable.

As I said earlier, as the tie has some meaning for people in cold countries, applying a *tilak* can also have meaning, but without first looking into it, it is utterly dangerous and wrong to call it a superstition right away — you may not have given any thought as to why a *tilak* is applied. People mostly apply it out of superstition; however, there *was* some scientific reason when people applied it for the first time. Actually, *tilak* is applied on the forehead at the spot between the two eyes where the *agya chakra*, the third-eye *chakra*, is located. Even with a little meditation this spot gets hot; however, it cools down with the application of sandalwood. The application of sandalwood is a highly scientific technique, but now it is lost; people are not concerned with that science any more. Now anybody goes on applying sandalwood whether he has any knowledge of the *agya chakra* or has ever done any meditation or not.

It is strange to find people wearing ties in hot countries. Wearing a tie can have a scientific basis in cold countries, and similarly, a *tilak* has a scientific meaning for one who meditates on the *agya chakra* because sandalwood cools that spot. Meditating on the *agya chakra*, stimulation occurs and heat is created in that area — and it needs cooling down or else it will harm the brain. But were we determined to remove the *tilak* altogether, we would of course take it away from those who are wearing it pointlessly, but we would also be removing it from the forehead of the poor guy who may have applied it for his own reason. And if he won't remove it, we will call him superstitious.

What I am saying is that there is no way you can determine what is superstitious and what is not. Actually, the same thing can be a superstition under one condition and scientific under different conditions. Something which might appear to be scientific under a certain condition may appear unscientific under a different set of conditions.

For example, in Tibet, there is a practice of taking a bath once a year — which is quite scientific, because there is no dust in Tibet and, being in a cold climate, people do not sweat. So they don't need to bathe. Taking a bath every day would simply harm their bodies; it would cause them to lose much body heat. And how are they going to replace that heat? It could prove very costly to stay uncovered in Tibet. If man were to keep his body uncovered for a whole day, he would need forty percent more food to replace the calories lost. In a place like India, if a man goes about without clothes, he is revered as a renunciate. Mahavira was sensible: he remained naked — and in a hot country like this, the more the heat leaves the body, the cooler it feels inside. But if a follower of Mahavira were to arrive in Tibet, naked, he would deserve to be admitted to a mental asylum. To appear in Tibet like this would be absolutely unscientific, stupid. But that's how it always happens.

When a Tibetan *lama* comes to India, he never bathes. Once I stayed with Tibetan *lamas* in Bodh Gaya. They were stinking so badly it was a torture to sit near them. When I asked why they were like that, they replied, "We follow the rule of bathing only once a year." This is where I make the distinction between superstition and science. That which is a science in Tibet is a superstition in India. Here, these *lamas* are stinking without realizing their bodies are perspiring heavily and that there is much dust all around.

We have no idea, but there are some countries where there is no dust at all. When Khrushchev first came to India he was taken to Agra to see the Taj Mahal, and on the way he saw a whirlwind of dust taking shape. He had the car stopped, got out, and stood right in the middle of the whirlwind. He was so happy. He said, "I am so lucky, I have never had such an experience before." We wouldn't feel lucky to be caught in so much dust. But where he comes from, there are piles of snow, not dust. It was a fascinating experience for him, as it is for us when we are in snow. How excited we feel when we walk on snow in the Himalayas. So don't get into breaking things simply believing them to be chains, without first taking into consideration the age, the conditions, and their usefulness.

A scientific mind is that which always hesitates. A man with a scientific mind never makes a decision in haste, saying, "This is right and that is wrong." Rather he always says, "Perhaps this may be right, but let me search more and more." Even at the end of his search he never comes to a decision and says with finality, "Okay, this is wrong, so destroy it." Life is so mysterious that nothing can be said in such definite terms. All we can say is, "So far, we have known this much, and based upon this knowledge such-and-such a thing appears to be wrong" — that's all. A man with a scientific attitude will say, "Based on the information available so far, such-and-such a thing does not seem to be right today; however, with added information it may appear right tomorrow. Something which is right today may prove to be wrong tomorrow." Such a man never makes a hasty decision about what is right and what is wrong. He always keeps on searching with an inquiring and humble mind.

There is fun in holding on to a superstition, and there is also fun in breaking it. The fun in holding on to a superstition is that it spares us the trouble of thinking — we believe what everyone else believes. We don't even want to ask the reason behind it, or why it's so. Who wants to bother? One simply follows the crowd. It's convenient to have superstitions.

And then there are people who are out to crack superstitions — that too is very convenient. The man who cracks them appears to be rational, without actually being rational. It's not easy to be rational; to see things rationally is to strain every nerve. This man looks into things so closely it becomes difficult for him to make any categorical statement. And so his statements are always conditional. He will say, "Under such conditions it is valid not to bathe in Tibet, while under other conditions it is utterly superstitious not to bathe in India." The man who thinks rationally will speak this kind of language.

On the other hand, a social reformer shows no concern for what he is saying: he is concerned with destroying things; he wants to destroy certain things. I say: go ahead and destroy — there are many things which have to be destroyed — but the first thing that has to be destroyed, however, is thoughtlessness. The tendency to act without first giving something rational thought is the primary thing that needs to be destroyed. So what it means is: if you destroy something without first giving it proper thought, then such destruction has no value. The tendency to think rationally has to be created, and the tendency to believe thoughtlessly has to be destroyed. This will lead us to see different contexts, deeper meanings. Then we will make an intensive search; we will think and reason. Then we will consider all the possibilities.

Psychoanalysis is very popular in the West and the interesting thing is that psychoanalysis is doing exactly the same kind of work as the good old witch doctor did in the villages. Nowadays, in France, there is an active sect created by Cuvier. Cuvier works on the same principles as the witch doctor did, except that Cuvier is a scientist and he uses scientific terminology — other than that everything is the same; there is no difference.

You will be amazed to know that when a *sadhu*, a mendicant, an ordinary man of the village, with no knowledge of medicine, gives a pinch of ash to a sick man in the name of God, we call it superstition. And yet, it works as effectively, and people are cured in the same proportion as with allopathic treatment. It is very interesting — the same ratio. Many experiments are being carried out in this area.

A unique experiment was conducted in a London hospital. A hundred patients with the same illness were divided into two groups. Fifty were given the regular injection, while the other fifty were injected with water. And the amazing thing is that the ratio of cured patients in both cases was the same. So the question was raised: what's going on?

In view of this experiment, it became necessary to examine the issue more closely. And what became clear was that the idea, the *feeling* that medicine is being given, works more than the medicine itself. Also, even the medicine, the dispensing of the medicine itself, does not work so much as does the idea of how expensive the medicine is and how well-known the doctor is. A lesser known doctor fails in his treatment not because he does not know his profession, but only because he is not very well-known. A well-recognized doctor impresses a patient at once. With his impressive attire, the overbearing set up, his fees, his big car, the long wait for an appointment, the crowd, the standing in line — you are already so impressed that whether he knows what he is giving you or not has very little effect.

The truth is that to be a good doctor you don't need a first class knowledge of medicine, what you need is an excellent knowledge of advertising. The question is how well you can publicize yourself. Publicity pays more, not the medicine.

Recently, a medical survey revealed that in France there are about eighty thousand physicians and about one hundred and sixty thousand quacks. When the patient gets tired of the practicing physicians, he is cured by those who have no knowledge of medicine. But they know the trick of how to treat a patient. That's why you see so many kinds of "pathies" prevalent. Can you imagine — all these different kinds of "pathies" abounding in this age of science? Even naturopathy works — a bandaging of mud on the stomach works; an enema with water works; the witch doctor's charms work. Even homeopathy, which consists of nothing but tiny sugar pills, works. These all work, and so does allopathy.

So the question arises: how does a patient get well? If a village quack prescribes a little dust

and cures his patients, then we will have to
think carefully; we will have to be concerned
about whether to break such superstitions or
not. The man with a stethoscope around his
neck and a big car is also able to cure patients
through his scientific means. But a magic is
working there too — the magic of the car, of the
stethoscope.

I know one quack. He has no degree from any
university, and yet he has cured many patients I
sent to him, patients who had otherwise been
pronounced incurable by other doctors. The
man is smart; he has a remarkable understanding of human nature. Actually, that's how one
happens to be a professional physician! So if you
go to his clinic for treatment, your diagnosis will
be conducted in such a way that half your illness
will go away while you are still being diagnosed.
He is an extremely clever doctor; all other doctors feel quite intimidated by him.

He has a large, impressive and serious-looking
consulting room with a big table on which he
makes the patient lie down. Above the patient's
chest hangs a thing which looks like a stethoscope. This contraption is connected to two trans-
parent tubes containing colored water. When he
applies the stethoscope-like contraption to the
patient's chest, the heartbeat causes the water in
the tube to jump. The patient looks at the jump-
ing water and is convinced he has come to a
great doctor indeed; he has never seen such a
doctor before. The thing he uses is a sort of
stethoscope, except that he doesn't connect it to
his ears, he watches the rising and falling of the
water in the tubes, and this assures the patient

that he is no ordinary doctor.

Do you know why an allopathic doctor writes prescriptions in such illegible handwriting? The reason is that if you could read it, you would find it is such an ordinary thing that you could even go and buy it in the market — and so, it is deliberately written with such skill that you are unable to read it. The truth is, if you were to take this same prescription back to the doctor, he himself wouldn't be able to figure out what he'd written. Another interesting thing is that the names of all medicines have to be written in Latin and Greek. The reason is simple: if he were to write in English, Hindi or Gujarati, you would never pay him ten or fifteen *rupees* for an injection; you would know it is nothing but a concoction of caraway seeds.

These are all magical tricks. It is the same as the villager who gives his patients a pinch of ash. But this will not be effective either if he looks like an ordinary man. If he is dressed, however, in an ochre robe, it will have more effect. And if the man is known to be honest, virtuous, kind and truthful, the pinch of ash will be far more effective. If it is known that he does not charge money, that he does not even touch money, the ash will have an electrifying effect. So, it is not the ash that works, it is the other factors which are at work. It needs careful consideration whether or not such cures be allowed to continue, because, if you ban this type of cure, others, equally as false, will have to be found to replace them. It never ends.

Man must be made to think so that he does not fall sick out of ignorance, so that he does not bring pseudo illnesses upon himself. As long as fake illnesses keep happening, fake doctors will keep on appearing as well. If you remove the old, pseudo methods, new ones will crop up — and if you then remove these, new ones will be born. There are so many types of treatment in the world, but there is no way to decide which one is right; they all claim to be successful in curing illnesses. And their claims are valid. They *do* cure illnesses.

The more we probe into the human psyche, the more it becomes clear that the disease exists somewhere in the human mind. As long as the disease exists in the human mind, the pseudo treatments will also continue to exist. Hence, I am not so much concerned with doing away with pseudo methods, I am more concerned with putting an end to the disease in the human mind. If the disease in the human mind disappears, if man's consciousness awakens, if he becomes discriminating, he will not be surrounded by annoying troubles. It is not that you go and collect ash because a man distributes it in a village — no, it is because you are eager to collect the ash; that's why someone has to distribute it.

No one becomes your leader on his own — but you cannot live for a second without one; that's why somebody has to become the leader. If you remove one leader, you will find another — and if he is removed you will find a third. And, in fact, while you are removing one leader, you will have first made sure who you want for your next. And so, leaders all over the world know very well the need for leading opposition parties. They know, with confidence, that when the people get fed up with one leader they will automatically elect the second, and when they get tired of the second they will replace him with the first. That's why two-party politics goes on all over the world. Everywhere, people are the same.

I was in Raipur during the last elections. A friend of mine, an old resident of Raipur, had been successively elected several times as a Member of Parliament, but this time he was defeated. Another friend of mine who was totally unknown and had recently settled in Raipur was elected in his place. I asked my friend how this happened. How did he lose and a total newcomer win the election?

He said, "It's very clear. People have become too used to me. This man is a new face; people don't know him yet. Don't worry, let him become a familiar figure and he will be defeated too. I will have to bide my time until then. By then I will be unfamiliar once again, and then I will have the upper hand."

Deep down, it is not a question of whether to remove this leader or that leader, whether to do away with this superstition or that superstition — that is not the issue. The question is to bring about a fundamental change in man. A scientific mind will not care much about superstition, but superstition will continue to exist as long as man is content with his blindness. If a man is not ready to open his eyes, then blindness is bound to exist.

And let me ask: who among us is really willing to open his eyes? None of us is willing to see with our eyes open, because with our eyes open we may see truths we don't want to see. That's why we close our eyes and see whatsoever we fancy. Have you ever opened your eyes and observed closely what life is like? Have you ever seen yourself with your eyes open? That you never want to do, because then you will see horrifying things.

Everyone considers himself to be absolutely pious, a *mahatma*. If he were to open his eyes and look closely, he would find, to his horror, the greatest sinner of all hidden within himself. He doesn't want to see that, of course, because then it will be difficult for him to be a *mahatma*. And so he shuts his eyes to himself. And not only that, in doing so he uses those people who can help him shut his eyes — around him he gathers all those people who come and tell him what a great *mahatma* he is. Thus he goes on gathering followers. Around him, he gathers all those people who cooperate in keeping him blind.

And there are many wonderful tricks for collecting people; incredible deceptions are practiced in this respect. One of the tricks for gathering people is to keep on shouting, "Don't come near me! I don't want anyone around me!" People are terribly impressed with this trick. They flock to such a man. The more he drives them away, the greater the *mahatma* they think he is. An ordinary *mahatma* would welcome people, but this one swings his staff and sends them away. He shows no concern for anyone.

I have heard about a man who had wandered a beach in California for years. He had become a kind of attraction. The story that went around about him was that he was such a simple man that if you offered him a ten-dollar bill and a dime, he would pick up the dime cheerfully. That's how innocent he was. Out of curiosity, a man visited him five or six times and always found him surrounded by a crowd. People would ask, "*Baba*, what do you want — this or that?" and he would pick up the dime at once, saying he liked it, he liked the shine of it. People found him such an innocent man.

The curious man found it hard to believe that even after so many years this fellow could not recognize a ten-dollar bill! That was too much innocence! One evening, after the crowd had disappeared, this curious man approached the fellow and said, "I have been watching you for the last twenty years, and I am astonished to find this game going on for so long. Do you still not recognize a ten-dollar bill?"

The fellow laughed, and said, "I knew it was a ten-dollar bill from the very first day! But if I had shown I recognized it, the game would have stopped right then and there. By not recognizing the bill, I have collected dimes from thousands of spectators. If I recognize it once, then that will be the only bill I'll ever have in my hand — no other bill will come from these people afterwards. So if I really want to make money, then I must spurn riches — and the bills will start piling up on their own. I have a good understanding of the whole thing; my job is going very well. During the day, I collect up to five hundred dollars from the crowd. The game will continue for sure."

The so-called *mahatma* also knows the value of money, although if you talk to him about money, he will say he never even touches it. But his disciple, sitting nearby, will pick up the offerings and put them in the safe — because the *mahatma* never touches money!

What can anyone do if a man wants to remain blind? Who will be stupid enough to do anything about it? That fellow on the beach is not the cause of mischief. The mischief-mongers are those people who approach him. It is because of their mischief the poor fellow has to put on the act. Let me tell you that if he had not done it, somebody else would have done the same thing. And people are stupid: wherever they can, they will continue to do what they did with this fellow; they want somebody to snatch their money away from them. Hence, such acts will continue. They can only be brought to an end when we begin to destroy the stupidity of man.

So don't worry too much about breaking the chains of superstition, because if the man who is wearing the chain remains the same he will make new ones. He cannot live without chains. The kind of man he is, he will create new chains.

All religions strive to break these chains, and every religion creates a new chain — so things remain the same. The world has seen so many religions. They were all founded to bring about reforms; they all proclaimed their intent to eradicate all prevailing superstitions, but in the process of destroying superstitions, nothing ever really gets destroyed. Of course, those who are fed up with the old superstitions replace them with new ones and are very happy, feeling they have brought about change.

In fact, an intelligent man never holds on to

anything — not even to any belief, let alone to superstition. He lives intelligently; he doesn't hang on to anything. He never creates any chain because he knows there is immense joy in living in freedom. Don't create any chains.

So the real question is to awaken enough consciousness in each individual that will create a desire in him to become free, to become intelligent, to become self-realized, to be filled with awareness. If the tendency to live blindly — to become a follower, a pursuer, a believer in somebody — could be reduced, all superstitions would crumble. But in that case it would not be that one kind of superstition would break down and another would survive — all would collapse; they would leave all at once. Otherwise, they will remain forever.

Actually, what needs to be understood is that nothing happens by merely changing clothes. Let anyone wear whatsoever he pleases. If someone wants to wear ochre-colored clothes, why stop him? If someone wants to wear black clothes, let him do so. What one needs to realize is that a change in clothes does not equal a change in one's life. Once this is realized, then there is no need to change clothes, because the man who will make you change your clothes will immediately replace them with clothes of a new kind.

A sannyasin, wearing ochre clothes, went to see Gandhi and told him he was very impressed with his ideas and would also like to serve the country. What Gandhi told him was highly significant. He said, "That's fine, but first you will have to give up your ochre clothes, because they will come in the way of your service. Generally, people serve those who wear ochre clothes rather than being served by them." This was very true. But then Gandhi, having made him drop the ochre clothes, made him wear clothes of *khadi,* of handspun cotton.

Now those who are wearing *khadi* are doing things even the people wearing ochre clothes never did before. What difference has it made? Now the *khadi* people are accepting service. The poor ochre people never accepted as much service as those who are wearing *khadi* are doing now. So *khadi* has proven to be very costly for this country. The sannyasin was very happy that his superstition about ochre clothing had dropped — but now he wears *khadi;* now he is holding on to the superstition of *khadi.* What's the difference?

The real question is not of letting people drop one thing and making them take on another. The question is to come to understand that very mentality which holds on to things. Gandhi did not sharpen that man's intelligence; he remained as stupid as ever. He simply made him change his clothes, and the man felt very happy to do so. But what difference did it make? This is how it has always been.

For the last five thousand years the story of humanity has been one of great misfortune. By an effort to break down a superstition we never change the man, we simply do away with the superstition — but then he creates a new superstition. Whatever we offer, he seizes upon it. "All right," he says, "let it be this. I'll drop the other superstition and hold on to this one!" And we feel very happy because he has accepted our superstition.

A young man used to visit me. Day and night he used to talk about the scriptures. He knew the *Upanishads*, the *Gita*, the *Vedas*, by heart. I told him, "Stop all this nonsense. You will gain nothing from it!" He became very angry with me, but nevertheless he continued to visit me. Someone who gets angry with you never stops visiting you, because anger also brings you into a relationship. He was certainly angry at me, yet he still kept coming. As the days went by and as he heard me more and more, something touched him. One day he came to me and said, "I bundled up the *Gita*, the *Upanishads*, the *Vedas*, and threw them all in a well."

"When did I tell you to throw them away?" I asked.

"I had to empty my shelf in order to make room for your books. Now I fully agree with your books," he said.

I said, "But this has made things more difficult. Nothing has changed. I was merely telling you not to agree with a book. I never asked you to throw that book away and grab on to my book. What difference has your doing so made?"

The so-called *gurus* feel very happy if their kind of superstition is held by people. This is how, even though superstitions keep changing, man himself continues to remain superstitious.

So I told the young man to throw my books into the same well too. He said, "How can that be possible?" He could never do that, he asserted. So I said, "Then the whole thing has remained as it was. Now *my* book has become your *Gita*. What was wrong with poor Krishna's *Gita*? If you needed to carry something, his *Gita* was sufficient — it served your purpose; it was much thicker than my book; it added enough weight to you. How are things different now? When did I ever blame Krishna? When did I ever say that Krishna was at fault?

This is how it has always been — and still is. What simply happens is that man remains the same, only his toys change. I feel very happy if someone takes my toy; I feel delighted that at last someone has taken my idea. My ego finds satisfaction in seeing that someone has started to believe more in me than in Krishna. But this does not bring about a change in humanity; humanity can never be benefited by this. What we need to be concerned about is how to break, from within, this human mentality that grabs on to things. How can man overcome his blindness?

I suggest to this friend: don't set about breaking down superstitions; instead, change the superstitious mind. Change that mind which breeds superstition, so that a new man can take birth. But it is an arduous task; it will require a great deal of effort. It is not an easy job. To be accomplished, it will require very scientific thought.

Don't be in such a hurry to deny the existence of ghosts and evil spirits. They are far more real than you. There is no falsity about their existence, but you will have to explore. And it so often happens that those who are scared of ghosts also begin to deny their existence. They say so, not because they have become very knowledgeable, the only reason is wish-fulfillment — they don't want ghosts to exist. Because if there *are* ghosts it will be difficult to walk down a dark alley. So, in a loud voice, they keep repeating, "There are no ghosts. Absolutely! It is all superstition; we will destroy the superstition!" What they are saying is they are very scared of ghosts. If there really are ghosts it will cause a lot of trouble, so they should not exist in the first place — that's the wish. Such a mind can never make ghosts non-existent.

If ghosts are, then they are. Whether you believe it or not, it makes no difference. What is, is, and it's better we investigate it — because whatever exists is related to us in one way or another; it is bound to be so. Hence it is more appropriate to understand them, to recognize them, and to find ways to establish contact with them, to figure out how to interact with them. It's not an easy matter.

The empty space you see between you and someone else may not necessarily be empty. There may be someone sitting there. You may not be able to see him; that's a different matter. But the idea that somebody might be sitting there can frighten you, so we don't leave an empty space, we stick together. We are always afraid of an empty space; that's why we fill our room with furniture, calendars, pictures of gods and goddesses, anything. Being in an empty space, being in an empty house, we are frightened. We fill them with people, with furnishings, so no empty space is left. Even then, there is plenty of empty space which is not altogether empty. And it has its own science.

If one wants to work in this direction, it can be

done. One can systematically work on this — it is an independent science; it has its own laws and methods. However, before you begin working in this area, never say whether these things exist or do not exist. It is better to suspend your judgment, to keep your conclusions in abeyance for a while — just say you don't know.

If asked whether there are ghosts or not, it will be characteristic of the scientific mind to answer, "I don't know, because I haven't looked into it yet. Also, I haven't even looked into myself yet. How can I find out whether or not there are ghosts? I am not even able to find myself as yet!" So never be in a hurry to answer "yes" or "no". Someone who gives a quick answer is superstitious. Keep thinking, keep searching. An intelligent man, in fact, will answer with great reluctance.

Once somebody asked Einstein how he differentiated between a scientist and a superstitious man. Einstein replied, "If you ask one hundred questions to a man of superstition, he will be prepared to offer a hundred and one answers. And if you ask one hundred questions to a scientist, he will claim absolute ignorance about ninety-eight of them. About the remaining two he will say, 'I know a little, but that knowledge is not ultimate; it can change tomorrow.'"

Remember, a scientific mind is the only artless mind. A superstitious mind is not. But in appearance, it looks the opposite. It looks as if a superstitious mind is very simple, but it is not; it is very complex and cunning. The greatest cunning of the superstitious mind is that it affirms things it has no knowledge of. A person with such a mind doesn't even know anything about a rock lying at his doorstep, but in his frenzy to prove his God is right and your God is wrong, he will go out and kill people. If, as yet, he cannot even explain what a rock is . . . And when he cannot prove that a rock is Mohammedan or Hindu, how will he be able to easily prove that God is Hindu or Mohammedan? But he will go ahead and kill people! And remember, resorting to violence shows that those things such acts are committed for must all be rooted in superstition.

People never come to blows over matters pertaining to knowledge; it is impossible. Wherever there is conflict, rest assured superstition is there — because a superstitious man wants to prove through conflict that he is right; he has no other means. If a man were to jump on me and put a sword to my throat saying, "Tell me I am right or I'll chop your head off" — he can chop my head off, of course, but that doesn't prove him right. No one has ever been proven right by chopping off somebody's head.

Even if all the Mohammedans get together and massacre all the Hindus, they will never be proven right — just as the Hindus will never be proven right if they all join together to slaughter all the Mohammedans. They will merely prove themselves stupid, nothing else. Has the sword ever proven anything right? But that's the only means available to the superstitious man. With what other means can he say that such and such a thing is right? He has no concept, he has never probed; he has no proof, he has no direction. He knows only one thing: might is right.

All over the world everyone is doing this. I am

not saying that only religious leaders are involved in such acts of violence, the politicians are no different. Whether Russia or America is right will be settled through the use of hydrogen bombs — obviously; there is no other means. It is exactly the same sort of foolishness. Is this how it can be resolved as to which of the two is right? How can it be determined whether Marx is right or wrong? Will it be by the use of the sword? Or by dropping the hydrogen bomb? Which will it be? It will have to be determined through the application of thought—but man is not yet free to think; he is still beset by superstition.

So remember, my emphasis is not on breaking the chains, my emphasis is on doing away with the superstitious mind that creates these chains. If that mind persists, then no matter how many chains you break it will create new ones. And remember, new fetters are far more attractive, more lovable, more worth holding on to. And remember this too: the new chain is always stronger than the old one, because by now our knowledge of how to make chains is also more developed, more advanced. It often occurs to me that those in the business of breaking down superstitions only succeed in providing much tougher superstitions as substitutes for the worn-out ones — they do nothing more than that.

The superstitious mind has to be discarded, or else it will keep on breeding superstition. Be cogitative, and make others cogitative also. "Be cogitative" means: think, search, be inquisitive. Speak only after you have the right experience, and still admit readily that your experience is not necessarily right. People may have other experiences tomorrow. You may even have to go through different experiences, and it is not certain that what you experienced was not an hallucination.

So until that experience has been verified by scores of experiences more, it is better not to say anything about it. That's why a scientist conducts an experiment, repeats it a thousand times, makes a thousand other people do it, and ony then does he arrive at some kind of a conclusion. And even then he never reaches a final conclusion. One who wants to reach a conclusion in a hurry, can never think. A man in a hurry to reach a final conclusion inevitably fills himself with superstition. And we are all in a great hurry.

A friend, in his question, has asked everything the whole of humanity is searching for and has not yet been able to find! He asks: *Does God exist or not? What is* jeevatman, *the individual soul? Where is* moksha? *Who created heaven? Is there a hell? Why has man appeared on the earth? What is the goal of life?*

He is in such a hurry he wants to know about all of this instantly. A man in such a hurry will undoubtedly become superstitious. Search requires great patience, tremendous patience: it doesn't matter if we don't find what we are looking for in one lifetime, but we will continue to search. In fact, for one who is cogitative, attaining is not important — searching is. For a man of superstition, attaining is important, seeking is totally unimportant.

A superstitious man is anxious to know; how can he attain? "Where is God?" he asks. He is not much concerned with first finding out whether there is a God or not. He is not interested in the pursuit of God; that is not his cup of tea. He says, "You seek him and then show me." That's why he is out looking for a *guru*.

Whosoever is looking for a *guru* is bound to end up being superstitious — he can't stop short of that. In fact, looking for a *guru* implies, "You have found, now please show us. Since you have already found, what is the point in our searching now? We bow down to your feet. Please give us what you have attained." The idea is for someone else to place his hand on your head and have you realize God. So people are wandering around accepting *mantras*, becoming initiates, paying fees, massaging feet, serving, in the hope that what someone has already attained can become their own. This can never happen. This shows clearly the hold of the superstitious mind.

Someone else's achievement can never become yours. That poor fellow went in search and found, and you want to have it free? And remember, if he has searched, then, while searching, he must also have realized that one attains through seeking, not by asking. And so he will not even create any disciples. Only those are after disciples who have themselves not yet attained. They are hanging on to some other *guru* above them. There is a long series of *gurus*, all hoping to gain from the other.

Many *gurus* are already dead, and yet people hang on to them in the hope they will give them something. There is a long chain of dead *gurus*, going back thousands and millions of years, and they are all hanging on to each other hoping someone may give something. This is the mark of a superstitious mind.

The characteristic of a searching mind, the indication of a reflective mind is, "If there is God, then I will search for him. If I succeed in finding him, then it will be because of my merit, my birthright. If I ever find him, then it will be because of my lifelong dedication, my sacrifice, my meditation. It will be the fruit of my effort."

And remember, if God does become available free, a cogitative individual will turn him down. He will say, "It is not right to accept something that has not come out of my own effort. I will attain through my own effort." And bear in mind there are certain things which can only be attained through one's own effort. God is not one of those things sold in the market, a piece of merchandise available anywhere. Truth is not one of those articles sold in a department store where you can go and purchase it. But such stores are open.

There are stores, there are bazaars, where a signboard hangs, saying "Real Truth Available Here". Even truth is of the real and artificial kind! On every shop the sign says, "The real Master lives here. The rest are all fake Masters; they live somewhere else. This is the only authentic shop. Buy from us! Give us the chance to serve you!" And once you have entered one of these shops, the owner won't want you to leave that easily. All this mischief is the creation of the superstitious mind.

I would like to say to you: have faith in seeking, not in begging. You will attain to God not by begging, but by knowing. Also, never believe what others say. Someone may have attained — it is possible of course — so don't disbelieve either, because that is superstition too. Neither believe nor disbelieve. If someone comes along and says he has attained God, say, "Congratulations. God has been very compassionate to you, allowing you to find him. But kindly don't show me. Let me find him also; otherwise I will remain a cripple."

If you are carried to a destination someone has already walked to, you will arrive as a cripple. Feet grow stronger by walking. Reaching a destination is not so important, the really important thing is the traveler becomes stronger in the pursuit. Attaining something is not as important as the transformation of the one who attained.

God, knowledge, or *moksha* are not ready-made things. They are the fruit of the offering of one's life, of a lifetime of effort and *sadhana*. It is like the ultimate flower which comes on its own. But if you go to the market you will find plastic flowers. They last longer. You just need to dust them — they last longer and create deception too. But whom do they deceive? Plastic flowers can deceive others — those walking on the street can be fooled; they may think the flowers in your window are real — but you can't be deceived because you bought them yourself.

For real flowers one has to sow the seeds, one has to put in effort, one has to raise the plants. Then, on their own, flowers bloom — they are not brought in. The experience of God is like the flower, one's *sadhana* is like the plant. Care for the plant and the flower will come by itself. But we are in a hurry. We say, "Forget the plant; just give us the flower!"

Sometimes when children go to school for an

examination, they don't solve the arithmetic problem, they look up the answer in the back of the arithmetic book and write it down. Even though the answer given is absolutely right, it is totally wrong. How can the answer of one who has not followed the method be right? His answer is absolutely right — he has written "five" —and those who followed the method have also written "five". But do you see the difference in the answer given by those who followed the method and those who stole it from the back of the book? And what difference does it make whether they have stolen it from the back of the *Gita* or the *Koran*?

Even though the answer given by both is the same, it is not the same; there is a fundamental difference. The real question is not finding the answer, the real question is not arriving at "five", the real question is learning how to arrive at the sum. And the one who looked in the back of the book didn't learn that. He didn't learn the arithmetic, he only got the answer.

And so, if you have learned something from somewhere, if you have received something from somebody, if you have heard something from someone and grabbed on to it — then such a God is stolen from the back of the book. Then such a God is lifeless, dead, useless, good for nothing, not alive. An alive religion comes into being by living it, not by stealing answers from the back of some book.

But we are all thieves. We scold little children and warn them not to steal. The teacher also makes it clear that his students must not look for answers in the back of the book, that they

should not steal their answers from somewhere
— but if he were to ask himself whether all his
answers were stolen or not, it would seem all his
answers were stolen as well.

The *guru* is a thief, the disciple is a thief, the
teacher is a thief. All life's answers are stolen.
From stolen answers one can never find peace or
joy. Joy is attained by going through the same
process by which flowers of answers bloom on
their own. They are not borrowed.

LOVE IS DANGEROUS

Morning
October 31, 1969

A friend has asked: *Why should we think of death at all? We have life, let us live it. Let us live in the present. Why do we bring in the thought of death?*

He has asked the right thing. But his very asking, "Why bring in the idea of death?" or "Let's just live and not even think of death" shows in itself that even he cannot escape thinking about death. Death is such an enormous fact it cannot be ignored; although, throughout our lives, we try not to think of death — not because death is not worth thinking about, but because the very thought of it is terrifying. The very idea that "I will die" sends chills up our spines. Of course, it will shake you up while dying; but even before that, if this idea takes hold of your mind, it will shake you to your very roots.

Man has always tried to forget about death, he has tried not to think about it. We have managed our entire system of life in such a way that death should not become visible. All man's efforts and plans towards falsifying death seem to be succeeding, but they never are successful — because death *is* there. How will you escape from it? Where will you escape? Even running away from it, you are ultimately going to run into it. No matter where you escape, no matter which direction you take, eventually you are going to end up there. Every day it approaches nearer — whether you think about it or not, whether you escape from it or not. One can never run away from a fact.

It is not that death is something which will happen in the future, so why think about it now? This too is a misapprehension. Death will not happen in the future — death is already happening every moment. Although it will come to its completion in the future, it is actually taking place every moment. We are dying this very moment. If we sit here for an hour, we will be dead one hour. It may take seventy years for us to die completely, nevertheless this one hour will be a part of it. During this one hour we will be dying too. It is not that, after seventy years, one dies all of a sudden; death never occurs instantaneously. It is not a sudden event; it is a growth that begins with birth.

In fact, birth constitutes one end of death, and death constitutes the other end. This journey begins with birth. What we call the birthday is actually the first day of death. It will take time, but the journey will continue.

For example, a man sets out from Dwarka for Calcutta. The very first step he takes will be as much to reach Calcutta as his last step. The final step will be as instrumental in bringing him to Calcutta as the initial step. And if the initial step can't bring him to Calcutta, the last step cannot either. This means that when he took his first step towards Calcutta, he began to reach Calcutta. With each step Calcutta drew nearer and nearer. You may perhaps say he took six months to arrive at Calcutta, but the fact is that it is only because he had started to arrive six months ago that he could arrive six months later.

The second thing I would like to say to you is: don't think that death is somewhere in the future, death is present every moment. And what is future? It is the sum total of all of our presents. We keep on adding to it. It is just like when we heat water. At the first degree the water warms up, but it hasn't turned into steam yet. And the same is the case when it heats up two degrees. The water will turn into steam when it heats to a hundred degrees; however, it started moving closer to becoming steam at the first degree, and then at the second, and the third and so on. But even when it's at ninety-nine degrees the water does not turn into steam; that will only happen when it reaches one hundred.

Has it ever occurred to you that the hundredth degree is also a degree, just as the first degree is also a degree? The journey from the ninety-ninth degree to the hundredth degree is the same as from the first to the second degree; there is no difference. And so, the one who knows will warn you, at the very first degree, that the water will turn into steam — although you never see water turning into steam anywhere. Of course, he may say the water is heating up, but where is it turning into steam? We can delude ourselves up to the ninety-ninth degree that the water is still not turning into steam, but at the hundredth degree it is bound to become steam. Each degree will keep bringing the boiling point closer.

Hence, it is meaningless to try to save yourself from death, or to postpone it, by saying that death is in the future. Death is happening every moment; we are dying every day. In fact, there is virtually no difference between what we call living, and dying. What we call living is just another name for dying gradually. I don't say think about the future, I say watch what is already happening now. I am not asking you to think, even.

This friend has asked, "Why think of death?" I don't say to think. Thinking will lead you nowhere. Remember this, no fact can ever be known by thinking. Actually, thinking is a tactful means of falsifying facts. Looking at a flower, if you begin thinking about it, you will never know the flower. Because the more you move into thinking about it, the further it will be removed from you. You will move ahead in your thoughts while the flower will remain, lying there. What has the flower to do with what you are thinking? A flower is a fact. If you want to know a flower, don't think about it — look at the flower.

There is a difference between thinking and seeing — and the difference is significant. The West puts great emphasis on thinking. That's why they have named their science of thinking "philosophy". Philosophy means conceptual thinking. *We* have named the same science *darshan. Darshan* means to see; *darshan* does not mean thinking. This needs to be understood a little. We have called it *darshan* while they have called it philosophy, and there is a fundamental difference between the two. Those who take philosophy and *darshan* to be synonymous know nothing. They are not synonymous. That's why there's nothing like "Indian philosophy" and nothing like "western *darshan*".

The West has a science of thinking — it consists of investigation, logic, analysis. The East cared for something else. The East has experienced that there are certain facts which can never be known by thinking about them. These facts will have to be seen, will have to be lived. And there is an enormous difference between living and thinking.

A man who thinks about love may perhaps write a thesis on it, but a lover lives it, sees it; it's possible he may not be able to write a thesis. And if someone asks a lover to say something about love, he may close his eyes, tears may start rolling down his cheeks, and he might say, "Please don't ask. What can I say about love?" One who has thought about love will explain it for hours, but he may not even know one iota of love.

Thinking and seeing are two altogether different processes. So I am not saying you should think about death. You can never know death by thinking about it. You will have to see it. What I am saying is: here is death, right now within you, and you have to see it. What I call the "I" is dying all the time. This phenomenon of death will have to be seen, this phenomenon of death will have to be lived, this phenomenon of death, that "I am dying, I am dying," will have to be accepted.

We try our best to falsify death; we have invented a thousand ways to falsify it. Of course we can dye our white hair, but that does not prove death a lie — it invariably comes. Even underneath the dyed color the hair is still white. They are the indications that death has started approaching, that it is sure to come. How can we falsify it? No matter how much we go on falsifying it, it makes no difference — it is approaching, non-stop. The only difference is that we can fail to know it.

What I am asking is: how will one who hasn't even known death yet know what life is? My point is: death is on the circumference; life is at the center. If we don't even know the circumference, how will we ever know the center? And if we run away from the circumference, we will never reach closer to the center. If you become frightened of the walls that make up the outer limits of a house, and escape, how will you ever enter the inner dwelling? Death is the periphery and life is the temple at the center of it. By running away from the periphery, we also run away from life. One who comes to know death will, by and by, uncover it and begin to understand life as well.

Death is the gateway to knowing life. Eluding death is eluding life as well. So when I say "Know death", recognize the facts — I am not asking you to think.

There is one more interesting thing that needs to be understood. Thinking means to repeat, in the mind, what we already know. Thinking is never original — although we ordinarily say that such-and-such a person's thoughts are highly original. No, thought is never original. Thoughts can never be original. *Darshan*, seeing, *can* be original.

Thoughts are always stale. If I ask you to think about this rose flower, what will you think? You will simply reiterate what you already know about a rose. What else would you do? What else can you do with thinking? Could even one single unheard-of and original viewpoint about a rose ever appear in your thoughts? How can it?

Thinking is nothing but reiterating a thought. You may say, "The rose flower is very beautiful," but how many times have you heard this before? How many times have you read this before? Or you may say, "The rose flower is just as beautiful as the face of my beloved." How many times have you heard this before too? How many times have you read it before? Or you may say, "The flower is very fresh" — but this too, how many times have you heard or read it before? What good are thoughts? How will you be able to enter the being of that rose flower by thinking about it? Thinking can only lead you into whatsoever is in your memory about a rose. That's why thinking is never original. There can never be an original thinker — only seers are original.

The first condition in looking at a rose flower is that the person looking at it should not think. He should remove thoughts from his memory; he should become empty, and live in that moment with the flower. Let the rose flower be on

one side and you be on the other, and let there
be no one between you — nothing you've ever
heard, nothing you've ever read, nothing you've
ever known. Nothing you've ever experienced
should be in between. No one should be between you two. Only then, the unknown seated
within the rose will begin to enter your being.
Finding no hindrance in between, it will enter,
and then you won't feel you want to know the
rose, you will feel you are one with the rose.
Then you will know the flower from its
interiority.

A seer penetrates inside an object, while a
thinker hovers around it on the outside — and
therefore a thinker has no achievement of his
own; only a seer enjoys achievement. A seer
penetrates within because there remains no wall
between him and the object before him — the
wall crumbles, disappears.

Once, Kabir asked his son Kamal to go to the
forest and bring some hay for their cattle. Kamal
went as he was told. It was morning when he
left, but when the sun was overhead and Kamal
had not yet returned, Kabir became worried.
And even by the waning hours of afternoon
there was no sign of Kamal. Kabir grew even
more worried. Soon it was evening, and the sun
was about to set, so finally, accompanied by a
few of his devotees, Kabir set out in search of
Kamal.

When they reached the forest they found
Kamal standing in the middle of the thick grass,
his eyes closed, swaying like a blade of grass in
the breeze. Kabir went over, shook him, and
asked, "What are you doing here?" Kamal

opened his eyes. He came to himself, realized what had happened, and immediately apologized. Kabir said, "But what have you been doing for so long? It's so late!"

Kamal answered, "I am sorry, but when I came here, instead of cutting the grass, I began to look at it. And just looking at it continuously, I don't know when, but I also became a blade of grass. Soon it was evening, and here I was, completely oblivious that 'I am Kamal who has come here to cut grass.' I became the grass itself. There was so much joy in being the grass, joy that, being Kamal, I never had before. It's good you came, because I didn't know what was happening. The breeze was not moving the grass, the breeze was moving me — the cutter and that which was to be cut had both disappeared."

Have you ever seen your wife, your son, with whom you have lived for so many years? Have you ever *seen* them? The things your wife did yesterday flash through your mind — and a thought comes in between you and her. You recall how she quarreled when you were about to leave for the office in the morning — and again the thought is present between you. What she said at the dinner table comes back to you — and the thought stands between you. You have always thought, you have never seen. And that's the reason there is no relationship between husband and wife, between father and son, between mother and son. Relationship happens where thought is no more and where *darshan*, seeing, has begun. That is really when a relationship takes place, because then no one exists to disrupt it.

Remember, a relationship does not mean there is a third factor binding the two. As long as there is something in between, to bind the two, the disrupter is also present. That which binds also breaks. The day nothing exists to bind, when only two remain, when nothing remains in between, that day what actually remains is only one; then there are not two.

A relationship does not mean we are joined with somebody, a relationship means that now, nothing exists between you and the other person, there is no one in between — not even to join you. There, the two streams disappear and merge into each other. This is love. Seeing leads you into love; seeing is the source of love. And one who has not loved has never known anything. No matter what a man may have set out to know, he has only known it through love.

So when I say death has to be known, I mean we will have to love death as well. We will have to *see* death. But the man who is afraid of death, who is eluding it — how can he love death, how can he have its *darshan*, how can he ever *see* death? When death appears before him, he turns his back on it. He shuts his eyes; he never lets death appear before him, face-to-face. He is afraid, he is frightened; that's why he is unable to see death at all, nor is he able to love it. And the man who hasn't been able to love death yet, how will he ever love life? — because death is a very superficial event and life is a far deeper phenomenon. One who turned away from the very first step, how will he ever reach the deep waters of the well?

That's why I say death will have to be lived, it

will have to be known, it will have to be seen. You will have to fall in love with it; you will have to look into its eyes. And as soon as a man looks into death's eyes, begins to watch it, penetrate into it, he feels astounded. To his great amazement, he realizes, "What a great mystery lies hidden in death! What I knew as death and kept running away from, actually conceals within itself the source of supreme life." Hence I say to you: enter into death willingly so that you may reach life.

There is an incredible saying of Jesus. Jesus has said, "The one who will save himself will perish; and the one who will efface himself — no one can ever destroy him. One who will lose himself shall find, and one who will save himself shall be lost." If a seed wishes to save itself, it will rot — what else? And if a seed annihilates itself in the earth, disappears, it will become a tree. The death of the seed becomes life for the tree. If the seed were to protect itself by saying, "I am scared. I could die. I don't want to disappear. Why should I disappear?" then the seed is bound to rot. In that case, it will not even remain a seed, let alone grow into a tree. We shrink with fear of death.

I would like to say one more thing that may not have occurred to you before. Only one who is afraid of death has ego, because ego means a constricted personality, a solid knot. One who has fear of death shrinks within. Anyone in fear has to shrink inside, and whatever shrinks turns into a knot. A complex is created inside the person.

The feeling of "I" is the feeling of a man afraid

of death. The man who penetrates death, who is not afraid of death, who does not run away from it, who begins to live it — his "I" disappears; his ego disappears. And when the ego disappears only life remains. We can put it this way: only the ego dies, not the soul. But since we continue to remain egos, a great difficulty is created. In fact, only the ego can die; only the ego has a death — because it is false. It will *have* to die. But we are holding on to it.

For example, a wave rises in an ocean. If the wave wants to survive as a wave, it cannot; it is bound to die. How can a wave survive as a wave? It will die. Unless, of course, it becomes ice. If it contracts, becomes solid, then it can survive. But still, in that sort of survival, the wave is no more and the ice remains — ice, which is a wave, closed, broken away from the ocean. Remember, as a wave it is not apart from the ocean, it is one with the ocean. As ice, it parts from the ocean, it separates, it becomes solid. In it, the wave has contracted; it has become frozen.

As a wave it was one with the ocean; however, if it becomes a chunk of ice, it will survive, of course, but then it will be cut off from the ocean. And how long will it survive in that state? Whatsoever is frozen will undoubtedly melt. A poor wave will melt a little sooner, while a rich wave will take a little longer — what else? The sunrays will take a little longer to melt a big wave, while a smaller wave will melt sooner. It is only a question of time, but melting is bound to happen. The wave will melt and it will make a big hue and cry, because as soon as it melts it will disappear. But if the wave, by falling back into the ocean, were to make itself cease to exist as separate, if it were to come to know that it *is* in fact the ocean, then there wouldn't be any question of the wave's disappearing. Then whether it disappears or remains, it still exists — because it knows that "I am not a wave, I am the ocean." When it disappears as a wave, it still exists — in a state of rest. When it rises, it is in a state of activity. And resting is no less enjoyable than being active. In fact, it is even more enjoyable.

There is a state of activity and there is a state of rest. What we call *samsara*, the world, is the state of activity, and what we call *moksha*, liberation, is the state of rest. It is like a restless wave which crashes against the wind and wrestles with it, and then it falls back into the ocean and disappears. It still exists. Whatever it was before in the ocean, it is now still the same, but it is at rest. However, if a wave were to assert itself as a wave, it would be filled with ego, and then it would want to break itself away from the ocean.

Once you get the idea that "I am", then how can you be with the rest of the all? If you choose to be with the all, then the "I" is lost. That's why the "I" insists, "Break away from the all." And how interesting it is, that breaking away from the whole makes you miserable. And then, once again, the "I" says, "Relate with the all" — such is the tortuous way of the "I". First the "I" says, "Break yourself away from the all, isolate yourself; you are different from the whole. How can you remain connected?" So the "I" snaps itself away; but then it gets into trouble — because, as soon as the "I" separates from the all, it becomes miserable; its end approaches. As soon as the wave comes to believe it is separate from the ocean, it begins to die, its death comes nearer. Now it will fall into the struggle to protect itself from death.

As long as it was one with the ocean, there was no death at all — because the ocean never dies.

Remember, an ocean can be without a wave, but a wave cannot exist without the ocean. You cannot conceive of a wave without the ocean — the ocean will be present in the wave. The ocean, however, can exist without a wave. When they are an integral part of the ocean, all waves exist in peace and rest. But the moment a wave strives to save itself from the ocean, difficulties arise — it cuts itself off from the ocean and its death begins.

This is the reason one who is to die wants to love. The reason all of us, who are going to die, are so eager to love is that love is the obvious means to connect. That's why no one wants to live without love and be miserable. Everyone is seeking love: somebody wants to receive your love, somebody wants to give you love. And for the man who does not find love, it becomes a problem. But have we ever wondered what the meaning of love is?

Love means: an attempt to reconstruct, once again, by putting different parts together, the relationship we have broken off with the whole. So one kind of love is the one where we attempt to rebuild our lost relationship with the whole by adding parts. This is what we call love. And there is another kind of love where we have stopped our attempts to break away from the whole. That is called prayer. Hence, prayer is absolute love. And this carries a totally different meaning. It does not mean that we are attempting to integrate the fragments; it means we have stopped breaking ourselves away from the whole. The wave has declared, "I am the ocean," and now it is not attempting to connect itself with each and every other wave.

Remember, the wave itself is dying, and the other waves nearby are dying too. If this wave tries to relate with other waves, it will get into trouble. That's why our so-called love is very painful, because it is a wave trying to relate with another wave. This wave and the other wave are both dying, and yet they get into a relationship with each other in the hope that, by joining with each other, they perhaps may save themselves. That's why we turn love into security. And so, a man is afraid to live alone. One wants a wife, a husband, a son, a mother, a brother, a friend, a society, an organization, a nation. These are all endeavors of the ego; these are attempts, by one who has broken himself away from it, to unite once again with the whole.

But all these efforts to unite are invitations to death—because the one with whom you are forming a union is as much surrounded by death, as much surrounded by the ego . . . The funny thing is that the other wants to become immortal by uniting with you, and you want to become immortal by uniting with the other. And the fact is that both of you are going to die. How can you become immortal? Such a union will double death; it will certainly not turn it into an elixir.

Two lovers long so much for their love to become immortal—they sing songs day and night. For eternity poems have been written about love becoming immortal. How can two people who are going to die desire immortality together? A union of two such people only makes death twice as real and nothing else. What else can it be? And both are melting, sinking, fading away; that's why they are frightened, worried.

The wave has created its own organization. It says, "I have to survive." It has created nations; it has created Hindu-Mohammedan sects—waves creating their own organizations. And the fact of the matter is that all these organizations are going to disappear—the ocean below is the only organization. And the organization of the ocean is a totally different thing. Belonging to it does not mean the wave joins itself with the ocean; rather, it means the wave knows that "I am not at all different from the ocean." And so I say that a religious man does not belong to any organization—he neither holds to a family, nor does he own a friend, a father or a brother.

Jesus has spoken some very strong words. In fact, only those who have attained to love can speak such strong words; people weak in love cannot utter them. One day Jesus was standing in the market surrounded by a crowd. His mother, Mary, came to see him. People began to make way for her. Somebody from the crowd shouted, "Make way, make room for Jesus' mother. Let her come." When Jesus heard him, he said in a loud voice, "If you are giving way to Jesus' mother, then don't do it, because Jesus doesn't have a mother." Mary stopped, stood there in shock.

Addressing the crowd, Jesus said, "As long as you have a mother, a father, a brother, you won't be able to come close to me." This is being very harsh. We can't even imagine a person like Jesus, so full of love, can utter such words as, "I have no mother. Who is my mother?" So Mary stood there in shock. Jesus went on, "Do you call this woman my mother? I have no mother. And remember, if you still have a mother, then you won't be able to come near me."

What seems to be the matter? The question is that if a wave is attempting to unite with another wave, it won't be able to come close to the ocean. Waves, in fact, unite with each other and create an organization mainly to save themselves from the ocean. On its own a wave feels more frightened that it may disappear, that it may really disappear. But the truth is, it is already disappearing.

Yet, when a few waves gather together, they feel more reassured—-some sort of organization is created; a crowd is created. That's why man likes to live in a crowd; he feels afraid if he is left alone. In its loneliness a wave is left totally by itself— slipping away, falling away, vanishing, close to disappearing, feeling alienated on both sides— the ocean on one; the rest of the waves on the other. Hence, it creates an organization, it creates a chain.

The father says, "I will disappear, but it doesn't matter—I will leave my son behind." The wave says, "I'll disappear, but I'll leave a little wave—it will survive after me, the chain will continue, my name shall remain." That's why a father feels unhappy if he doesn't have a son—it means he couldn't arrange his immortality. He will, of course, be gone, but he wants to create another wave which will continue further on, which will at least identify the wave it came from. So it's all right for the former wave to disappear—it leaves another one behind.

You may or may not have noticed that people who are engaged in a creative activity—a painter, a musician, a poet, a writer—are not too concerned with having sons, simply because they have found a substitute. Their paintings will survive, their poetry will survive, their sculptures will survive—they don't care about having a son. That's why scientists, painters, sculptors, writers and poets are not overly concerned with having sons. There is no other reason except that they have found a different kind of son. They have created a wave which will remain long after they are gone. Actually, they have found a son that will last even longer than yours, because even when your son has disappeared, the writer's book will still remain.

A writer doesn't care much about having a son, about having an offspring. This does not mean, however, that he is carefree; it simply means he has found a long-lasting wave; he stops worrying about smaller waves. Hence he is not interested in having a family; he has created a different kind of family. He is also striving for the same degree of immortality. So he will say, "Money will be lost, wealth will be lost, but my work, my scripture will survive"—and that is precisely what he wants.

But scriptures also become lost. No scripture lasts forever, although, of course, it lasts a little longer. Who knows how many scriptures have already been lost, and how many get lost everyday.

Everything will be lost. In fact, in the world of waves, no matter to what extent a wave may prolong itself, ultimately it is bound to be lost. To be a wave means to face extinction—prolonging makes no difference.

So if you look upon yourself as a wave you will want to avoid death—you will remain afraid, scared. I say to you: look at death—neither should you avoid it nor be afraid of it, nor run away from it. Look at it. And just by looking at it you will find that what seemed like death from this end, as you enter into it a little, the same thing turns out to be life.

Then the wave becomes the ocean; its fear of extinction disappears. Then it doesn't want to become frozen ice. Then, for whatever time it has, it dances in the sky, rejoices under the rays of the sun, is happy. And when it falls back into the ocean, it is equally happy in its state of rest. Thus it is happy in life, it is happy in death—because it knows that "that which is" is never born nor does it ever die. That which is, is; only forms keep changing.

We are all waves risen above the ocean of consciousness. Some of us have turned into ice—most of us have. The ego is like ice, as hard as a rock. How amazing it is that a fluid like water can become hard like ice and rock. If a desire to freeze arises in us, the consciousness, otherwise so simple and fluid, freezes and becomes an ego. We are all filled with desire to freeze, and so we employ many kinds of means to see how we can become frozen, solidified.

There are laws under which water turns into ice, and there are also laws which cause the formation of the ego. Water has to cool down in order to become ice, it has to lose its heat, it has to turn cold. The colder it gets, the harder it becomes. The man who wants to create ego has to become cold as well; he has to lose his warmth. That's why we say "a warm welcome". A welcome is always warm; a cold welcome has no meaning.

Love means warmth; a cold love carries no meaning. Love is never cold; it contains warmth. Actually, life is sustained by warmth; death is cold, below zero. That's why the sun is the symbol of life, the sun is the symbol of warmth. When it rises in the morning, death departs; everything becomes warm and hot. The flowers bloom and the birds begin to sing.

Warmth is the symbol of life. Cold is the symbol of death. So, one who wants to create an ego has to become cold, and in order to become cold he has to lose all those things which give warmth. He has to lose everything that gives warmth to his being. For example, love gives warmth, hatred brings coldness. So, for the sake of the ego, one has to give up love and cling to hatred. Mercy and sympathy bring warmth; cruelty and ruthlessness bring cold.

Just as there are laws for the freezing of water, there are laws for the freezing of human consciousness. The same law works: keep on becoming cold. Sometimes we say that such-and-such a person is very cold—there is no warmth in him; he becomes hard like a rock. And remember, the warmer a person is, the more simple he is. Then his life has a liquidity that enables him to flow into others and allows others to flow into him. A cold person becomes hard, unable to flow, closed from all sides. No one can enter into him, nor can he enter into anyone. The ego is like frozen ice and love is like water, fluid, flowing. The man who is afraid of death will run away from it. He will go on freezing, because the fear that he may die, that he may disappear, will make him contract—and his ego will remain, growing harder, stronger.

I was a guest at a friend's house for a few days. He is quite rich, with a great deal of property. But I was puzzled about one thing: he would never speak kindly to anyone; otherwise he was a good man. I was very puzzled to see that, inwardly, he was very soft, but very hard on the outside. The servant trembled before him, his son trembled before him, his wife was scared to face him. People thought about it a good deal before they called on him. Even when they came to his door, they hesitated to ring the bell, wondering whether they should go in or not.

When I stayed with him and came to know him closely, I asked him what all this was about. I said, "As such, you are a very simple man." He said, "I am very scared. It is dangerous to form a relationship, because if you form a relationship with somebody then sooner or later he starts asking for money. If you remain courteous and loving to your wife, the expenditures shoot up. If you don't remain stiff with your son, his pocket money goes on increasing. If you talk to your servant gently, he also tries to behave like a boss."

So a solid wall of coldness had to be erected all around—that would scare the wife, that would scare the son. How many fathers have done this?

The truth of the matter is that there is hardly any home where the father and the son meet each other lovingly. The son goes to the father when he needs money, the father goes to the son when he wants to give him a sermon; otherwise, the two don't meet, the meeting never happens. There is no meeting point between a father and a son. The father is afraid, and he has surrounded himself with a solid wall. The son is also afraid; he sneaks by his father. There is no harmony anywhere between the two. The more a person is afraid, the more he worries about his security, the more solid he becomes. There is great danger in being fluid, there is insecurity in it.

This is the reason we are afraid of falling in love. Only after we have scrutinized the person and become totally reassured, do we ever fall in love. That means, first we make sure there is no cause for danger from the person, then we fall in love. That's why we invented marriages—first we marry, first we take all the necessary measures, then we fall in love—because love is dangerous. Love is fluid—a man might find his way into anyone. It is dangerous to fall in love with a stranger, he may sneak off at night with all your valuables! So, first, we make absolutely certain who the man is, what he does, where his parents are from, how his character is, what his qualities are. We take all the measures, we take the full social precautions; only then do we accept the individual in marriage.

We are a frightened people; we want to make everything secure first. The more we secure ourselves, the harder and colder the wall of ice is all around us, and it shrinks our entire being. Our separation from God has happened because of one reason alone: we are not liquid, we have become solid. This is the only cause of separation: we are not flowing, we have become like blocks; we are not like water, we are like frozen ice. Once we become fluid-like, the separation will no longer exist; but we will only become fluid-like when we agree to see and to live death, when we accept that death exists.

Once we have seen and recognized that death exists, why should there be any fear? When death is surely there, when the wave knows for certain she is bound to disappear; if the wave has found out that birth itself contains death, if the wave has come to know that its disintegration began the very moment it was created, the matter is finished. Now why turn into ice? Then it will accept being a wave as long as it has to be, and it will accept being the ocean as long as it has to be. That's it! The matter is over! Then everything is accepted. In that acceptance the wave becomes the ocean. Then all worry over its disappearance is gone—because then the wave knows it existed before its extinction, and it will continue to exist even after it has vanished—not as the "I", but as the boundless ocean.

When Lao Tzu was about to die, somebody asked him to reveal a few secrets of his life. Lao Tzu said, "The first secret is: no one has ever defeated me in my life." Hearing this, the disciples became very excited. They said, "You never told us this before! We also wish to be victorious. Please show us the trick." Lao Tzu answered, "You made a mistake. You heard something different. I said no one could ever defeat me, and you are saying you too want to be victorious. The two things are totally opposite, although they look similar in meaning. In the dictionary, in the world of language, it has one meaning—that a person who has not faced defeat is victorious. I simply said no one could defeat me, while you are talking about becoming victorious. Get out of here! You will never understand what I am saying."

The disciples pleaded, "Even then, please explain to us. Please show us the technique. How were you never defeated?"

Lao Tzu said, "No one could defeat me because I always remained defeated. There is no way to defeat a defeated man. I was never defeated because I never wished for victory. In fact, no one could pick a fight with me. If anyone ever came to challenge me, he found me already defeated, so he couldn't have any fun defeating me. The joy is in defeating one who desires to be victorious. What fun can there be in defeating someone who doesn't even want to win?"

Actually, it gives us pleasure to destroy somebody's ego because doing so strengthens our own. But if a man has already effaced himself, what fun can there be in destroying such a person? Our ego wouldn't get any kick out of it. The more we succeed in breaking the other's ego, the stronger ours becomes. The other's broken ego becomes the strength of our own. But the ego of this man we are talking about is already broken.

For example, you go out to defeat a man, and before you knock him down he lays himself down on the ground; and before you sit on him he invites you and lets you sit on him. What will your state be then? You would want to run away from there! What else could you do? People watching would laugh and say, "Go on, sit on him; sit comfortably. Why are you running away?" Who would look stupid?—the one who sat on the man, or the man who kept laughing and whose laughter resounded throughout your life?

So whenever somebody went to challenge this man, he would immediately lie down on the ground and say, "Come on, sit on me. You have come for that, haven't you? So go ahead. Don't take too much trouble, don't bother too much; there's no need to exert yourself—just come and sit on me."

Lao Tzu went on to say, "But you are asking something else. You want me to tell you the technique of winning. If you think of winning, you will lose. One who harbors the thought of winning is always the loser. In fact, defeat begins with the very idea of victory." And Lao Tzu said further, "And no one has ever been able to insult me."

"Please tell us its secret also, because we do not like to be insulted either," a disciple said.

"Once again you are making a mistake. No one could insult me because I never desired honor. You will always be insulted because you are filled with the desire for recognition. I was never kicked out from any place, because I always sat near the entrance where people remove their shoes. I was never asked to move from a place because I always stood at the end, where no one could push me further back. I was very happy to be at the end; it saved me from all sorts of trouble. No one ever forced me out of there or pushed me aside; nor did anyone say, "Get lost!" because that was the last place. There was no place beyond that. No one ever wanted to be in that spot. I was the lord of my own place; I have always been the lord of my own place. Where I stood, no one ever came to throw me out."

Jesus also says, "Blessed are those who are ready to stand in the last row." What does this mean?

For example, Jesus says, "If a man slaps your right cheek, offer him the left." What this means is: don't even give him the trouble of turning your other cheek—you do it for him. Jesus says, "When someone comes to defeat you, be defeated readily. If he makes you lose one round, lose two instead." And Jesus says, "If a man snatches your coat, also give him your shirt immediately." Why? Because it is possible the man may feel embarrassed taking the shirt away from you. And Jesus says, "If someone asks you to carry his load for a mile, at the end of the mile ask him if he would like you to carry it further."

What does this mean? This means that by accepting the facts of life totally, concerning insecurity, failure, defeat, and finally death, we conquer them all. Otherwise, these facts eventually lead us nowhere but death. In the final analysis, death is our total defeat. Even in the biggest defeats, you still survive; although defeated, you still continue to exist. But in death even you are annihilated as well.

Death is the biggest defeat of all; that's why we want to kill our enemy—there is no other reason. Death is the ultimate defeat; after that there is no possibility for the enemy to win, ever. The urge to kill an enemy comes from our desire to inflict on him the ultimate defeat. After that there is no way he can ever be a winner, because then he exists no more.

Death is the final defeat, and we all want to run away from it. And remember also, the man who attempts to escape his own death will continue to work towards the killing of others. The more he succeeds in killing others, the more alive he will feel. Hence, the reason for all the violence in the world is totally different from what people ordinarily take it to be. The reason for this violence is not that it is caused because people don't drink unstrained water or they eat after sunset, no, it is nothing of that sort.

The fundamental reason for violence is that man kills others to forget about his own death. Killing others, he believes no one can kill him, because now, he himself has the power to kill. Hitler, Genghis Khan, and such other people, killed millions in order to assure themselves that "No one can kill me, since I kill millions myself." By killing others we try to be free of our own death, we want to confirm our independence. The assumption is that, when we ourselves are capable of killing people, who can kill us?

Deep down, this is avoiding death. Deep down, a violent man is an escapist from death. And one who wants to save himself from death can never be non-violent. Only he who declares, "I accept death, for death is one of the facts of life; it is a reality," can be a non-violent person. One can never deny death. Where will you run from it? Where will you go?

The sun begins to set the moment it rises. A

sunset is as much a reality as the sunrise—the difference is only of direction. At sunset, the sun
reaches exactly where it was at sunrise—but at
sunrise it is in the east, whereas at sunset it is in
the west. Birth is on one side, death is on the
other. That which is ascending on one side is de-
clining on the other. The rising and the setting go
together—the setting, in fact, lies hidden in the
rising. Death lies hidden in birth. One who
knows that such is the case, there is no way he
can ever deny it. Then he accepts everything.
Then he lives this truth. He know it, he sees it,
and he accepts it.

With acceptance comes transformation. When I
say "triumph over death", I mean that as soon as
a person accepts death, he laughs—because he
comes to know there is no death. Only the outer
sheath is formed and unformed. The ocean has
always been—it is only the wave which has taken
form and then disintegrated. Beauty was always
around—the flowers bloomed and withered
away. Light always shone—the sun rose and set.
And that which shone with the rising and setting
of the sun was forever present—before sunrise
and after sunset. But this we will come to see only
when we have seen death, when we have had the
vision of death, when we have encountered
death face-to-face—never before.

So the friend asks: "Why should we think
about death? Why not forget it? Why not just
live?" I would like to say to him that, forgetting
death, no one has ever lived, nor can anyone ever
live. And one who ignores death also ignores life.

It is just as if I have a coin in my hand and I say,
"Why bother about the reverse side of the coin?

Why not just forget it?" If I give up the reverse side, then I will lose the front side of the coin too, because both make two sides of the same coin. It isn't possible to save one side of the coin and throw the other side on the street. How can this be possible? With the one I keep, the other side will automatically be saved. If I throw away one, both will be thrown away; if I save one, both will be saved. Actually, both are aspects of the same thing. Birth and death are two aspects of the same life. The day one realizes this, not only does the sting of death depart, the thought of not dying disappears as well. Then one comes to know that birth is there and so is death. Both comprise bliss.

We get up every morning and go to work. Somebody goes and digs ditches . . . Different people do different jobs—people sweat the whole day. There is a joy in getting up in the morning, but isn't it equally joyful to sleep at night? If a few madmen were to start convincing people not to sleep at night, then getting up in the morning would also stop—because the man who wouldn't sleep, wouldn't be able to wake up in the morning either. The whole of life would come to a halt. One might feel afraid to go to bed, arguing, "It is such a joy to wake up in the morning, it is better not to fall asleep or else it will spoil the whole charm of waking up." But we know this is ridiculous—sleeping is the other side of waking up.

One who sleeps right will wake up right. One who wakes up right will sleep right. One who lives properly will die properly. One who dies properly will take the right steps in his future life. One who does not die in a right manner will not live rightly. One who does not live rightly will not die rightly. It will be a mess; everything will become ugly and distorted. The fear of death is responsible for creating the ugliness and the distortion.

If a fear of falling asleep were to overtake somebody, it would make life difficult. An old lady was brought to me by her son. He said his mother was too afraid to fall asleep. I asked him, "How did this happen?"

He said, "She has been ill lately, and she feels she may die in her sleep, so she is afraid of falling asleep. She fears she won't wake up once she goes to sleep, so she keeps trying to stay up the whole night. We are in big trouble. She isn't recovering from her illness because she stays up all night, afraid she may not wake up alive. Please do something and save her from this fear; otherwise I am in great trouble."

In a way, sleeping is like dying every day. The whole day we are alive; the whole night we are dead. This is like dying in parts, dying a bit every day. We dive within ourselves at night and come out refreshed in the morning. By the time we are seventy or eighty, the body is worn out. Then death takes over. And with that, this body goes through a complete change. But we are very scared of death, although it is nothing more than a deep sleep.

Do you know that the body undergoes change overnight and comes out different every morning? The change is so minimal you don't notice it. The change is not total, it is a partial transformation. When you go to bed at night, tired and weary, your body is in one state, and when you wake up in the morning it is in a different state. In

the morning the body feels fresh and rejuve-
nated; it is filled with energy, ready to face
another day of activity. Now, once again, you can
sing new songs, something you couldn't do the
previous evening. Then you were tired, broken,
worn out. You have never wondered however,
why there is so much fear of death.

When you wake up in the morning you feel
happy, because only a part of your body changes
in sleep—but death, on the other hand, brings
about a complete change. The whole body becomes useless and the need arises to acquire a
new body. But we are scared of death and so our
whole life has become totally crippled. Every moment is filled with fear of death. Because of this
fear we have created a life, a society, a family
which lives the least but fears death the most.
And one who fears death can never live—both
things cannot exist together. The man who is
ready to meet death with absolute spontaneity,
he alone is ready to live as well. Life and death
are both aspects of the same phenomenon. That's
why I say: look at death. I am not asking you to
think about death, because such thinking will
mislead you. Thinking about death, what will
you do?

A sick and miserable man may find it gratifying
to think that everything ends in death. The
thought is gratifying to this man not because it is
right. Remember, never believe that what seems
pleasing to you is necessarily true, because what
feels pleasing does not depend on what is true, it
depends on what you think of as convenient. A
person who is miserable, troubled, sick and in
pain feels he should meet a total death, that

nothing should be left behind—because if any part of him does survive, then it would obviously mean *he* would survive, he, the miserable, sick individual.

A friend has asked: *Some people commit suicide. What do you have to say about them? Are these people not afraid of death?*

They are afraid of death too. But they are more afraid of life than of death. Life seems more painful to them than death; hence they want to finish it. Putting an end to their lives does not mean they find any joy in death, but since life appears worse than death to them, they prefer death. One who is miserable, living in pain, will readily believe that death takes everything away—including the soul—that death leaves nothing behind. He obviously does not want to save any part of himself, because if he does he will be saving nothing but his misery and pain.

One who is afraid of death and wants to save himself, readily accepts the belief in the immortality of the soul. These are all conveniences. It does not show understanding, it merely shows our concern for convenience. This sort of acceptance feels comfortable, that's all. That's why we change our beliefs many times. A man who was an atheist in his youth becomes a theist in his old age. In fact, the truth is that beliefs change with headaches.

When the head has no pain we follow one set of beliefs; with a headache these beliefs are replaced by another set. It is hard to say how much the scriptures affect your belief system and how much your liver does! One can't be sure whether *gurus* or the liver affect it more! What goes on inside the body has a greater effect. When the stomach is upset one feels like becoming an atheist, and when the stomach is okay one feels like believing in God! How in the world can a man believe that there is a God when he has a headache? If God exists and so does the headache, how can you connect the two?

We can run an experiment. Take fifty men and infect them with chronic diseases, and keep the other fifty in good health. Let the first fifty live in misery and let the other fifty live happy lives. You will find that atheism will increase in the former group and theism will increase in the latter group. It is not that happiness is caused by believing in God, a miserable mind inevitably becomes atheistic. Hence, remember, if you see atheism increasing around the world, know well that misery must be on the increase too. If you see an increasing number of people believing in God, you should know that more and more people are becoming happy.

I say to you, therefore, that in the next fifty years there is a great possibility that Russia will become theistic and India will become even more atheistic. Beliefs don't mean anything. In Russia people read Marx, while in India you read Mahavira—this makes no difference. The works of Mahavira and Marx cannot make the least difference. If people were to go on becoming happier in Russia, then in the next fifty years theism would revive there and the bells would begin to ring in Russian temples. Lamps would be lit and prayers would be chanted. Only a happy mind rings bells in the temple, kindles lamps, and chants prayers. People would begin to thank God. Only a happy mind wishes to thank somebody, and who else should one thank?—because a man can find no reasons for the presence of inner happiness, so he thanks the unknown; it must be because of it.

An unhappy mind wants to express its anger. And when the person finds no cause for being unhappy, then who should he be angry at? He obviously becomes filled with bitterness towards the unknown. He says, "The whole mess is because of that unknown one, because of God. Either he does not exist, or he has gone mad." What I am saying is that our theism and our atheism, our beliefs—all of them—are the products of conveniences that suit our conditions.

One who wants to escape from death will inevitably grab hold of some belief. Similarly, someone who wishes to die will also grab on to some belief. But neither of them is eager, anxious to know death. There is a vast difference between convenience and truth. Never think too much about convenience. A thought is always about convenience. A vision is always of truth; a thought is always of convenience.

One man is a communist. He makes a lot of noise—there should be a revolution, the poor should be poor no longer, property must be divided, and so on. Now just give him a car, a big bungalow, and a beautiful girl to marry, and in fifteen days you will see a totally different man. You will hear him say, "Communism, et cetera—it's all nonsense!" What happened to this man? What was convenient to him shaped his thinking.

The other day it was convenient for him to

think that the property be divided; now it is inconvenient to think that property be divided. Now the division of property would mean dividing his car, dividing his bungalow.

The man who doesn't have a beautiful woman can very well say that women should also be socialized. Why should some men have a monopoly over beautiful women? Women should belong to all. There are people who think this way. There are people on this earth who propound, "Today, property; tomorrow, women." And there is nothing wrong in it, because all along you have been treating women as your property anyway.

If one says, "It is wrong that one man should live in a big house and the other in a shanty," then what is the problem in questioning, "Why should one man have a pretty woman and another man not? The division should be equal." These are danger signals. Sooner or later such questions will surely come up. The day property is distributed, the question of sharing women is bound to arise. But the man who has a beautiful woman will certainly protest. He will say, "How can this be possible? What nonsense are you talking about? This is all wrong!"

So, convenience shapes our thinking; our thoughts are formed out of convenience. All our thoughts either foster our convenience or remove our inconvenience. A vision is something else. A vision has nothing to do with convenience. Remember, therefore, that having a vision is a *tapascharya*, a deep personal commitment to knowing the truth. *Tapascharya* means one is not concerned with conveniences; instead, one has to know whatever is, whichever way it is.

So the fact of death has to be seen, not thought about. You will think according to your convenience; your convenience determines your thinking. It is not a question of convenience. We have to know what death is, see it as it is. Your conveniences and inconveniences make no difference. Whatsoever is, that has to be known. As soon as you come to know it, a transformation happens in your life—because death is not. The moment you know death, you come to realize that it is not. You believe in its existence only as long as you have not known it. The experience of ignorance is death; the experience of awareness is immortality.

I TEACH DEATH

Evening
October 31, 1969

A friend has asked: *Are you teaching people how to die? Are you teaching death? You should teach life instead.*

He is right, I am indeed teaching people how to die. I am teaching the art of dying, because one who learns the art of dying becomes an expert in the art of living as well. One who agrees to die becomes worthy of living a supreme life. Only those who have known how to erase themselves also come to know how to be.

These may seem like opposite things because we have taken life and death to be opposing each other, contradictory, but they are not. We have created a false contradiction between the two, and that has produced fatal results. Perhaps nothing has caused so much harm to the human race as this contradiction. Subsequently, this contradiction has had ramifications on many levels. If we divide things which are essentially one into separate parts — not only separate but contradictory parts — the ultimate result can be nothing but the creation of a schizophrenic, insane man.

Let's assume there is a place where mad people live. Great difficulty and trouble would arise if these people were to believe that cold and hot were not only separate but contradictory things — for the simple reason that cold and hot are not contradictory, they are different degrees of qualifying the same thing. Our experience of cold and hot is not absolute, it is very relative. A little experiment will make this clear.

We always find things which are hot and things which are cold. We also see that something which is hot is hot, and something which is cold is cold — we cannot believe the same thing can be hot and cold at the same time. Now, when you go back home, do a little experiment. Take a pot containing hot water, a pot containing cold water, and a pot containing water at room temperature. Put one hand in the hot water and another hand in cold water. Now take both hands out and place them in the water at room temperature. One hand will feel the water is cold and the other will feel the same water is hot. Is that water hot or cold? One hand will say it is hot, the other will say it is cold. Then what is the nature of the water really? If, simultaneously, one hand feels it is hot and the other feels the same water is cold, then we will have to realize the water is neither hot nor cold — its feeling hot or cold is relative to our hands.

Hot and cold are degrees of the same thing —

they are not two different things. The distinction between them is of quantity, not of quality.

Have you ever thought about the distinction between childhood and old age? Ordinarily we think they are opposite to each other — childhood on the one hand, old age on the other. But what is the distinction between childhood and old age really? The difference is only of years, the difference is only of days; the difference is not qualitative, it is only quantitative.

For example, there is a child aged five. We can call him "an old man of five" — what's wrong with that? It is simply linguistic usage that we say "a child five years of age". If we want to, we can call him — as is done in English — "five years old", which can also mean "an old man of five". One is just an old man of seventy, while there is someone who is five years old. What is the difference? If we want, we can call a seventy-year-old man a seventy-year-old child — after all, a child grows into an old man. But when we look at them separately they seem like two contradictory things. It seems like childhood and old age are contrary to each other, but if they are, then no child can ever become old. How can he? How can two contrary things be the same? Have you ever been able to note the day a child turned into an old man? Or, which night? Can you note on a calendar that on such-and-such a day this man was a child and then on such-and-such a day he became old?

In fact, the problem is . . . For example, there are steps leading to the terrace. You can see the lower steps and you can see the steps on the top as well, but you may not be able to see the steps in the middle section. It may look as if the lower steps and the steps on top are separate, far away from each other. But one who can see the whole staircase will deny such a distinction. He will say, "The difference between the steps below and the steps above only appears because of the steps in between. The very step at the bottom is connected with the step on the top."

The difference between hell and heaven is not of quality, the difference is only of quantity. Don't think hell and heaven are contrary, diametrically opposite to each other. The difference between hell and heaven is the same as between cold and hot, between the lower rung and the higher rung, between a child and an old man.

The same sort of difference exists between birth and death; otherwise one who is born will never be able to die. If birth and death were contrary to each other, how could birth end in death? We can only reach to a point of our natural growth. Birth grows into death — this means birth and death are two ends of the same thing. We sow a seed, it grows into a plant, and then it becomes a flower. Have you ever believed there was any opposition between the seed and the flower? The flower grows out of the seed itself and becomes a flower. Growth is in the seed.

Birth turns into death. God knows from what kind of foolishness and during what unfortunate times the idea became fixed in the human mind that birth and death are dichotomous, that life and death are two separate things. We want to live; we don't want to die — but we don't know that death is already part of life. Once we decide we don't want to die, it becomes a certainty, that very moment, that our lives will be filled with problems and difficulties.

The whole of mankind has become schizophrenic. Man's mind is split into parts, into fragments, and there is a reason for this. We have taken the totality of life as if it were made up of parts, and we have pitted each part against the other. Man is the same, but we have created divisions inside him and, as well, have determined that these divisions are contrary to each other. We have done this in all spheres. We tell a person, "Don't be angry, be forgiving," without realizing that the difference between anger and forgiveness is, again, only of degrees — as it is between cold and hot, between childhood and old age. We can say that anger, reduced to the lowest, is forgiveness — there is no dichotomy between them. But all the age-old precepts of mankind teach us, "Get rid of anger and adopt forgiveness" — as if anger and forgiveness are such opposite things that you can drop anger and retain forgiveness. Such a thing can only result in splitting man into fragments and in bringing him trouble.

All of our past belief systems say that sex and *brahmacharya*, celibacy, are contrary to each other. Nothing can be more erroneous than this. The lowest point of sex is *brahmacharya*. Sex, dropping downward, decreasing, is *brahmacharya*. The distance between the two is not one of enmity and contradiction. Remember, in this world there is nothing at all like contradiction. In fact, there can never be anything like contradiction in the world, because if there were, there would be no way to unite the opposites. If birth and death were separate entities, birth would move along its own course and death on its own — nowhere would they meet. Just as two parallel lines don't meet anywhere, no meeting would ever take place between birth and death.

Birth and death are intertwined, they are two ends of a continuum. When I say this, what I am actually saying is that if man must be saved from going insane in the near future, we will have to accept life in its totality. We can't afford any longer to create divisions and to pit one part against the other.

It is so strange that one who says, "Sex is contrary to *brahmacharya*, so let's get rid of sex," will himself be ultimately destroyed in his attempts to get rid of sex. Such a person can never attain *brahmacharya*. Striving to cut off sex from his life, his mind will remain fixed on sex alone — there is no way he can ever attain *brahmacharya*. His mind will be in great tension and trouble forever — right there, that's his death. His life will become too onerous. He will become heavy and won't be able to live at all — not even for a moment. He will be in great trouble.

If you look at it this way — and this is the fact — then what I am saying is that sex and *brahmacharya* are related to each other, just as the lowest and the highest rungs are. As man moves up the ladder of sex, he enters into *brahmacharya*. *Brahmacharya* is nothing but sex reduced to its lowest degree. One reaches to a point where it almost feels as if everything has become empty — it is reaching to the ultimate end. Then there is no contradiction in life, no tension. Then there is no restlessness in life. Then we can live a natural life.

What I am talking about is how to live a most natural life, in all its aspects. We don't live naturally at any level, because we have learned the ways of living life unnaturally. If you were to tell a person, "Walk only with your left foot, because the left foot stands for religion, righteousness. Don't walk on your right foot because the right foot represents unrighteousness." If the man were to believe this . . . And there are lots of people who would believe this — people to believe in such stupid ideas have always been found. So you would come across people who would agree that to walk on the left foot is righteous, and to walk on the right foot is unrighteous. Then they would begin cutting their right foot off and trying to walk on the left foot. They would never be able to walk.

We can only walk with the combined movement of both legs. By itself, a leg never walks alone, although only one leg moves forward at a time. Walking, you only lift one leg at a time too, which may create the wrong impression that you walk on one foot. But don't forget that the one at a standstill, the one in repose, is as important as the one in motion. The day one attains *brahmacharya*, the sex in repose is instrumental in that attainment — in the same way the stationary right leg is instrumental in the left leg's moving forward. The left leg would not be able to move without the help of the right one.

Sex, which has become still, becomes the foothold for the arising of *brahmacharya*. One can take the step of *brahmacharya* only when sex has ceased to move. Uprooting the foothold of sex, breaking it, will certainly result in cutting off sex, but that won't help in achieving *brahmacharya*. Instead, man will remain hanging in limbo — in the same way all the age-old teachings have left humanity hanging in limbo. What we see around us in life is nothing but the movement of the left and the right step, of the left and the right foot.

In life everything is integrated. The apparent diversity is like the notes of a great symphony. If you cut anything out, you will find yourself in difficulty. Someone may say the color black signifies evil. That's why no one is allowed to wear black at marriages; black is allowed at somebody's death. There are people who believe black is a sign of evil, and there are people who believe white is a sign of purity. In a symbolic sense, it is all right to have such distinctions, but if someone were to say, "Let's get rid of black, let's remove black from the face of the earth," then remember, with the removal of black, very little white will be left behind — because the whiteness of white stands out in all its sharpness only against a black background.

The teacher writes on a blackboard with white chalk. Is he out of his mind? Why doesn't he write on the white wall? Of course, one can write on a white wall, but the letters won't stand out. White manifests because of the black background; black is, in fact, causing the white to stand out. Remember, the white of the man who invites enmity with black will inevitably grow dull, insipid.

One who is against showing anger, his

forgiveness will be impotent. The strength of forgiveness lies in anger; only one who can be angry has the power to be forgiving. The more fierce the anger, the far greater will be the magnanimity of forgiveness. The power of anger itself will lend luster to the act of forgiveness. In the absence of anger, the forgiveness will appear totally lackluster, absolutely lifeless, dead.

If a person's sex is destroyed — and there are means to destroy sex — then, remember, that will not make him a *brahmacharya*, a celibate, he will simply turn into an impotent person. And there is a fundamental difference between these two things. There are ways to do away with sex, but a man cannot become a *brahmacharya* by doing away with sex, he can only become impotent. By transforming sex, by accepting it, by moving its energy towards a higher level, one can certainly attain *brahmacharya*. But remember, the brilliance you see in the eyes of a *brahmachari*, a celibate, is the brilliance of sex energy itself. The energy is the same, but transformed.

What I am saying is that what we call opposites are not opposites — life consists of a very mysterious order. In this mysterious order opposites have been created so that things can exist. You must have seen a heap of bricks piled up in front of a house under construction. All the bricks are the same. Then the architect, the engineer, in order to make an arch for a doorway in the house, lays the bricks in opposing order. The bricks are the same, but, making the doorway, he places them opposite to each other so they can hold each other. He wouldn't be able to make the arch if he placed them in the same order — the doorway would fall immediately.

Bricks laid in the same order carry no strength; there is no resistance in them. Wherever resistance occurs a strength is created. All strength comes with opposition; all energy is produced from friction. In life, the principle of polarity is behind the creation of energy, power. The bricks are all alike, but they are placed in opposite order.

God, the divine architect of life, is very intelligent. He knows that life will become cold immediately, will dissolve right away if the bricks are not laid in opposition to each other. So he has placed anger opposite forgiveness, sex opposite *brahmacharya*, and because of the resistance present between them, an energy is created. And that energy is life. He has put the bricks of birth and death together, facing each other, and thus, of both, a gateway to life is created. There are people who say, "We will only accept the brick of life, we won't accept the brick of death." That's fine. Suit yourself. But if you don't accept death you will die that very moment, because then all the bricks that are left will be alike. Only the bricks of life will be left — and they will collapse right away.

This mistake has been repeated many a time. For the last ten thousand years man has been badly afflicted with and troubled by this mistake. He insists on placing bricks that are all alike; he doesn't want opposing bricks. "Remove the polarity," he says. He says, "If we believe in God, then that's all we'll believe in. Then we won't believe in *samsara*, in the mundane world.

If God is, then there is no *samsara;* then we can never accept the mundane life. We can't be in the marketplace, we can't attend to our businesses; because we believe in God we'll become monks and retire to the forests." That man would like to create his world with the bricks of God. Can you imagine what the consequences would be if, by mistake, worldly people were to go crazy and become monks? From that very day, things wouldn't move an inch; from that day the whole world would be in ruins.

In fact, the man who is a monk has no idea that he is surviving, that his left foot moves forward, because someone, a worldly man, is running a store in the marketplace out there. One foot is rooted there; that's why the monk's foot is free to move. The monk's very life-breath comes from the worldly man. He is under the illusion that he is living on his own, but the fact is, all his nourishment comes from the mundane world. And yet he goes about cursing the worldly man; he goes on telling him, "Renounce the world and become a monk." He doesn't realize he is creating a situation for universal suicide this way — a situation even he can't escape from: he will die as well. He is thinking of using bricks that are all alike.

There are also people who say the opposite. They say, "There's no God, there's just this world and nothing else. We only believe in matter." And, believing only in matter, they also tried to create a world of their own. They too have landed in trouble. Where they have arrived, suicide will happen there as well — because if there is only matter and no God, then everything that lends savor to life, that makes life charming, that gives movement to life, that creates the desire to rise, will be gone.

If one were to believe there is no God, that there is nothing but matter, then what meaning is there in life? Then life becomes totally useless. That's why people like Sartre, Camus, Kafka and others talk so much about meaninglessness in the West. Today, with one voice, all western philosophers are saying that life is meaningless. What Shakespeare once said has become relevant all of a sudden, and, about life, western thinkers are now reiterating it: "A tale told by an idiot, full of sound and fury, signifying nothing." There cannot be any significance, any meaning, because you have put together only bricks of matter, and of matter alone. Meaning is bound to disappear absolutely. Just as there being only monks would take meaning away from the world, there being worldly people alone would also take meaning away.

It is interesting that the worldly man survives with the help of the renunciate and the renunciate survives with the help of the worldly man — in the same way the left foot is dependent on the right foot and the right foot is dependent on the left foot. On the surface this dependence appears as a contradiction, but deep down it is not. Both feet are part of the same being: one keeps it rooted; the other causes it to move.

No one can experience the whole truth of life without understanding this contradiction correctly. A person who, in his opposition, insists on cutting out the half of it has not yet attained enough intelligence. You can do away with the half, of course, but as soon as that happens, the remaining half will die as well — because, unquestionably, the latter half received its life energy from the first half and from nowhere else.

I have heard . . . Two monks were involved in an ongoing dispute. One believed it is good to have some money on you, that it can be useful in emergencies. His friend, the other monk, used to argue, "Why do we need money? We are renunciates, what do we need money for? Only worldly people keep money." Both used to put forward arguments in support of their respective views, and it seemed like their arguments were correct.

The great mystery of this universe is that you can present an equal number of arguments in support of any of the opposing bricks used in its creation. And the dispute can never end because both bricks are used equally. Anyone can point out, "Look, the universe is created of *my* bricks," while someone else can argue against this, saying, "No, the universe is made of *my* bricks."

And life is so vast that very few people evolve enough to see that the whole doorway is made of opposing bricks. The rest merely see the bricks that fall within the range of their view. They say, "You are right, the universe is a creation of sannyas. You are right, *Brahman* is the source of the universe. You are right, the universe is made of *atman*." Other people say, "The universe is made of matter, it is made of nothing but dust. Everything will eventually turn into dust — 'Dust unto dust.'" These people can also show only the bricks that fall within their particular view. In this whole affair neither the theist nor the atheist wins the argument; neither the materialist nor the spiritualist wins. They cannot. Their statements are coming from a dichotomized view of life.

So there was a great dispute between these monks. One maintained it is necessary to have money, while the other disagreed. One evening, in a great hurry, they arrived at a river. It was close to nightfall. One of the monks approached the boatman, who was tying up his boat for the night, and said, "Please don't tie your boat up yet, bring us across the river. Night is approaching and we must reach the other side."

The boatman said, "Sorry, I am finished for the day and now I have to go back to my village. I'll take you across in the morning."

The monks said, "No, we can't wait until morning. Our *guru*, with whom we lived, who taught us what life is all about, is close to dying. The news is, he will be dead by morning. He has summoned us. We can't stay overnight."

The boatman said, "Okay, I'll take you over for five *rupees*." The monk who had argued in favor of carrying money laughed and, looking at the other monk, said, "What do you think, my friend? Is carrying money worthless or meaningful?" The other monk simply kept laughing. The monk paid five *rupees* to the boatman — he had won. After reaching the other shore, the monk said again, "What do you say, my friend? We would have been unable to cross the river if we hadn't had the money."

The second monk laughed uproariously. He

said, "We crossed the river not because you *had* money, but because you could *part* with it! We were able to cross the river not because you had money but because you could let go of it." So the argument remained. The second monk continued, "I always said a monk must have the courage to let go of money. We could give it up; that's why we could cross the river. If you had kept holding on to it, if you had not let it go, how could we have crossed the river?"

So the problem remained. The first monk also joined in the laughter. They came to their *guru*. They asked him, "What shall we do? This has become quite a problem. What happened today illustrates our differences succinctly. One of us believes we crossed the river because we had money on us, while the other says we were able to cross because we let money go. We are firm in our beliefs, and we both seem to be right."

The *guru* laughed a belly laugh. He said, "You are both crazy. You are committing the same kind of foolishness mankind has done for ages."

"What is that foolishness?" the monks asked.

The *guru* said, "Each one of you is looking at one side of the truth. It is true you could hire the boat and cross the river only because you let go of money — but the other side is equally true: you could part with your money because you had money to part with. It is true, of course, that you were able to cross the river because you had money on you. But the other part is equally true. Had you not had any money you wouldn't have been able to cross. You crossed because you let go of money. So both things are right. There is no contradiction between them."

But we have created such dichotomies in all levels of our lives. And a belief in either of the two parts can provide a convincing argument in its support. It is not difficult, because after all, a man has at least half of life to draw upon — he is living half his life; that's not a small matter. It is more than enough to argue for. So nothing will be solved by arguing. Life will have to be investigated, known in its totality.

I certainly teach death, but that does not mean I am against life. What it means is: death is the gateway to know life, to recognize life as well. What it means is: I don't see life and death as contrary to each other. Whether I call it the art of dying or whether I call it the art of living — both mean the same thing. It depends on how we look at it. You may ask, "Why don't you call it the art of living?" There are reasons for it.

The first thing is, we have become extremely attached to life. And this attachment has become very unbalanced. I can call it the art of living too, but I won't, because you are too attached to life. If I should say, "Come learn the art of living," you would come running because you would want to strengthen your attachment to life. I call it the art of dying so you can regain your balance. If you learn how to die, then life and death will stand before you equally; they will become your left and right foot. Then you will attain to the ultimate life. In its ultimate state life contains neither birth nor death, but it *is* made of the two aspects we call birth and death.

Of course, if there is a town where people are suicidal, where no one wants to live, I won't go there and talk about the art of dying. There I will say, "Learn the art of living." And as I tell you, "Meditation is the gateway to death," I would tell the people of that town, "Meditation is the gateway to life." I would tell them, "Come, learn how to live, because unless you have learned how to live, you won't know how to die. If you wish to die, then let me teach you how to live — because once you have learned how to live, you will have learned how to die as well." Only then would the people of that town come to me. Your town is just the opposite: you are residents of a town where no one wants to die, where everyone wants to live, where people want to cling to life so hard they can keep death away forever. Therefore, I am compelled to talk to you about death. It has nothing to do with me; because of you I am calling it the art of dying. I have been saying the same thing all along.

Once Buddha entered a village. It was early morning and the sun was just about to appear on the horizon. A man came to him and said, "I am an atheist, I don't believe in God. What do you think? Is there God?"

Buddha said, "God alone is. There is nothing but God everywhere."

The man said, "But I was told that you are an atheist."

"You must have heard wrongly," said Buddha. "I am a theist. Now you have heard it from my own lips. I am the greatest theist ever. There is God, and nothing but God." The man stood there under the tree with an uneasy feeling. Buddha moved on.

Another man came at noon and said, "I am a theist. I am an absolute believer in God. I am an enemy of atheists. I have come to ask you, what do you think about God's existence?"

Buddha said, "God? Nor is there one, nor can there ever be one. There is absolutely no God."

The man couldn't believe his ears. "What are you talking about?" he exclaimed. "I heard a religious man had come to this village, so I came to ask whether God is. And what's this you are saying?"

Buddha said, "A religious man? A believer in God? I am the greatest atheist ever."

The man stood there utterly confused. We can understand this man's confusion — but Ananda, a disciple of Buddha's, was in a terrible suspense; he had heard both conversations. He became very restless; he couldn't figure out what was going on. It was all right in the morning, but by afternoon it became a problem. "What has happened to Buddha?" Ananda wondered to himself. "In the morning he said he was the greatest theist, while in the afternoon he said he was the greatest atheist." He made up his mind to ask Buddha in the evening, when he would be alone. But by evening Ananda was in for yet another surprise.

By the time it was evening another person came to Buddha and said, "I don't understand whether there is God or not." The man must have been an agnostic, one who says he doesn't know whether God is or not. No one knows, and no one can ever know. So he said, "I don't know whether there is God or not. What do you say? What do you think?"

Buddha replied, "If you don't know, then I

don't know either. And it would be good if we both remained silent."

Listening to Buddha's answer, this man was confounded as well. He said, "I had heard you are enlightened, so I thought you must have known."

Buddha said, "You must have heard wrong. I am an absolutely ignorant man. What knowledge can I have?"

Just try to feel what Ananda must have gone through. Put yourself in his shoes. Can you see his difficulty? When it was night and everyone had left, he touched Buddha's feet and said, "Are you trying to kill me? What are you doing? I almost lost my life! Never have I been so upset and restless as I have been today. What is this you have been saying and doing the whole day? Are you in your right mind? Are you sure you know what you said today? In the morning you said one thing, in the afternoon another, and in the evening you gave an entirely different answer to the same question."

Buddha said, "I did not give these answers to you. I gave my answers to the people concerned. Why did you listen to them? Do you think it is right to hear what I say to others?"

Ananda said, "Now this tops it all! How in the world could I not hear? I was present, right there; my ears were not clogged! And could it ever be possible I wouldn't want to hear you speak? I love to hear you speak, no matter who you talk to."

Buddha said, "But why are you upset? I didn't answer *you*!"

Ananda said, "Maybe not, but I am in a quandary. Please answer me, right now. What is the truth? Why did you give three different answers?"

Buddha explained, "I had to bring the three of them to a point of balance. The man who came in the morning was an atheist. Being an atheist only he was incomplete, because life is made of opposites."

Keep this in mind: a truly religious person is both — an atheist on one hand, and as well, a believer in God on the other hand. His life contains both aspects, but he brings harmony between the two opposites. Religion is in that very harmony. And one who is only a believer in God lacks religious maturity. He has not yet attained a balance in his life.

So Buddha said, "I had to bring a balance to his life. One side of him had become very heavy, so I had to put some rocks on the other scale. And besides, I also wanted to unsettle him, because somehow he had become convinced there is no God. His conviction needed to be shaken up, because one who becomes certain, dies. The journey must go on; the search must continue.

"The man who came in the afternoon was a theist. I had to tell him I was an atheist because he had become lopsided too; he had lost his balance as well. Life is a balance. One who attains this balance attains the truth."

The reason I say to you, you should learn the art of dying is because your life has become lopsided. You are sitting very solidly on the scale of life, and so everything has turned to rock. Life has become solidified; the balance is gone.

Go ahead. Invite death as well. Say, "Come

and be my guest too. We'll stay together." The day life agrees to live with death, it is transformed into life supreme. The day one welcomes death, gives it a hug, embraces it, the matter is over! That day the sting of death departs. The sting lay in our running away from death, in our being afraid of it. When a person comes forward and embraces death, death loses, death is conquered, because the man who embraces death becomes immortal. Now death can't do anything to him. What can death do when the man himself is ready to disappear?

There are two types of people — one whom death seeks and the other who seeks death. Death seeks those who run away from it. And there are those who seek death, but it keeps eluding them. They search endlessly but can't find death. What kind of a person would you like to be — the one who runs away from death or the one who embraces it? A person eluding death will continue to be defeated; his entire life will be a lifelong story of defeat. One who embraces death will instantly triumph over it; defeat will no longer exist in his life. Then his life becomes a triumphant journey.

Yes, I teach the very art of dying. I am teaching you how to die so you may attain life. Do you know a secret? The man who learns how to live in darkness — the moment he accepts the totality of darkness, the darkness turns into light for him. Do you know that the man who takes poison lovingly, joyfully, as if he were taking nectar — the poison becomes nectar for him? If you don't, then you must find out. One of the most profound truths of life is that the man who accepts poison lovingly, the poison no longer remains poison for him — it turns into nectar. And the man who has accepted darkness itself, whole-heartedly, finds to his astonishment that darkness has become light. And one who greets pain with open arms, finds there is no pain at all — only happiness remains for him.

For one who accepts his state of agitation and agrees to live with it, the doors of peace and tranquility are thrown open. This seems contradictory. Remember, however, that one who says he wants to attain peace can never become peaceful, because to say "I want to attain peace," is, in fact, looking for disturbance. Man is restless as he is, and yet there are some who create a new restlessness by saying, "We want to be peaceful."

Once a man came to me. He said, "I have been to the Ramana Ashram in Pondicherry, and to the Ramakrishna Ashram — they are all full of hypocrisy. I couldn't find anything else there. I am looking for peace, which I find nowhere. I have been wandering in search of it for the last two years. In Pondicherry someone mentioned your name. I have come straight from there. I want peace."

I said, "Get up and walk out that door right this moment, otherwise I shall be proven to be a hypocrite as well."

He said, "What do you mean?"

I said, "Simply get out. And don't ever look back in this direction again. It is better I save myself before I am called a hypocrite as well."

"But I have come to find peace," the man said.

"Simply get lost," I said. "And let me ask you

this: who did you go to and ask how to be in agony? Which *guru* has initiated you into agitation? Which ashram did you go to, to learn how to be restless?"

"I went nowhere," the man replied.

Then I said, "You are such a clever fellow, you can even create mental disturbance for yourself. Then what is there for me to teach you?" The way you have created your agitation, take an opposite route and you will find peace. What do you want from me? Don't tell anyone you came to see me too, even by mistake. I have nothing to do with what's happening to you!"

The man said, "Please show me the way to find peace."

I told him, "You are looking for ways of becoming agitated. There is only one way to attain peace: be at peace with restlessness."

One who accepts restlessness in its totality, one who says, "Come, stay with me. Be my guest in this very home," suddenly finds the restlessness has left him. With the change in our state of mind the restlessness departs. One who accepts even the restlessness itself, his mind quiets down. How can restlessness last if the mind is attuned to peace?

Even though it may be a non-acceptance of restlessness, the very restlessness itself is the product of our attitude of non-acceptance. One who says he will not accept being restless will continue to be restless, because this very non-acceptance is, itself, the root of restlessness. A man says, "I won't accept restlessness, I can't accept suffering, I can't accept death, I can't accept darkness." That's just fine, don't accept them —

but you will continue to be surrounded by what you will not accept. Instead, see what happens by accepting, by agreeing to something no one else wants to. And to your great surprise you will find what you considered your enemy became your friend. If you invite your enemy to be your guest, what other course is there for him but to become your friend?

The reason for my discussing these issues with you for three days was because I saw you came here with the desire to conquer death. You must have thought I would let you in on some trick so you would never die.

A friend has written a letter in which he says, *Are you going to show us how to rejuvenate our bodies? Are you going to show some alchemical method to become young again? If that's the case then it's worth spending our money to come there.*

Maybe you have come here with the same idea too. If so, you will be disappointed, because I am teaching the art of dying here. I say unto you: Die! Learn how to die. Why run away from death? Accept it, welcome it. And remember, I am giving you the very key to be victorious over death. Rejuvenation is not the key for attaining victory over death. No matter how much you go through a process of rejuvenation, you will still have to die. The body is sure to die. Rejuvenation can only push death a little further away; death can be avoided a little longer. It only means your problems will be extended over a longer period — instead of dying in seventy years, you might be able to die in seven hundred years. The suffering you could have otherwise finished with in seventy years will be prolonged for seven hundred years — what else? The troubles of seventy years will extend to seven hundred. The quarrels of seventy years will continue up to seven hundred. The problems of seventy years will spread over seven hundred years — they will be stretched that much, multiplied. What else do you think will happen?

This may not have occurred to you, but if you really should come across someone who could give you a potion and say, "Take this and you will live for seven hundred years," you would tell him, "Wait a minute, let me think it over." I don't believe any one of you would agree to take a potion that would extend life for seven hundred years. So what does that mean? That means "I will continue to be as I am. This very 'I' will now have to live for seven hundred years." And that would prove to be very costly; it would have very grave consequences.

Should scientists someday discover how man can live infinitely — and such a discovery is possible; it is not difficult — remember, people will start looking for a *guru* to teach them how to die quickly. Just as, now, people are looking for *gurus* who can rejuvenate their bodies, people then will look for someone who will show them the secret, the technique of dying, so that even scientists will not be able to save them. They will try to cheat the government so they can ease themselves out of life.

We have absolutely no idea that an extended life has no meaning. The meaning of life comes with living. An individual can live so totally in one moment — more totally than another man could, even in an infinite number of lives. It's a matter of living, and only a man who has no fear of death can live — otherwise how can he live? The fear of death keeps man trembling — he never stands still; he keeps running all the time.

Have you noticed that speed is continuously on the increase in the world? Everything is speedy. In one respect a rocket is better than a bullock cart — because a rocket can take us places faster — but why so much insistence on speed? You may not have realized this, but all man's attempts at speed are attempts to escape where he is. Where he is, he is so scared, he is so afraid, he wants to get away. He feels he would be better off anywhere except where he is.

All over Europe and America weekends and holidays have become a great nuisance. People get more tired on these days than ever. The idea is to jump into the car and dash off — fifty miles, a hundred miles, two hundred miles — to escape to a picnic spot, to a mountain, to a hill resort, to the beach. The motivation for rushing off so fast is because others are running off, are in a hurry too — they might reach first. If one asks where they want to reach, they don't know. One thing is certain, however: they want to get away from where they are — away from the house, away from the wife, away from their work.

Man is unable to live; that's why there is so much running about. He wants to go on putting more power into his vehicles so he can run faster. Ask where he is going, where he wants to reach, and his answer will be, "I can't tell you right now; I don't have time. I have to get there soon. We have to land on the moon; we have to land on Mars." All our lives we are running. What are we running from? What is the fear? The fear is that on the one hand we are unable to live fully, and on the other hand the fear of death is imminent, present. Both things are interconnected. The man who is afraid of death will not be able to live his life; he will remain terrified of death. Then what is the answer?

You ask me, "What's the answer? What's the solution?" I say: accept death. Invite death and say, "Come on, I'll worry about living later — first you come. Let me first be finished with you so the matter is over for once and for all. After that I'll live at leisure. Let me take care of you first, then I'll settle down and live comfortably." Meditation is the means to accept death with this attitude. To extend such an invitation to death, meditation is the means, meditation is the answer. One who accepts death in this way comes to a halt immediately. His speed disappears.

Have you ever watched? When you are angry and you are cycling, you pedal faster. When you are angry and driving a car, you press the accelerator harder. Psychologists say car accidents happen, not because of bad roads but because of the man on the accelerator — there is something wrong with the man. His teeth are clenched in anger and he is pressing the accelerator harder, and somehow or other he is wishing to have an accident. He is filled with the desire to crash into something. Life seems so dull and useless to him that he wants to bring some excitement, some juice into it — at least by crashing against something, if nothing else. He thinks he'll get some thrill out of it, will feel good about it. He feels he'll have the satisfaction that something happened in his life, that it was not a total waste.

Many criminals in Europe and America have given statements in court, saying they had nothing against the person they killed — they just wanted to see their names in print, and that was the only way. A good man's name never appears in the papers; you only see names of murderers and criminals. There are two types of murderers: those who commit a single murder for personal reasons, and those who commit collective murder — the politicians. Only their names are printed in the newspapers, the rest are ignored. Although you may be a good citizen, your name will not be in the papers — but stab a person and it will create headlines.

A criminal confesses in the court, "I had no enmity with the person, I had never seen the man before. I just looked at his back and plunged a knife into it. When the blood gushed out of the victim I felt satisfied that finally I had done something people would talk about, that my life had not passed in vain. The newspapers are filled with the story. The courts, the big judges and lawyers in their black gowns are discussing my case with great seriousness. Looking at all this, I feel I have also done something, I am not an ordinary man."

A man who is evading death, who is scared of death, has become so frustrated, so sad and bored that he is ready to indulge in anything. The one thing he is not doing, however, is welcoming death. As soon as a man welcomes death, accepts death, a new door opens in his life — a door that leads him to the divine.

The word "Die" is inscribed on the temple of God, whereas, inside, the stream of life is overflowing. Looking at the signboard "Die", people turn back. No one goes inside. It's a very smart idea, a very clever idea, otherwise there would be a crowd inside and it would be difficult to live — so the temple of life has the signboard "Die" hanging outside. Those who become frightened looking at it, run away. That's why I said one has to learn how to die.

The biggest secret of life is to learn how to die, how to accept death. Let the past die every day. Let us die every day. We don't let the yesterday's past die. A seventy year-old man keeps the happy memories of his childhood alive. His childhood is not yet dead. He still carries the desire to return to his childhood. The man is too old to move about, he is bedridden, but his youth is not yet dead. He is still thinking about the same things. He is still dreaming of the female movie stars of his youth, although none of them are the same now. The pictures are still moving before his eyes; nothing has died. In fact, our yesterday never dies. We never gather the courage to die; we never let anything die, and consequently, everything piles up. We don't let the dead be dead; instead, we amass it like a heavy load. And then it becomes impossible to live under its weight. So one of the keys to the art of dying is: let the dead be dead.

As Jesus was passing by a lake, a wonderful incident took place. It was early morning — the sun was about to rise; the horizon had just turned red. A fisherman had thrown his net in the lake to catch fish. As he began pulling the net out, Jesus placed his hand on the fisherman's shoulder and said, "My friend, would you spend all your life catching fish?"

The same question had crossed the fisherman's mind many times before. Is there any mind in which it doesn't? Of course, the fish may be different, the net may be different, the lake may be different, but nevertheless, the question arises, "Am I supposed to spend the whole of my life catching fish?"

The fisherman turned around to see who the man was who was raising the same question he had in his mind. He looked at Jesus. He saw his serene, laughing eyes, his personality. He said, "There is no other way. Where else can I find a lake? Where else can I find fish and throw my net to catch them? I ask myself too, 'Will I go on catching fish the rest of my life?'"

Then Jesus said, "I am a fisherman too. But I throw my net in some other ocean. Come, follow me if you wish, but remember, only a man can throw a new net who has the courage to give up his old net. Leave the old net behind."

The fisherman must have really been a courageous man. There are very few courageous people like him. Right there, he dropped the net filled with fish. A desire must have occurred in his mind to at least pull out the net that was already filled, but Jesus said, "Only they can throw the new net into the new ocean who have the courage to leave the old net behind. Drop your net right there." The fisherman let go of his net and asked, "Tell me where I have to go?"

Jesus said, "You seem to be a man of courage. You have the potential to go some place. Come with me!" As they reached the outskirts of the village, a man came running. He caught hold of the fisherman and said, "You madman, where are you going? Your father, who was ill, has died. Where were you? We went looking for you at the lake and found your net lying there. Where are you going?"

The fisherman said, "Please let me take your leave for a few days to perform my father's last rites. Then I'll come back."

Jesus' words in reply to the fisherman are tremendously wonderful. He said, "You fool, let the dead bury the dead! What need is there for you to go? Come. Follow me. Now one who is dead is already dead, why even bother to bury him? These are all tricks to keep him alive. So one who is now dead, is dead forever. And there are many dead people in the village. They will bury the dead. You come with me."

The fisherman hesitated for a moment. Watching him, Jesus said, "Perhaps I wrongly understood you could leave your old net behind." The fisherman paused for a moment and then followed Jesus. Jesus said, "You are a courageous man. If you can leave the dead behind, you can indeed attain to life."

Actually, that which has died in the past should be dropped. You sit in meditation but then you always come and tell me it never happens, that thoughts keep coming. Thoughts don't come like that. The question is, have you ever left them? You always keep holding on to them, how can they be at fault? If a man keeps a dog, feeds him, ties him in his house and then suddenly one day sets him loose, turns him out;

if the poor dog comes back to the man again and again, would the dog be at fault?

All these days you fed the dog, petted him, loved him, played with him, tied a collar around his neck, kept him in your home. And then all of a sudden you decide to meditate and tell the dog to get lost. How can that be? The poor dog has no idea what has happened to you so suddenly, so he wanders around for a while and then comes back to you. He thinks maybe you are having some kind of fun with him, hence the more you drive him out the more playful he becomes, the more he keeps coming back to you. He feels something new is happening, that maybe the master is in a good mood, so he takes more and more interest in the game.

You come and tell me thoughts won't leave you. How can they? You have nourished them with your own blood. You have tied them to yourself; you have put a collar around their necks with your name on it. Just tell someone what he thinks is wrong — he will jump back at you, saying, "What do you mean what I think is wrong? My thoughts can never be wrong!" So the thought with a collar with your name on it comes back to you. How is your thought supposed to know you are meditating? Now you say to your thought, "Get out! Scram!" The thought is not going to go away like this.

We nourish thoughts. We nourish thoughts of the past, we keep tying them to ourselves. And then, one day, you want them to leave you all of a sudden. They won't leave you in one day. You will have to stop feeding them; you will have to stop rearing them.

Remember, if you want to drop thoughts, stop saying, "My thoughts". How can you leave something you claim as yours? If you want to get rid of thoughts, then stop taking interest in them. How will they depart unless you stop taking interest in them? Otherwise, how will they know you have changed, that you are no longer interested in them?

All our memories of the past are thoughts. There is a whole network of them we are holding on to. We don't allow them to die. Let your thoughts die. Let the dead remain dead; don't try to keep it alive. But we are keeping it alive.

This is also a part of the art of dying. Keep this key in mind too: if you want to learn the art of dying then let the dead be dead. Let the past be past. It no longer exists, let it go. There is no need even to preserve it in your memory. Say goodbye to it, let it depart. Yesterday was finished yesterday; now it is no more — and yet it keeps its hold over us.

There is another small question. A friend has asked, *What is a mind filled with illusions? What is a very confused mind? What is clarity of mind?*

This needs to be understood, because it will be useful for meditation as well as in learning the art of dying. He has asked a very significant question. He asks, "What is a confused mind?" But here we make a mistake. We say, "disturbed mind", "confused mind". This is where the mistake is. What is the mistake? The mistake is we are using two words — "confused", "mind" — and the truth of the matter is that there is no such thing as a "confused mind". Rather, the very state of confusion itself is mind. There is nothing like a confused mind.

Mind is confusion. Mind is another name for confusion. And when there is no confusion does not mean that the mind has become peaceful, then there is no more mind at all.

For example, there is a storm at sea, the sea is restless. Would you call it a "restless storm"? Would anyone call it a "restless storm"? You would simply call it a storm, because a storm is just another name for restlessness. And when the storm dies down, do you now say the storm has become peaceful? You simply say the storm no longer exists.

In understanding the mind, remember too, mind is just another name for confusion. When peace descends it does not mean the mind becomes peaceful; rather, the mind does not exist at all. A state of no-mind appears. And when the mind is no more, then what remains is called the *atman*. The sea exists even when there is no storm. When the storm disappears, the sea remains. When the confused mind ceases to exist, then what remains is *atman*, soul.

Mind is not a thing, it is a state of disorder, a state of chaos. Mind is not a faculty, it is not a substance. The body is a substance, the *atman* is a substance — and existing as a state of confusion that becomes a link between the two, is mind. In a state of peace, the body remains, the *atman* remains, but the mind is no more.

There is no such thing as a "peaceful mind". This error in expression is because of the language we have created. We say an "unhealthy body", a "healthy body". This is okay. There is an unhealthy body, of course, and there is a healthy body as well. With the disappearance of unhealthiness, a healthy body remains. But this is not true in the case of the mind. There is no such thing as a "healthy mind", an "unhealthy mind". Mind by itself is unhealthy. Its very being is confusion. Its very being is unhealthy. Its very being is a disease.

So don't ask how you can save the mind from becoming confused, ask how you can get rid of this mind. Ask how this mind can die. Ask how you can do away with this mind. Ask how you can let go of this mind. Ask what can be done so that the mind will exist no more.

Meditation is a way to be finished with the mind, to part with the mind. Meditation means to step out of the mind. Meditation means to move away from the mind. Meditation means cessation of the mind. Meditation means to stay away from where the confusion is. By moving away from the confusion, the confusion stills— because it is our very presence that creates it. If we move away, it ceases to be.

Say, for instance, two people are having a fight. You have come to fight with me and the fight is on. If I were to step aside, how would the fight continue? It would stop, because it can only continue if I make myself a part of it. We live on a mental plane; we are present right where the disorder, where the trouble is going on. We don't want to get away from there, and yet we want to bring peace there. Peace cannot be there. Just be kind enough to step aside; that's all.

As soon as you step aside, the turmoil will

come to an end. Meditation is not a technique to bring peace to your mind; rather, it is a technique to move away from the mind. Meditation is a means to slip away, to turn away from the waves of confusion.

Yet another friend has asked a question which is related to the previous one. It would be good to understand that as well. He has asked, *What is the difference between to be in meditation, and to do meditation?*

It is the same difference I am already explaining to you. If a person is "doing" meditation, he is trying to make a confused mind peaceful. What will he do? He will attempt to make his mind quiet. When an individual is *being* in meditation, he is not trying to quiet down his mind; instead, he is slipping away from it.

If it is sunny outside, you may see a man trying to open his umbrella—and umbrellas can be stretched outside in the sun; one may stand under its shade, or any other shade—but such umbrellas, however, can never be stretched within the mind. The only kind of umbrellas there can be in the mind are of thoughts—but they make no difference. It is as if a man were to stand in the sun with his eyes closed, thinking that an umbrella is over his head and that he is not feeling hot now. But he is bound to feel hot. This man is trying to cool down the sun. He is trying to "do" meditation. Now there is another man. When it is sunny outside, he merely gets up, walks inside the house and relaxes. He is making no effort to cool down the sun, he is merely moving away from the sun.

Doing meditation means making an effort, an effort to change the mind. And to *be* in meditation means not making any effort to change the mind but, instead, moving within without a sound.

You must take into account the distinction between the two. If you make an effort to meditate, meditation will never happen. If you try to make a conscious effort, if you sit down, strain your muscles, force yourself, become determined to calm your mind no matter what, it won't work. Because, after all, who will be doing all this? Who will be showing determination? Who else but you?

As it is, you are already confused, restless. Now you try to calm yourself down—that means you will be adding one more headache. You are sitting uptight, ready, disregarding everything. The more stiff you become, the further you get into difficulty, the more you go on becoming tense. This is not the way. I ask you to meditate because meditation is relaxation. You have not to do anything, just be relaxed.

Make sure you understand. Let me explain a little further through one small principle. Keep it in mind finally. A man is swimming in the river. He says he wants to reach the other side. The current of the river is swift, and he flaps his arms and legs, trying to swim across. He is getting tired, worn out, broken, but he keeps on swimming. This man is making an effort to swim. To swim is an effort for him. *Doing* meditation is an effort too. Then there is another man. Instead of swimming he just keeps floating. He has let himself go in the river. He does not throw his arms and legs about; he is simply lying in the river. The river is flowing and, along with the river, so is he. He is not swimming at all, he is just floating. An effort is not required to float; floating is merely no-effort.

The meditation I am talking about is like floating, it's not like swimming. Watch a man swimming and a leaf floating in the river. The delight and the joy of the floating leaf is simply out of this world. There is no trouble, no hindrance, no quarrel, no bother for the leaf. The leaf is very smart. And what's its smartness? The smartness of the leaf is that it has made the river its boat and is now riding on it. The leaf is ready and willing to go wherever the river takes it. The leaf has broken all the strength of the river. The river can do it no harm because the leaf is not fighting against the river. The leaf doesn't want to create any resistance, it's just floating.

So the leaf is in complete accord. Why is that so? It is because now, it is not trying to fall in accord with the river, it is simply floating; that's all. Wherever the river wants to take it, so be it. So keep the floating leaf in mind. Can you float like this in the river? There should not be even a thought of swimming, not even the feeling of it; there should be no mind at all.

Have you ever observed that a living man can drown in a river whereas a dead man floats on the surface? Have you ever wondered what this is about? A living man drowns, but never a dead man. He comes to the surface right away. What's the difference? The dead body enters into a state of no-effort. The dead body does nothing; it cannot even if it wished to. The body comes to the surface and floats. A living man can drown because a living man makes an effort to stay alive. Attempting to do that, he gets tired— and as he gets tired, he drowns. His fighting drowns him, not the river. The river can't drown the dead man because he doesn't put up any fight. Since he doesn't fight, losing his strength is out of the question. The river can do no harm to him. So he floats in the river.

The meditation I am talking about is like floating, not like swimming. You just have to float. When I say relax your body, I mean you should let the body float. Now one does not maintain any hold over the body; now one does not tether oneself to the shore of the body—you let it go, you float. When I say to let go of the breath as well, then do not cling to the shore of breathing. Then leave that too, then float with it also. Then where will one go? If you let go of the body, you will move within; if you hold on to the body, you will come out.

How can one enter the river if he holds on to the shore? He can only be back on the shore. If one leaves the shore, he will go straight into the river. So a stream of life, a stream of divine consciousness is flowing within us, but we are grabbing on to the shore, on to the shore of the body.

Let go of it. Let go of breathing too. Let go of thoughts as well. Now all the shores are left behind. Where will you go now? Now you will begin to float in that stream which flows within. One who allows himself to float in that stream reaches the ocean.

The stream within is like a river, and one who starts floating in it reaches the ocean. Meditation is a kind of floating. One who learns how to float reaches the divine. Do not swim. One who swims will go astray. One who swims will, at the most, leave this shore and reach the other. What else will he do? What more can a swimmer do? He will go from one shore to the other. This shore brings you out of the river, and so does the other shore. A poor man, after a great deal of swimming, may become a rich man at most— what more? After swimming a great deal, a man occupying a small chair may sit on a high chair in Delhi—what more will happen?

This shore takes you out of the river, the same as that shore does. The shore of Dwarka is as outside the river as the shore of Delhi is—it makes no difference. A swimmer can only reach the shore. But what about the one who is floating? No shore can prevent a floater, because he has let himself go in the stream. The stream will carry him. It is sure to carry him and bring him to the ocean.

The very goal is to reach the ocean—the river becomes the ocean and the individual consciousness becomes the divine. When a drop is lost in the vast ocean, the absolute meaning of life, the supreme bliss of life, the paramount beauty of life is attained.

The ultimate thing is: the art of dying is the art of floating. One who is prepared to die never swims. He says, "Take me where you will. I am ready!"

What I have talked about these four days has pertained to this. Some friends, however, believed I was merely answering questions. They have written over and over again, "Please say something of yours. Don't simply answer questions . . ."—as if someone else were giving the answers!

The problem is that pegs become more important than the clothes hanging on them. What they are saying is, "Just show us the clothes. Why are you bothering to hang them on pegs?" But what am I hanging on the pegs anyway? Whatever I have to say, I will be hanging it on the pegs of your questions. But that's how our minds are.

I have heard . . .

There was a circus. Every day, the owner of the circus used to give four bananas to the monkeys in the morning and three in the evening. One morning it happened there weren't enough bananas in the market, so he gave them three bananas. The monkeys went on strike. They said, "This is impossible, we want four bananas in the morning."

The owner said, "I'll give you four in the evening, take three now."

The monkeys insisted, "This has never happened before. We have always had four bananas in the morning. We want four bananas now!"

The owner said, "Have you gone crazy? You'll have seven bananas altogether anyway."

The monkeys persisted, "We don't care about your arithmetic. All we care about is that we have been getting four bananas every morning. We want four bananas right now!"

On and on friends write to me, "Please say something of your own. Don't answer questions." Indeed I will speak, but the question is: what will I speak? The questions merely serve as

pegs; whatever I have to say, I hang on them.
Whether I speak or whether I answer questions,
what difference does it make? Who is it that will
be answering? Who is it that will be speaking?
But they feel I must speak my own stuff because
they have been getting four bananas every
morning.

In each meditation camp there used to be four
discourses and four question-and-answer sessions. This time it has happened that you have
turned all the meetings into question-and-answer sessions. But this makes no difference.
Keep the arithmetic of seven bananas in mind.
Add them together. There is no need to count
one by one—that there are four in the morning
and three in the evening, or vice versa. I have
given you all seven bananas. If you get mixed
up, counting, you might miss the point. That's
why, at the end, I have said there are seven
bananas. What I had to say, I have said it all.

BOOKS PUBLISHED BY
RAJNEESH FOUNDATION
INTERNATIONAL

BOOKS PUBLISHED BY
RAJNEESH FOUNDATION
INTERNATIONAL

For a complete catalog of all the books published by
Rajneesh Foundation International, contact:

Rajneesh Foundation International
P.O. Box
Rajneeshpuram, USA
(503)

THE BAULS
The Beloved (2 volumes)

BUDDHA
The Book of the Books (volume 1 & 2)
the Dhammapada

The Diamond Sutra
the Vajrachchedika Prajnaparamita Sutra

The Discipline of Transcendence (4 volumes)
the Sutra of 42 Chapters

The Heart Sutra
the Prajnaparamita Hridayam Sutra

BUDDHIST MASTERS
The Book of Wisdom (volume 1)
Atisha's Seven Points of Mind Training

The White Lotus
the sayings of Bodhidharma

EARLY DISCOURSES
And Now, and Here (volume 1)

Beware of Socialism

The Long and the Short and the All

The Perfect Way

TANTRA

The Book of the Secrets (volumes 4 & 5)
Vigyana Bhairava Tantra

Tantra, Spirituality & Sex
Excerpts from The Book of the Secrets

Tantra: The Supreme Understanding
(Tilopa's Song of Mahamudra)

The Tantra Vision (2 volumes)
the Royal Song of Saraha

TAO

The Empty Boat
the stories of Chuang Tzu

The Secret of Secrets (2 volumes)
the Secret of the Golden Flower

Tao: The Golden Gate (volume 1)

Tao: The Pathless Path (2 volumes)
the stories of Lieh Tzu

Tao: The Three Treasures (4 volumes)
the Tao Te Ching of Lao Tzu

When The Shoe Fits
the stories of Chuang Tzu

THE UPANISHADS

I Am That
(Isa Upanishad)

The Ultimate Alchemy (2 volumes)
Atma Pooja Upanishad

Vedanta: Seven Steps to Samadhi
Akshya Upanishad

Philosophia Ultima
Mandukya Upanishad

WESTERN MYSTICS

The Hidden Harmony
the fragments of Heraclitus

The New Alchemy: To Turn You On
Mabel Collins' Light on the Path

INITIATION TALKS
between Master disciple

Hammer On The Rock
(December 10, 1975 - January 15, 1976)

Above All Don't Wobble
(January 16 - February 12, 1976)

Nothing To Lose But Your Head
(February 13 - March 12, 1976)

Be Realistic: Plan For a Miracle
(March 13 - April 6, 1976)

Get Out of Your Own Way
(April 7 - May 2, 1976)

Beloved of My Heart
(May 3 - 28, 1976)

The Cypress in the Courtyard
(May 29 - June 27, 1976)

A Rose is a Rose is a Rose
(June 28 - July 27, 1976)

Dance Your Way to God
(July 28 - August 20, 1976)

The Passion for the Impossible
(August 21 - September 18, 1976)

The Great Nothing
(September 19 - October 11, 1976)

God is Not for Sale
(October 12 - November 7, 1976)

The Shadow of the Whip
(November 8 - December 3, 1976)

Blessed are the Ignorant
(December 4 - 31, 1976)

The Buddha Disease
(January 1977)

What Is, Is, What Ain't, Ain't
(February 1977)

The Zero Experience
(March 1977)

For Madmen Only (Price of Admission: Your Mind)
(April 1977)

This Is It
(May 1977)

The Further Shore
(June 1977)

Far Beyond the Stars
(July 1977)

The No Book (No Buddha, No Teaching, No Discipline)
(August 1977)

Don't Just Do Something, Sit There
(September 1977)

Only Losers Can Win in this Game
(October 1977)

The Open Secret
(November 1977)

The Open Door
(December 1977)

The Sun Behind the Sun Behind the Sun
(January 1978)

Believing the Impossible Before Breakfast
(February 1978)

Don't Bite My Finger, Look Where I am Pointing
(March 1978)

Let Go!
(April 1978)

The Ninety-Nine Names of Nothingness
(May 1978)

The Madman's Guide to Enlightenment
(June 1978)

Don't Look Before You Leap
(July 1978)

Hallelujah!
(August 1978)

God's Got a Thing About You
(September 1978)

The Tongue-Tip Taste of Tao
(October 1978)

The Sacred Yes
(November 1978)

Turn On, Tune In, and Drop the Lot
(December 1978)

Zorba the Buddha
(January 1979)

Won't You Join the Dance?
(February 1979)

You Ain't Seen Nothin' Yet
(March 1979)

The Shadow of the Bamboo
(April 1979)

The Sound of One Hand Clapping
(March 1981)

OTHER TITLES

The Book
an introduction to the teachings of
  Bhagwan Shree Rajneesh
  Series I from A to H
  Series II from I to Q
  Series III from R to Z

A Cup of Tea
letters to disciples

The Orange Book
the meditation techniques of
  Bhagwan Shree Rajneesh

Rajneeshism
an introduction to Bhagwan Shree Rajneesh and His
  religion

The Sound of Running Water
a photobiography of
  Bhagwan Shree Rajneesh and His work, 1974-1978

This Very Place The Lotus Paradise
a photobiography of
  Bhagwan Shree Rajneesh and His work, 1978-1984

BOOKS FROM OTHER PUBLISHERS

ENGLISH EDITIONS
UNITED KINGDOM

The Art of Dying
(Sheldon Press)

The Book of the Secrets (volume 1)
(Thames & Hudson)

Dimensions Beyond the Known
(Sheldon Press)

The Hidden Harmony
(Sheldon Press)

Meditation: The Art of Ecstasy
(Sheldon Press)

The Mustard Seed
(Sheldon Press)

Neither This Nor That
(Sheldon Press)

No Water, No Moon
(Sheldon Press)

Roots and Wings
(Routledge & Kegan Paul)

Straight to Freedom (Original title:
Until You Die)
(Sheldon Press)

The Supreme Doctrine
(Routledge & Kegan Paul)

The Supreme Understanding (Original title:
Tantra: The Supreme Understanding)
(Sheldon Press)

Tao: The Three Treasures (volume 1)
(Wildwood House)

UNITED STATES OF AMERICA

The Book of the Secrets (volumes 1-3)
(Harper & Row)

The Great Challenge
(Grove Press)

Hammer on the Rock
(Grove Press)

I Am The Gate
(Harper & Row)

Journey Toward the Heart (Original title:
Until You Die)
(Harper & Row)

Meditation: The Art of Ecstasy
(Harper & Row)

The Mustard Seed
(Harper & Row)

My Way: The Way of the White Clouds
(Grove Press)

Only One Sky (Original title:
Tantra: The Supreme Understanding)
(Dutton)

The Psychology of the Esoteric
(Harper & Row)

Roots and Wings
(Routledge & Kegan Paul)

The Supreme Doctrine
(Routledge & Kegan Paul)

Words Like Fire (Original title:
Come Follow Me, volume 1)
(Harper & Row)

BOOKS ON BHAGWAN

The Awakened One: The Life and Work
of Bhagwan Shree Rajneesh
by Swami Satya Vedant
(Harper & Row)

Death Comes Dancing: Celebrating Life
with Bhagwan Shree Rajneesh
by Ma Satya Bharti
(Routledge & Kegan Paul)

Drunk On The Divine
by Ma Satya Bharti
(Grove Press)

The Ultimate Risk
by Ma Satya Bharti
(Routledge & Kegan Paul)

Dying For Enlightenment
by Bernard Gunther (Swami Deva Amitprem)
(Harper & Row)

Neo-Tantra
by Bernard Gunther (Swami Deva Amitprem)
(Harper & Row)

FOREIGN LANGUAGE EDITIONS
DANISH

TRANSLATIONS

Hemmelighedernes Bog (volume 1)
(Borgens Forlag)

Hu-Meditation Og Kosmisk Orgasme
(Borgens Forlag)

BOOKS ON BHAGWAN

Sjælens Oprør
by Swami Deva Satyarthi
(Borgens Forlag)

DUTCH

TRANSLATIONS

Drink Mij
(Ankh-Hermes)

Het Boek Der Geheimen (volumes 1-5)
(Mirananda)

Geen Water, Geen Maan
(Mirananda)

BOOKS ON BHAGWAN

Bhagwan Shree Rajneesh: De Laatste Gok
by Ma Satya Bharti
(Mirananda)

Oorspronkelijk Gezicht,
Een Gang Naar Huis
by Swami Deva Amrito (Jan Foudraine)
(Ambo)

FRENCH

TRANSLATIONS

L'éveil à la Conscience Cosmique
(Dangles)

Je Suis La Porte
(EPI)

Le Livre Des Secrets (volume 1)
(Soleil Orange)

La Meditation Dynamique
(Dangles)

GERMAN

TRANSLATIONS

Auf der Suche
(Sambuddha Verlag)

Das Buch der Geheimnisse
(Heyne Taschenbuch)

Das Orangene Buch
(Sambuddha Verlag)

Der Freund
(Sannyas Verlag)

Sprung ins Unbekannte
(Sannyas Verlag)

Ekstase: Die vergessene Sprache
(Herzschlag Verlag, formerly Ki-Buch)

Esoterische Psychologie
(Sannyas Verlag)

Rebellion der Seele
(Sannyas Verlag)

Ich bin der Weg
(Rajneesh Verlag)

Intelligenz des Herzens
(Herzschlag Verlag, formerly Ki-Buch)

Jesus aber schwieg
(Sannyas Verlag)

Jesus -der Menschensohn
(Sannyas Verlag)

Kein Wasser, Kein Mond
(Herzschlag Verlag, formerly Ki-Buch)

Komm und folge mir
(Sannyas Verlag)

Meditation: Die Kunst zu sich selbst zu finden
(Heyne Verlag)

Mein Weg: Der Weg der weissen Wolke
(Herzschlag Verlag, formerly Ki-Buch)

Mit Wurzeln und mit Flügeln
(Edition Lotus)

Nicht bevor du stirbst
(Edition Gyandip, Switzerland)

Die Schuhe auf dem Kopf
(Edition Lotus)

Das Klatschen der einen Hand
(Edition Gyandip, Switzerland)

Spirituelle Entwicklung
(Fischer)

Vom Sex zum Kosmischen Bewusstsein
(New Age)

Yoga: Alpha und Omega
(Edition Gyandip, Switzerland)

Sprengt den Fels der Unbewusstheit
(Fischer)

Tantra: Die höchste Einsicht
(Sambuddha Verlag)

Tantrische Liebeskunst
(Sannyas Verlag)

Die Alchemie der Verwandlung
(Edition Lotus)

Die verborgene Harmonie
(Sannyas Verlag)

Was ist Meditation?
(Sannyas Verlag)

Die Gans ist raus!
(Sannyas Verlag)

BOOKS ON BHAGWAN

Rajneeshismus - Bhagwan Shree Rajneesh und
seine Religion
Eine Eiufuhrung
Rajneesh Foundation International

Begegnung mit Niemand
by Mascha Rabben (Ma Hari Chetana)
(Herzschlag Verlag)

Ganz entspannt im Hier und Jetzt
by Swami Satyananda
(Rowohlt)

Im Grunde ist alles ganz einfach
by Swami Satyananda
(Ullstein)

Wagnis Orange
by Ma Satya Bharti
(Fachbuchhandlung fur Psychologie)

Wenn das Herz frei wird
by Ma Prem Gayan (Silvie Winter)
(Herbig)

Der Erwachte
by Vasant Joshi
(Synthesis Verlag)

Rajneeshpuram - Fest des Foiedeus und der Liebe
(Sannyas Verlag)

GREEK

TRANSLATION

I Krifi Armonia (The Hidden Harmony)
(Emmanual Rassoulis)

HEBREW

TRANSLATION

Tantra: The Supreme Understanding
(Massada)

ITALIAN

TRANSLATIONS

L'Armonia Nascosta (volumes 1 & 2)
(Re Nudo)

Dieci Storie Zen di Bhagwan Shree Rajneesh
(Né Acqua, Né Luna)
(Il Fiore d'Oro)

La Dottrina Suprema
(Rizzoli)

Dimensioni Oltre il Conosciuto
(Mediterranee)

Estasi: Il Linguaggio Dimenticato
(Riza Libri)

Io Sono La Soglia
(Mediterranee)

Il Libro Arancione
(Mediterranee)

Il Libro dei Segreti
(Bompiani)

Meditazione Dinamica:
L'Arte dell'Estasi Interiore
(Mediterranee)

Nirvana: L'Ultimo Incubo
(Basaia)

La Nuova Alchimia
(Psiche)

Philosophia Perennis
(Alkaest)

La Rivoluzione Interiore
(Mediterranee)

La Ricerca
(La Salamandra)

Il Seme della Ribellione (volumes 1-3)
(Re Nudo)

Tantra: La Comprensione Suprema
(Bompiani)

Tao: I Tre Tesori (volumes 1-3)
(Re Nudo)

Tecniche di Liberazione
(La Salamandra)

Semi di Saggezza
(SugarCo)

BOOKS ON BHAGWAN

Rajneeshismo
una introduzione a
  Bhagwan Shree Rajneesh a sua religione

Alla Ricerca del Dio Perduto
by Swami Deva Majid
(SugarCo)

Il Grande Esperimento:
  Meditazioni E Terapie Nell'ashram
Di Bhagwan Shree Rajneesh
by Ma Satya Bharti
(Armenia)

L'Incanto D'Arancio
by Swami Swatantra Sarjano
(Savelli)

JAPANESE

TRANSLATIONS

Dance Your Way to God
(Rajneesh Publications)

The Empty Boat (volumes 1 & 2)
(Rajneesh Publications)

From Sex to Superconsciousness
(Rajneesh Publications)

The Grass Grows by Itself
(Fumikura)

The Heart Sutra
(Merkmal)

Meditation: The Art of Ecstasy
(Merkmal)

The Mustard Seed
(Merkmal)

My Way: The Way of the White Clouds
(Rajneesh Publications)

The Orange Book
(Wholistic Therapy Institute)

The Search
(Merkmal)

The Beloved
(Merkmal)

Tantra: The Supreme Understanding
(Merkmal)

Tao: The Three Treasures (volumes 1-4)
(Merkmal)

Until You Due
(Fumikura)

Rajneeshism
an introduction to
  Bhagwan Shree Rajneesh and His religion

PORTUGUESE (BRAZIL)

TRANSLATIONS

O Cipreste No Jardim
(Soma)

Dimensões Além do Conhecido
(Soma)

O Livro Dos Segredos (volume 1)
(Maha Lakshmi Editora)

Eu Sou A Porta
(Pensamento)

A Harmonia Oculta
(Pensamento)

Meditacão: A Arte Do Extase
(Cultrix)

Meu Caminho:
   O Comainho Das Nuvens Brancas
(Tao Livraria & Editora)

Nem Agua, Nem Lua
(Pensamento)

O Livro Orange
(Soma)

Palavras De Fogo
(Global/Ground)

A Psicologia Do Esotérico
(Tao Livraria & Editora)

A Semente De Mostarda (volumes 1 & 2)
(Tao Livraria & Editora)

Tantra: Sexo E Espiritualidade
(Agora)

Tantra: A Supreme Comprensao
(Cultrix)

Antes Que Voce Morra
(Maha Lakshmi Editora)

Extase: A Linguagem Esquecida
(Global)

Arte de Morrer
(Global)

SPANISH

TRANSLATIONS

Introducción al Mundo del Tantra
(Colección Tantra)

Meditación: El Arte del Extasis
(Colección Tantra)

Psicológia de lo Esotérico:
La Nueva Evolución del Hombre
(Cuatro Vientos Editorial)

¿Qué Es Meditación?
(Koan/Roselló Impresions)

Yo Soy La Puerta
(Editorial Diana)

Sòlo Un Cielo (volumes 1 & 2)
(Colección Tantra)

El Sutra del Corazon
(Sarvogeet)

Ven, Sigueme (volume 1)
(Sagaro)

BOOKS ON BHAGWAN

El Riesgo Supremo
by Ma Satya Bharti
(Martinez Roca)

SWEDISH

TRANSLATION

Den Väldiga Utmaningen
(Livskraft)

RAJNEESH MEDITATION CENTERS, ASHRAMS AND COMMUNES

RAJNEESH MEDITATION CENTERS, ASHRAMS AND COMMUNES

There are hundreds of Rajneesh meditation centers throughout the world. These are some of the main ones, which can be contacted for the name and address and telephone number of the center nearest you. They can also tell you about the availability of the books of Bhagwan Shree Rajneesh — in English or in foreign language editions. General information is available from Rajneesh Foundation International.

A wide range of meditation and inner growth programs is available throughout the year at Rajneesh International Meditation University.

For further information and a complete listing of programs, write or call:

Rajneesh International Meditation University
P.O. Box 5, Rajneeshpuram, OR 97741 USA
Phone: (503) 489-3328

USA

RAJNEESH FOUNDATION INTERNATIONAL
P.O. Box 9, Rajneeshpuram, Oregon 97741.
Tel: (503) 489-3301

UTSAVA RAJNEESH MEDITATION CENTER
20062 Laguna Canyon Rd., Laguna Beach, CA 92651.
Tel: (714) 497-4877

DEVADEEP RAJNEESH SANNYAS ASHRAM
1430 Longfellow St., N.W., Washington, D.C. 20011.
Tel: (202) 723-2188

CANADA

ARVIND RAJNEESH SANNYAS ASHRAM
2807 W. 16th Ave., Vancouver, B.C. V6K 3C5.
Tel: (604) 734-4681

SHANTI SADAN RAJNEESH MEDITATION CENTER
P.O. Box 374, Station R, Montreal, Quebec H2S 3M2.
Tel: (514) 272-4566

AUSTRALIA

PREMDWEEP RAJNEESH MEDITATION CENTER
64 Fullarton Rd., Norwood, S.A. 5067. Tel: 08-423388

SATPRAKASH RAJNEESH MEDITATION CENTER
4A Ormond St., Paddington, N.S.W. 2021
Tel: (02) 336570

SAHAJAM RAJNEESH SANNYAS ASHRAM
6 Collie Street, Fremantle 6160, W.A.
Tel: (09) 336-2422

SVARUP RAJNEESH MEDITATION CENTER
303 Drummond St., Carlton 3053, Victoria. Tel: 347-3388

BELGIUM

VADAN RAJNEESH MEDITATION CENTER
Platte-Lo-Straat 65, 3200 Leuven (Kessel-Lo).
Tel: 016/25-1487

BRAZIL

PRASTHAN RAJNEESH MEDITATION CENTER
Caixa Postal No. 11072, Ag. Cidade Nova,
Rio de Janeiro, R.J. 20251.
Tel: 222-9476

PURNAM RAJNEESH MEDITATION CENTER
Caixa Postal 1946, Porto Alegre, RS 90000.

CHILE

SAGARO RAJNEESH MEDITATION CENTER
Golfo de Darien 10217, Las Condes, Santiago.
Tel: 472476

DENMARK

ANAND NIKETAN RAJNEESH MEDITATION CENTER
Stroget, Frederiksberggade 15, 1459 Copenhagen K.
Tel: (01) 139940, 117909

EAST AFRICA

AMBHOJ RAJNEESH MEDITATION CENTER
P.O. Box 59159, Nairobi, Kenya

GREAT BRITAIN

MEDINA RAJNEESH BODY CENTER
81 Belsize Park Gardens, London NW3.
Tel: (01) 722-8220, 722-6404

MEDINA RAJNEESH NEO-SANNYAS COMMUNE
Herringswell, Bury St. Edmunds, Suffolk 1P28 6SW.
Tel: (0638) 750234

HOLLAND

DE STAD RAJNEESH NEO-SANNYAS COMMUNE
719 Prinsengracht, 1017 JW Amsterdam
Tel: 020-221296

INDIA

RAJNEESHDHAM NEO-SANNYAS COMMUNE
17 Koregaon Park, Poona 411 001, MS. Tel: 28127

ITALY

VIVEK RAJNEESH MEDITATION CENTER
Via San Marco 40/4, 20121 Milan. Tel: 659-0335

JAPAN

SHANTIYUGA RAJNEESH MEDITATION CENTER
Sky Mansion 2F, 1-34-1 Ookayama, Meguro-ku, Tokyo 152.
Tel: (03) 724-9631

UTSAVA RAJNEESH MEDITATION CENTER
2-9-8 Hattori-Motomachi, Toyonaki-shi, Osaka 561.
Tel: 06-863-4246

NEW ZEALAND

SHANTI NIKETAN RAJNEESH MEDITATION CENTER
119 Symonds Street, Auckland. Tel: 770-326

PUERTO RICO

BHAGWATAM RAJNEESH MEDITATION CENTER
Box 2886, Old San Juan, PR 00905.
Tel: 765-4150

SWEDEN

DEEVA RAJNEESH MEDITATION CENTER
Surbrunnsgatan 60, S11327 Stockholm. Tel: (08) 327788

SWITZERLAND

KOTA RAJNEESH NEO-SANNYAS COMMUNE
Baumackerstr. 42, 8050 Zurich. Tel: (01) 312 1600

WEST GERMANY

BAILE RAJNEESH NEO-SANNYAS COMMUNE
Karolinenstr. 7-9, 2000 Hamburg 6. Tel: (040) 432140

DORFCHEN RAJNEESH NEO-SANNYAS COMMUNE
Dahlmannstr. 9, 1000 Berlin 12. Tel: (030) 32-007-0

SATDHARMA RAJNEESH MEDITATION CENTER
Klenzestr. 41, 8000 Munich 5. Tel: (089) 269-077

WIOSKA RAJNEESH NEO-SANNYAS COMMUNE
Lutticherstr. 33/35, 5000 Cologne 1. Tel: 0221-517199

RAJNEESH INTERNATIONAL MEDITATION UNIVERSITY

Rajneesh International Meditation University offers over sixty-five innovative and dynamic workshops, programs and training courses — and individual sessions — covering the whole spectrum of human possibility, human growth, human flowering.

On beautiful Rancho Rajneesh in central Oregon, Rajneesh International Meditation University is a unique opportunity to explore yourself, to know yourself, to love and celebrate yourself, to soar beyond your self — all in the radiance of a Buddhafield, of a community inspired by the understanding, love and grace of the living enlightened Master, Bhagwan Shree Rajneesh.

"The radiance of the soul, the flowering of the soul, the health of the soul, is what I mean by flowering. And when one has come to flower in the innermost core of one's existence, one knows who one is. That knowing triggers an infinite sequence of knowing; then one goes on knowing more and more about the mysteries of life and death. Just open the first door of self-knowledge and many doors start opening on their own."

Bhagwan Shree Rajneesh
From: *Won't You Join the Dance?*

For information or a complete descriptive catalog:

**Rajneesh International Meditation University
P.O. Box 5,
Rajneeshpuram, OR 97741, USA
Tel: (503) 489-3328**

RAJNEESH
FOUNDATION
INTERNATIONAL
NEWSLETTER

- Bhagwan's message for today's world
- Latest developments in the living religion of Rajneeshism
- Twice a month
- Illustrated

Annual Subscription Rates:

USA (bulk rate)	$20.00
USA, Canada (1st class)	$30.00
Mexico and Central America	$40.00
Europe, South America, North Africa	$45.00
Rest of World	$50.00

Please make payment to:
Rajneesh Foundation International
P.O. Box 9
Rajneeshpuram, OR 97741 USA

BEWARE OF SOCIALISM

by
Bhagwan Shree Rajneesh

Five discourses given at Cross Maidan, Bombay—April 1970.

"Men are not equal. And so, if we impose equality on man with force, it will only destroy him. Man should have full opportunity to be unequal and different; he should be free to differ, to dissent, to deny, to rebel. Then only will he grow and blossom and bear fruit."

$3.95 paperback   ISBN 0-88050-706-3

Please make payment to:
Rajneesh Foundation International
P.O. Box 9
Rajneeshpuram, OR 97741   USA